Agequake

Agequake

*Riding the Demographic Rollercoaster
Shaking Business, Finance and
our World*

Paul Wallace

NICHOLAS BREALEY
PUBLISHING

LONDON

First published by
Nicholas Brealey Publishing Limited in 1999

36 John Street
London
WC1N 2AT, UK
Tel: +44 (0)171 430 0224
Fax: +44 (0)171 404 8311

1163 E. Ogden Avenue, Suite 705-229
Naperville
IL 60563-8535, USA
Tel: (888) BREALEY
Fax: (630) 428 3442

http://www.nbrealey-books.com

ISBN 1-85788-192-3

British Library Cataloguing in Publication Data
A catalogue record for this book is available from the
British Library.

Printed in Finland by WSOY.

Contents

Preface

As we approach the millennium, there is inevitably a sense both of excitement and of foreboding. Calendars matter: they mark off eras. What I argue in this book is that the twenty-first century will be remarkable for something quite unanticipated in most science fiction: a new age when we will no longer be young.

Through the long vistas of history, we have been remarkably young. Our average age has been around 20 or less. But in the current generation's lifetime, the average age of the world will nearly double from 22 in 1975 to 38 in 2050, according to the UN's latest projection issued at the end of 1998. Under another projection, it could reach over 40 as early as 2040. Many countries will reach average ages of 50 or more.

This is an epochal change by any reckoning, which is why I call it the agequake. The tremors from the agequake are already reaching into every corner of our lives, from stocks and shares to our love lives, from the property market to the new generational faultlines in society, from the future of youth culture to the growing importance of immigration. Many of the changes are welcome. We are living longer and remaining healthier. The falls in fertility that are driving global ageing mean that the specter of unstoppable population growth is receding. But the transition from an era of youthful and fast-growing populations to one of older and often declining ones requires radical adjustment, not least in our attitudes and expectations. A new age calls for a new mindset.

My goal in writing this book has been to show how this dramatic shift in the age profile of populations will affect key aspects of our lives, from business and finance to housing and pensions, from marketing and communications to the workplace. Throughout, I try to spell out what these changes may mean for individuals, sketching out a routemap through the unfamiliar demographic landscape that lies ahead.

The agequake is not confined to one country, nor is it about the fate of one generation, like the baby boomers born in the two decades after the Second World War who attract so much attention. It is above all a global phenomenon. In the West, countries are ageing from the middle of the age pyramid; in developing countries, from the bottom of the age pyramid as fewer children are born. There are many books, particularly in the US, that focus on baby boomers. What I seek to do is to convey the crucial international dimension to the agequake that will make it so powerful a force in all our lives in the years ahead.

This has been an ambitious project and I am well aware of how much ground I have tried to cover. In researching and writing this book, I have accumulated many debts. I owe particular gratitude to economists Roger Bootle, Tim Congdon and David Miles for reading and commenting on the manuscript; and to demographer David Coleman of Oxford University for similar assistance. I would also like to thank George Masnick, an American demographer, for his helpful comments on one of the chapters. I have also been helped by several officials in government departments and international organizations. I would like to acknowledge the assistance of Chris Shaw and Steve Smallwood at the Government Actuary's Department, Harri Cruijsen, formerly of Eurostat, Joseph-Alfred Grinblat at the UN and Nick Vanston at the OECD. Press officers Robert Dececco at the Office for National Statistics and Nicole le Vourch at the OECD have also been extremely helpful. Any shortcomings that remain are entirely my own.

Throughout the project, my publisher Nicholas Brealey has been a source of inspiration and clear thinking. I also owe a big debt to my agent Sara Menguc for her always helpful advice on the book. Sally Lansdell has been a wonderful editor. But most of all I want to thank my family – my mother, Bridget and Peter; Sylvia and Gunter; Joseph and Imogen who have got thoroughly fed up with their absentee father; and above all Shirley.

Part One

Faultlines

1

Boom, bulge and bust

THE DEMOGRAPHIC FOUNDATIONS OF WESTERN ECONOMIES THAT WE take for granted – an ever-expanding and youthful population – are slipping beneath our feet. As people live longer and have fewer children, a seismic shift is under way in the age profile of populations: the *agequake*.

Just as earthquakes are sometimes preceded by warning foreshocks, so with the agequake. The signs of the times are all around us – for those who choose to discern them. The early rumblings of the agequake are already starting to shake business and finance along with lifestyles and attitudes.

At present, the age profile of western populations is bulging in the center as the bumper postwar baby-boom generation becomes middle aged. This has helped stock markets levitate in the 1990s and created the incongruous spectacle of fifty-something rock stars.

But within 20 years, the boomer bulge will have moved into the older age brackets. The swelling number of retired people will put economies under severe pressure, undermining pension systems and stock markets alike. The long journey from postwar baby boom threatens to terminate in economic bust.

An extraordinary crossover is already starting to occur as older people outnumber younger people for the first time in human history. In the early twenty-first century, this tilt from young to old will take on a new dimension. It will go hand in hand with the onset of population decline in many developed nations as they experience the first sustained demographic reverse in centuries. We will no longer be facing that old bogey, world overpopulation, but 'the increasing *under*population of the developed countries', says management guru Peter Drucker.[1]

If the past is another country, so too is the future. Take a trip and see what kind of world the agequake is creating. It's one where more than half of western populations will be over 40 but fitter and healthier than ever before, where still youthful developing countries overhaul ageing and declining western populations, where well-educated workers can have their pick of jobs all over the world, and where the US is the second largest Spanish-speaking country. But it is also a world where house prices no longer rise inexorably, where governments are forced to renege on their pension commitments and where we could face the biggest bear market in history.

In the immediate future, the agequake will strike advanced countries most intensely. In the late 1990s, Japan became the first country ever with an average age of 40. In 2007 its population will reach a peak and then start falling. Italy will follow suit soon after. By 2025 there will be more Italians over 50 than under that age. Populations in Europe generally are poised to plunge on a scale not seen since the Black Death in 1348.[2]

There is, understandably, intense focus in the West on the ageing of the baby boomers born in the 20 years after the Second World War. But the agequake is bigger than the fate of an individual generation, however vociferous. It is above all a global phenomenon. Where the West is leading, the rest of the world is following.

Demographers have been taken aback in recent years at unheralded reductions in birth rates which could well stabilize the overall world population before the middle of the twenty-first century. Although the global population count is still increasing by leaps and bounds, the *growth rate* actually peaked at the end of the 1960s and is now falling sharply.

A triumph for humanity, many would say, given longstanding concerns about an overpopulated world. But hand in hand with the demographic slowdown comes ageing. The two are inextricably linked, since it is new births that rejuvenate populations. That is why global ageing will be the *leitmotif* of the twenty-first century. Indeed, the speed of the fertility declines in developing countries means that they will age much more quickly than the West: a daunting challenge. China, home of the one-child policy, will be one of the most rapidly ageing societies in 20 years' time.

Many of the changes are positive. The World Health Organization struck an optimistic note in its 1998 *World Health Report*: 'the most important pattern of progress now emerging is an unmistakable trend towards healthier, longer life.' In the West, the falling number of young people in the population has helped stem the crime wave. The 1990s have seen unexpected falls in recorded crime in many developed countries, including the US, France, Britain and Denmark. Home Office research for England and Wales has pinpointed a clear link between the number of young men and the extent of property crime.[3]

In many other respects, the agequake presents an immense economic and social challenge. There is no sign of a let-up in the financial strain on couples with children as they also support a retired population that is living so much longer. GenXers – the generation born in the late 1960s and 1970s – are entering working life saddled with debt as governments cut back spending on higher education to meet the bill for today's pensioners.

All this brings home to us that the impact of ageing is here and now, as much as in the distant future. There is a natural tendency to equate ageing with the growing number of old people that lies ahead in the twenty-first century. Since this prospect lies some way in the future, we close our minds to it and try to get on with our lives. But ageing is already happening today, affecting everything from stock markets to our lifestyles, as the swollen ranks of the baby-boom generation turn 40 and 50.

When we were young

The new millennium closes the first chapter in human history: when we were young. When Jesus was born 2000 years ago, he could expect, like other babies in the Roman Empire, to live for only around 25 years. Herod could have spared the innocents, since infant diseases could be relied on to massacre them. A thousand years later, nothing had changed. Even at the start of the twentieth century, life expectancy in Britain and the US was still under 50. But a baby girl born in England in the year 2000 will live on average for 80 years. A baby boy can expect to live about five years less than his sister, but even 75 is still far more than the average lifespan of our ancestors.[4]

We tend to think this improvement in life expectancy is mainly restricted to the developed world; not so. According to the World Health Organization, at least 120 countries with a total population above five billion – five-sixths of the world total – now enjoy a life expectancy at birth of more than 60 years. The global average has risen by a third in the past forty years to 65 and is projected to reach 70 years in the 2010s (see Figure 1).[5]

As well as people living longer, birth rates are plummeting around the world. In the late 1990s, fertility rates were already at or below replacement level – 2.1 children per woman – in 61 countries with almost half the world's population. From Singapore to Australia, Denmark to Portugal, younger generations are no longer being fully replenished. Now the same process is at work in developing countries. By around 2010, a further 28 developing nations, including India, Indonesia and Egypt, are expected to fall to replacement level or below.

The combination of rising longevity and declining fertility is relentlessly pushing up our average age. Throughout history, humanity has been extraordinarily young. In 1850, the average age of Americans was just 19. In other words, only half the population was 19 or more; the other half consisted of children. With that age profile, you can see why the word teenager hadn't yet been coined. In 1900, the average age in the US was still only 23; in England it was 24. Even today, western

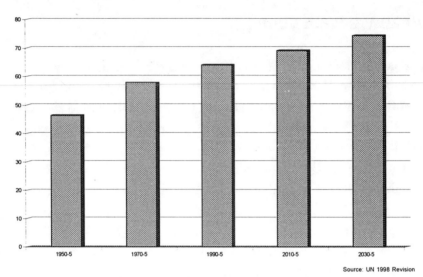

Source: UN 1998 Revision

Figure 1 World average life expectancy at birth

societies are still only in their mid- to late thirties – one reason that youth culture remains all conquering.

All this is set to change dramatically, as the UN's 1998 projection of world population makes clear. For example, the average age of Italians will rise by 10 years in the early twenty-first century. This trend isn't confined to the developed world. In 1980, the average age of the Chinese population was 22; by 2030 it will hit 41 (see Figure 2). In Hong Kong, it will rise to 49.

Under the UN's central projection, the average age of the world's population will reach 38 by 2050 – up from 22.5 in 1980. Under another one of the three scenarios, it will rise to 43.5 – six years *more* than in the UK today.[7]

The ageing of humanity across the world is a defining stage in history. It will change everything from business and finance to society and culture.

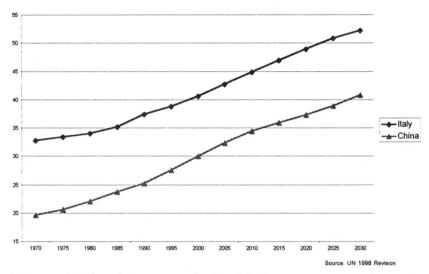

Figure 2 The ultimate trend: the global rise in average age

When pyramids flip...

Throughout the past, the age structure of the population has resembled a pyramid. It has a broad, youthful base and a small, elderly top. This remains the characteristic age profile of most developing countries.

In rich countries today – and even more so in some East Asian countries – the age structure looks like a Chinese lantern: it bulges in the middle. While this lasts it is the ideal economic shape, since it maximizes the number of people of working age.

In the twenty-first century, however, the age pyramids of developed countries will flip: the elderly top (broadly defined) will be wider than the working age middle, which in turn will be wider than the youthful base.

Turn a pyramid upside down and it falls over. Our extraordinary experiment in inverting age pyramids will prove just as unstable. The switch in dependency from young to old will create unprecedented economic strains. The old are far more expensive to maintain than children and the burden is shouldered to a far greater degree by society rather than individual families. The story of the next 20 to 30 years will be how we respond to the challenge of age pyramids as they flip.

...and populations implode

As if topsy-turvy pyramids were not enough, the agequake will be accompanied by the most dramatic demographic reverse in centuries. Not only will the age structure shift, but populations in the rich industrial democracies are poised to decline, drastically in several countries. The UN's central projection is that the population of Germany, where births have been running well below replacement level in the past 25 years, will fall by 10 percent in the first half of the twenty-first century. Italy's population will decline by over a quarter.

Populations are like supertankers. They seem to take forever to turn around. The enduring effects of high fertility in the past, together with immigration and declines in mortality, have for example kept European populations growing for decades, disguising the fact that birth rates had plunged below replacement level. Now, however, the tanker is about to go into reverse, first in Japan and Europe, but ultimately throughout the world.

Remember the early 1970s, when free love reigned and the bombs rained down on North Vietnam? That was the time when World Bank President Robert McNamara, who had presided over the bombing campaign as Lyndon Johnson's Defense Secretary, compared the continuing increase in the world's population to the threat of nuclear war. He was wrong, just as he had been wrong in Vietnam, although his worries about overpopulation were widely shared, both then and now.[8]

It turns out that we've been worrying about the wrong thing. One of the forces driving global ageing – lower fertility – is set to turn the global population supertanker around. The world's population will continue rising into the twenty-first century, but will peak much sooner than anyone could have predicted.

Until very recently, such a view was heresy in the population establishment. But establishments have to bow to facts. Fertility is declining across developing countries far faster than had been anticipated. Between 1996 and 1998, the UN lopped off half a billion people in its central estimate of world population in 2050. Even in the big number

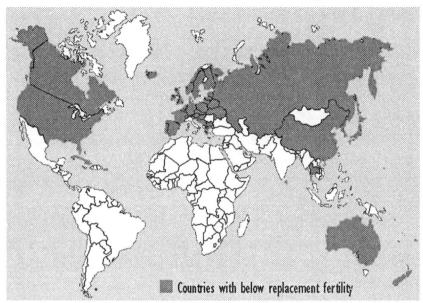

Figure 3 The spread of low fertility around the world
Total fertility rates below replacement in 1995–2000
Source: UN 1998 Revision

currency of demographics, that's more than small change: it's the same as the entire global population in 1500.

Low fertility is no longer confined to the developed world (see Figure 3). Countries where birth rates fell below replacement level in the 1990s included China and Thailand. Brazil is expected to reach replacement fertility in 1999. In Iran, the fertility rate dropped like a stone in the 1990s, halving to a rate of 2.8 births per woman. As recently as 1996, the UN believed it would take until 2015 for Iranian fertility to fall this low.[9]

In 50 countries where fertility was already quite low in 1975, it has declined further in all but three. In Australia and Singapore it fell by a sixth in the following two decades. Many other countries, including South Korea and Ireland, saw still more dramatic declines of over two-fifths. In Hong Kong and Spain, the fertility rate plunged by over a half.[10]

These precipitate and sustained declines suggest that the UN's low projection for population is now more likely than its central one. The central case is that the world's population will rise from 6 billion in the year 2000 to 8.9 billion by 2050, eventually stabilizing at around 10 billion in the following century. Under the low fertility scenario, however, the world's population will peak as early as 2040 at 7.5 billion.

Immigration to the fore

Increased immigration is sometimes regarded as a possible solution to ageing populations because immigrants tend to be young. But the scale of the ageing pressures is such that it would require inconceivably high admissions to counter the agequake.

One estimate is that immigration would have to rise tenfold from current already high levels to neutralize ageing in western countries. What is more, these higher inflows would have to be sustained indefinitely. With political opposition to immigration gathering around the world, this is a solution too far. Looking further ahead to the inexorable advance of global ageing, immigration cannot be a solution: it simply redistributes people around the world.

Yet set against a background of stagnant or declining populations, even the present levels of immigration will have an astonishing impact on the make-up of many countries. California will become a 'majority minority' state as early as 2001, official demographers revealed at the end of 1998. On current trends, the US will become the third biggest Spanish-speaking nation in the world by 2010 and the second by 2020. Already Latinos' buying power in the US is larger than Mexico's economy. Hispanic culture will move to center stage. Businesses will have to tailor their strategies to such new ethnic realities if they want to survive.[11]

The hidden hand of demographics

These changes are momentous by any reckoning. They herald an equally momentous economic and social revolution. What is more, unlike so many other forecasts, the agequake is inherently *predictable*.

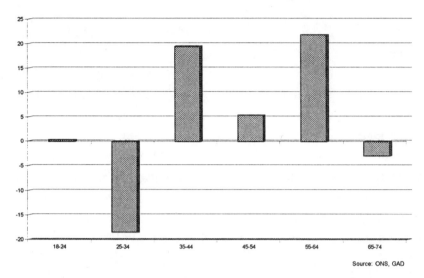

Figure 4 Cutting a new age profile
Percent change in size of age groups in the UK population, 1995–2005

Adam Smith talked of the invisible hand that coordinates market economies. But there is another invisible hand that guides their course: demographics. This point is often overlooked because the vital statistics of demography – births, deaths and population increase – usually change quite gradually. Like a gliding swan, however, demographic trends are deceptive. Nothing very much seems to be happening at first sight. Look below the surface at what is happening to individual age components of the population, however, and there is some furious paddling going on.

The UK's population, for example, hardly grows at all between 1995 and 2005 – by just 2.5 percent, assuming continuing immigration. But the size of some age groups changes by far more. The 55–64 age bracket increases by a fifth, as does the 35–44 age group. Meanwhile, the number aged 25–34 *falls* by the same amount (see Figure 4).

Projecting the age structure of a population – over a period of two to three decades – can be done with a fair degree of certainty. You start with a known quantity: the existing population. Every year, everyone already born who stays alive gets a year older. That simple fact of life allows us to project the age structure of today's population long into the future using the same techniques that insurers deploy to make money out of our desire to protect against the chance of misfortune. Because the pattern of mortality follows a much more stable path than that of fertility, you can have a pretty good idea about the way in which the age profile of a population will develop over time.

Intelligently used, demographics can predict not just the changing age profile of a population but associated changes in behavior. We know, for example, that you are much more likely to migrate in your twenties than at any other age. We also know that as you get into your thirties and start to raise a family, you are likely to move out of city centers and into the suburbs. So looking forward, we can anticipate key shifts in social behavior.

For example, if the British government had been mugging up on its demographics, it would have been able to anticipate the consumer spending spree and house price rises in the 1980s. The postwar baby boom peaked in 1964 so, 20 years on, a bulging number of 20-year-olds in the population was entering the labor market and buying homes for the first time. People in their twenties run up debts not because they're improvident but because they are purchasing houses and consumer durables like cars.

Such age-related spending patterns reflect the fact that however much we might resist the notion, a good deal of our behavior tracks our age. A good deal – but not all. As new generations age, they don't necessarily follow in their parents' footsteps. This means that predicting future behavior on the basis of known demographic trends is an art rather than a science. You have to weigh up whether people, as they age, will behave like today's older generations or whether they will break new ground.

Membership of a generation counts. When you are born can determine your life chances as much as all the certificates you get at college. That's something that Eastern astrologers also believe. There was a marked dip in Japanese births in 1966, for example, because it was the year of the fire horse, seen as an especially unlucky sign for girls, combining fire with fire.

This kind of superstition does work, but in exactly the opposite direction laid out by the astrologers. The lucky ones are those born in the unlucky year and vice versa. The year of your birth does matter – because of the company you keep. If you're born in a baby-boom year, you can expect heightened competition throughout your life, in school, at work, in the housing market. By comparison, if you're born in a baby-bust year, you can expect to coast it.

Why Bridget Jones can't find her Darcy

The baby booms and busts creating the agequake send waves rippling out in all directions. One effect is to change the odds in the marriage market. *Bridget Jones's Diary*, written by baby boomer Helen Fielding, has been a bestseller in the UK and US. The book, a *Pride and Prejudice* of our times, recounts Bridget Jones's quest for true love, acknowledging that universally acknowledged truth of the 1990s that a single, thirty-something woman in possession of a good career must be in want of a partner.

Its sales owed much to the fact that there were so many of these women around. In 1996, over a quarter of women in their early thirties were single – a far higher proportion than in the recent past. Even taking into account the fact that many are cohabiting, why have women in their thirties apparently been finding it more difficult to get hitched?[12]

One reason that is normally overlooked is the effect of baby booms and busts. When birth rates are rising, as they were in the 1950s and early 1960s, there will be more girls born in later years compared with the number of boys in preceding years. Three decades on, this simple fact tilts the balance of power towards men, since women tend to marry men who are older than themselves. At any given stage, there will be fewer potential male suitors compared with the number of eligible women.

There's good news ahead, however, for women born after the peak of the baby boom. That's because the position is already starting to reverse thanks to the delayed impact of the baby bust. As birth rates declined to a trough in the late 1970s, so with every year that passed there were fewer girls born compared with the number of boys two or

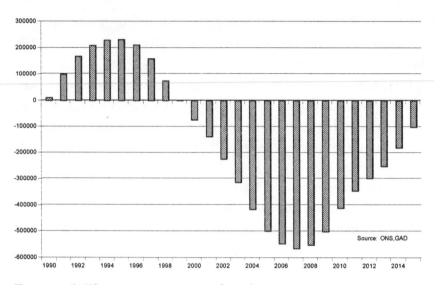

Figure 5 The coming revenge of Bridget Jones
The surplus/deficit of women aged 30–39 over men aged 33–42

three years earlier. Wind the clock forward and the result is an excess of Darcys and sweet revenge for Bridget Jones (see Figure 5).

How to survive – and profit from – the agequake

The first tremors of the agequake are already reverberating through our lives. What you want to know is to how to deal with them. That is what I have set out to do in this book. It is a survivor's guide to the most elemental force to affect your life now and in the future, one that is sending shockwaves through the world of work, your finances – and your love life. Don't kid yourself: you will almost certainly survive a lot longer and in much better shape than you ever imagined. So relax: you might even enjoy it.

Revolution is an overworked word, but the World Health Organization hits the mark when it describes ageing as 'a quiet, almost unseen social revolution that is gradually gaining pace and will accelerate and become ever more evident in the next 25 years'. The WHO

says that 'its influence will be felt at every level, from family life and living arrangements, employment, the provision of health services and
pension systems, to the state of the economy'.[13]

This book anatomizes the revolution. In the next chapter, I outline
the powerful demographic forces that lie behind the agequake. In Part
Two, I look ahead over the next 10 or so years as ageing starts to reshape
our lives in earnest. Part Three looks further ahead to a time when we
will have to cope with the potential downside of ageing in the West
and an increasing number of countries elsewhere in the world. I trace
the impact of the agequake in six main areas: finance, property, business, society and culture, jobs and pensions.

Financial rollercoaster

▼ The delayed impact of the baby boom is pushing up the numbers
of people in their peak years for savings and financial investment.
The result has been a goldrush for financial services as baby
boomers turn prospectors in the Klondike of the world's equity
markets.

▼ The strategy of investing in emerging economies took a cold shower
when financial markets collapsed in Asia and elsewhere in the developing world. But, looking ahead, demographics are on the side of
the bold investor who persists with emerging markets in the twenty-
first century.

▼ There is the prospect of 'the longest and deepest bear market in history' in the early twenty-first century as baby boomers try to liquidate
their savings in order to provide an income for their retirement.[14]

The new property game

▼ The days when house prices were buoyed up by a rising tide of first-
time buyers are over. First-time buyers, typically in their twenties
and early thirties, are in short supply because of the baby bust of the
1970s.

▼ The new property game of the next 10 years is about hot spots and
black holes. Hot spots are those areas and kinds of homes favored by

new types of households, mainly single people, and baby boomers trading up to larger accommodation. Black holes are mainstream starter homes on the wrong side of town.

▼ Immigration is becoming a key driver of housing markets, particularly in the US.

The new business game

▼ As for housing, so for business. The demographic rollercoaster is soaring for some sectors, plunging for others. Business strategies everywhere are having to adapt to the shifting age structure of the population.

▼ The runaway success of the impotence drug Viagra is a pointer to the potential of an ageing population for drugs companies. The pharmaceuticals sector is one sure-fire winner as demographics boost the markets for new products generated by the scientific revolution in molecular biology. Expect, too, a surge in the leisure industry as the number of well-heeled 50-year-olds soars.

▼ By contrast, companies that have ridden the long upswing of the postwar baby boom are in for a rougher ride. From fast food to denim jeans, firms that have failed to read the demographic runes are in trouble.

Cultural revolution

▼ With western populations ageing fast, the obvious inference is that the era of youth culture is drawing to an end. Obvious but wrong: youth culture has got legs. Baby boomers may be turning middle aged, but they don't want to be categorized as such. Mid-youth is the term favored by some marketers. It sounds absurd, but there's a kernel of substance to the euphemism.

▼ While the concept of youth becomes conveniently elastic, generational differences are coming to the fore. As the old class faultlines disappear, new generational ones are replacing them. These new generational distinctions are just one way in which ageing societies will differ distinctly from those in the past.

▼ The increasing importance of immigration in population change will make ethnic minorities more important than ever. We are moving away from monolithic mass cultures dominated by households bringing up children, to rainbow societies with a plethora of lifestyles and a much more diverse spectrum of social identities.

Work makeover

▼ You can paint an optimistic scenario in which weight of numbers batters down ageism in the workplace, allowing people to work longer under more flexible conditions and so relieving the pressure on pension schemes. But if anything, it is the smaller number of younger people who will benefit most as companies enter into a bidding war for their services. Scarcity, not a glut, confers power in markets.

▼ The waves of downsizing and delayering in the 1990s are likely to continue as companies shake out an excess of middle-aged managers.

▼ The opportunities for many older workers will lie as subcontractors to large companies, whether as individual freelancers or by setting up small businesses. For some this will be the opportunity to make good and win independence. For many it will mean entering the world of the contingent worker, with variable earnings and no security.

Pensions crunch

▼ State pensions stand in the demographic firing line. In many countries, public pension promises are unaffordable and will have to be broken. The alternative is a quite unacceptable escalation in contributions, overburdening the working population that will ultimately have to find the resources to honor the promises.

▼ Across the western world and in Japan, governments have accepted the need for reform. This is an early indication of the way in which population ageing is already starting to dominate politics as well as economics. But most of the changes made so far have barely scratched the surface of the problem. There has been no response yet that measures up to the scale of the potential increase in longevity that lies ahead.

▼ The imbalance between pension liabilities among the different states of the European Union is potentially the most serious threat to the long-term success of the euro.

The new demographics will also lead to a new international pecking order. The US will remain the preeminent economic superpower through the first half of the twenty-first century, not least because of continuing population growth through immigration. But the postwar winners of Japan and Germany will turn losers as their economies stagnate or even decline because of falling working-age populations.

By contrast, Britain, the also-ran of the postwar era, is better placed to survive the agequake than most countries in Europe. The Irish Republic is particularly well placed for the future within the EU thanks to its relatively young population.

However, all countries in the West will find their weight in the world diminishing. Favorable demographics will foster fast progress in developing countries, while many western economies will be hit by declining labor forces. This is the real new world order, brought to you not by the collapse of communism but by the power of demography.

2

The future that's happened

ON 4 AUGUST 1997, JEANNE CALMENT DIED IN ARLES, THE CITY IN Provence where Vincent Van Gogh painted some of his most exceptional pictures, like *Starry Night*. Unlike Van Gogh, there was nothing exceptional about Jeanne Calment – except her age. She lived to 122, the longest life ever reliably recorded.

Stop a moment and think about that long stretch of human history. Jeanne Calment was born on 21 February 1875, just four years after *l'année terrible* when France was crushed by the Prussian juggernaut and a year after the first Impressionist exhibition. She was 15 when Van Gogh committed suicide; in her forties during the First World War; in her sixties during the Second World War. When youth took over the streets of Paris in 1968, she was already 93.[1]

Calment was a pioneer of the long life revolution. One of the stories she liked to tell was how she outwitted a local lawyer thanks to her extraordinary longevity. In 1965, at the tender age of 90, she made a deal that must have had him rubbing his hands with glee. He agreed to pay her handsomely for the rest of her presumably short life. In return, he would receive her flat when she died. But she had the last laugh: he died first, having lost out financially as well. She lived independently until she was over 110 and remained mentally alert to the end of her life.[2]

Jeanne Calment's long life is as nothing compared to biblical feats. Methuselah supposedly lived for 969 years, perishing only in the year of the flood. Noah, his grandson, clocked up a mere 950 years. According to the rather more reliable source of modern demography, however, no one ever lived for 110 or more years until the twentieth century. The first accurately documented case was Katherine Plunket, who died aged 111 in 1932. Only one other person other than Jeanne Calment is believed to have lived to 120 – Shirechiyo Izumi, a Japanese man who died in 1986. James Vaupel, a demographer who specializes in the study of old age, believes that earlier centenarians were a lonely bunch. These Robinson Crusoes of longevity were few and far between, with perhaps one person in the world notching up 100 years in any one century.[3]

But now the desert islands are becoming increasingly crowded. In 1950, there were only 200 centenarians in France. By 2000, the number will have risen to 8500 and by 2050 it is projected to reach 150,000. Worldwide, over 150,000 centenarians will see in the new millennium, said the UN in late 1998 in its first ever projection to feature this age group. By mid-century there will be over two million. By that time Calment's record will assuredly have been broken.[4]

Modern Methuselahs

The certainty of global ageing is part of what management guru Peter Drucker calls 'the future *that has already happened*'. Tomorrow's old have long been born: they are now baby boomers in their prime. No one can be precisely sure about the *scale* of ageing that lies ahead, but there is a strong likelihood that it will be even more extreme than currently anticipated.[5]

Ageing is driven by two forces: rising longevity and falling fertility. Start with the trend to greater longevity. Although life expectancy has been rising for over a century because of declining mortality, it has only recently started to make populations older – which means that its effects will be more far-reaching in the future. The reason for this delay is that the falls in mortality were initially concentrated among younger people and also allowed the vast majority of women to live throughout their reproductive years, so boosting fertility.[6]

It is only recently – now that mortality declines are more and more concentrated at older ages – that longer lifespans have started to play a major role in the ageing of the West. One way of measuring this effect is by comparing trends in life expectancy at birth and at age 60. Between 1901 and 1961, male life expectancy at birth in the UK rose by more than twenty years; but for men aged 60 it rose by less than two years. Improvements were much more evenly shared between 1961 and 1991 as life expectancy for 60-year-olds rose at three times the rate earlier in the century (see Figure 6). Looking forward, the increase in life expectancy will be still more concentrated among older people.

These continuing sharp rises in life expectancy, particularly among older people, caught everyone by surprise. Neither demographers nor governments anticipated this outcome. In the US, the National Center for Health Statistics suggested that life expectancy might have reached a limit in the early 1960s. A decade later, the 1974 projections of the Social Security Trust Fund assumed that mortality rates would stop

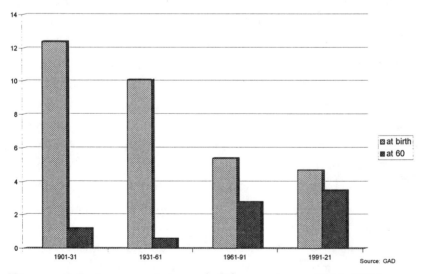

Figure 6 Improvements in male life expectancy 1901–2021

falling by 2000. This error was a key reason that the system needed radical reform in the early 1980s.[7]

You might think, therefore, that today's demographic projections would incorporate a generous allowance for a further big jump in longevity. Not so. Official forecasts do assume some increase, but on nothing like the same scale as has actually occurred in the past three decades.

For example, life expectancy at birth in the US, Germany and the UK rose by two years a decade from the early 1960s to the early 1990s. However, the UN now projects it to increase by just one year a decade after 2000. Japanese life expectancy at birth rose by over three years a decade from the early 1960s to the start of the 1990s. But from 2000 on, it is projected to increase by *under* a year a decade.

Elastic lifespans

These downbeat projections arise partly because of official caution about the sustainability of recent improvements in life expectancy among older people, which owe much to rapid reductions in heart and circulatory diseases. But they also reflect the influential view that there is a fixed limit to average human lifespans. A rule of thumb – based on past observations of mortality rates at different ages – has been that the maximum average life expectancy is around 85. Just as a car decelerates as it approaches its maximum speed, so you would expect increases in life expectancy to taper away as we approach its full potential.

The idea that maximum life expectancy is around 85 is in turn based on a biological model of why we grow old and eventually die. Taking its cue from evolutionary theory, this argues that we only exist in order to pass on our immortal genes. Once we have reproduced we become genetically irrelevant; there is no reason for natural selection to improve our life chances at ages beyond reproduction. We have therefore evolved in order to maximize our fitness during the reproductive period, rather than to extend our own individual lives.[8]

According to this mainstream theory, there are diminishing returns to further medical advances. As one disease is stamped out, so another takes its place. This is the gloomy but realistic notion of 'competing diseases': you've got to die of something. The theory insists that there is a mountain to climb if longevity is to rise much further. For American men to achieve a life expectancy of 85 would require mortality rates to fall by two-thirds at all ages. To achieve a life expectancy of 100, 84 percent of all individuals would have to survive until 85, as opposed to 31 percent today.[9]

By contrast, an increasingly influential revisionist school argues that the genetic gloom is overdone. In a striking analogy, demographer James Vaupel compares the evolutionary paradox of rising longevity to unmanned space probes that carry on working after their initial mission is completed. The Voyager spacecraft, launched in 1977, were designed with a five-year lifespan to fly past Jupiter and Saturn. However, their engineering has allowed them to continue working and sending back information as they exit the solar system, and NASA expects them to return valuable data for another 20 to 30 years.[10]

So with humans: the design may simply be to meet the demands of successful reproduction, but it is sturdy enough to allow many years of 'surplus' living. As if to make the point, 1998 saw the triumphant return to space of astronaut-turned-senator-turned-ageing-guinea-pig John Glenn at the age of 77. The evolutionary paradox can also be turned on its head. The 'grandmother hypothesis' suggests that the emergence of long-lived grandmothers, who could help provide food for children, may have been crucial in human evolution.[11]

The revisionists are much more open-minded about the potential for medical advances, along with healthy behavior, nutrition and prosperity, to increase maximum life expectancy. They reject the gloomy notion that evolution stacks up a host of malfunctioning genes for our post-reproductive years, pointing out that such mutations would in practice be rare. Instead of a single, universal process of ageing, they regard ageing as having multiple causes and multiple manifestations. On this basis, advances against a particular disease do not simply open up a vacuum filled by other diseases; they lead to worthwhile increases in life expectancy.[12]

One strong argument that the revisionists can use is the existing longevity gap in advanced countries. For example, projections for the US and the UK suggest that it will take until the 2020s to achieve the life expectancy *currently* enjoyed by the Japanese – even though both countries enjoyed higher life expectancy than Japan in the early 1960s.

Further support for the revisionist school comes from the experience of particular subgroups within populations in recent years. Death rates of physically active Harvard alumni aged 60 or over are half those of the same age group among American white males in general. The long life of these select Americans is likely to be a forerunner of more general improvements in health and prosperity affecting the whole population. A study in the journal *Demography* shows how older Americans are benefiting from improvements in nutrition, commercial food processing and conservation practices, and in public health way back in the early twentieth century. There is no reason to suppose that these improvements were one-offs: other studies show that this trend stretches back well into the nineteenth century. The implication is that mortality will fall still further as Americans born later in the twentieth century benefit in old age from a healthier start to life.[13]

For my money, the revisionist school has the edge. During the 1950s and early 1960s, the conventional wisdom was that further mortality reductions would be hard won once the big gains from controlling infections and parasitic disease had been achieved. Then came the dramatic reduction in strokes and heart disease that began at the end of the 1960s: death rates sank by 50 percent between 1975 and 1995. A UN working group reported in 1997 that 'a paradigm shift has occurred in the past few years regarding the biological potential of life prolongation'. An investigation into longevity by the American National Research Council was notable for its scepticism about imminent limits to longevity and its stress on the plasticity of human lifespans.[14]

Genetic elixirs

It would be complacent to take future improvements in longevity for granted. In Britain, for example, the decline in smoking halted in the 1990s. New scourges like AIDS have surfaced and old diseases like TB are making a comeback. There is increasing concern about the rise of anti-biotic resistance in bacteria. On the other hand, pharmaceutical compa-nies are fighting back in this particular arms race: research into new vaccines to ward off bacterial infections is exploding, according to drugs giant SmithKline Beecham, which has about a quarter of the world market.[15]

There is another compelling reason that lifespans can be expected to stretch still further in the future: the scientific and medical profes-sions are zeroing in on ageing as never before. Research is advancing on a wide front. One principal objective is to map out the links between genetics and ageing. The US National Institute on Aging has launched an initiative to identify the genes affecting the rate of ageing in humans. Longevity does appear to run in families; Jeanne Calment came from long-lived stock. US scientists have already identified 'Methuselah genes' in worms, showing that two of them work together to multiply their lifespan. A longevity gene has been tracked down in yeast. Genetics have also been shown to determine how long fruit flies live. At the University of California, Irvine, evolutionary biologist Michael Rose has doubled the lives of fruit flies through selective breeding.[16]

In addition, researchers are making important discoveries about the biochemistry of ageing. One theory of ageing points the finger at free radicals, the highly reactive by-products of normal metabolism that damage proteins, membranes and DNA. Enzymes like superoxide dis-mutase (SOD) have been shown to play a role in preventing such oxidative attacks. Inserting extra copies of the SOD gene into fruit flies extends their lifespan. Hormones, too, have been linked to ageing. Doses of the hormone DHEA have produced dramatic anti-ageing effects in animals.[17]

Scientists have also made some remarkable findings about the beneficial effects of calorie-restricted diets. Rats fed 30 percent fewer calories live 30 percent longer and are healthier. The research has now been extended to monkeys. It shows that calorie restriction raises 'good' cholesterol levels, so reducing the risk of cardiovascular disease, and slows down the age-related decrease in DHEA.[18]

As important, medicine is on the verge of significant new victories in the two scourges of older people, cancer and cardiovascular diseases. In evidence to Congress in 1998 from the National Institutes of Health (NIH), the US government's medical research organization, there were encouraging dispatches from the war against mortality as people grow older. NIH director Dr Harold Varmus said that 'revolutionary discoveries in many fields – especially genetics, neuroscience, cell biology, bioengineering and computer sciences – have the power to transform the practice of medicine'.[19]

New therapies for cancer should be one spectacular pay-off from advances in molecular and genetic science. Dr Varmus told the American Association for the Advancement of Science that 'the near-term prospects for advances against cancer seem to be exceptionally strong'. US cancer rates started to fall in the 1990s for the first time since records began to be collected in the 1930s. The number of drugs entering clinical trials for cancer has increased fivefold in the 1990s. Worldwide, the WHO says that that stomach, cervical and liver cancers will become less common because of improved food conservation and dietary changes, screening and immunization against hepatitis B virus respectively.[20]

Despite massive reductions in the past 30 years, cardiovascular diseases remain the other main killer of older people. Also giving evidence to Congress in 1998 was Dr Claude Lenfant, director of the National Heart, Lung and Blood Institute. He was just as upbeat as Dr Varmus: the Institute was 'poised to make a quantum leap in our understanding of many basic issues that govern health and disease'. For example, research into atherosclerosis – the clogging of arteries with fatty deposits – had shown that the size of these plaques is less important than other characteristics making them susceptible to erosion and rupture. 'Millions of heart attacks may ultimately prove preventable if we can unravel this mystery and develop effective interventions.'[21]

Peter Pan and the fountain of youth

As if to reinforce the general mood of optimism, American scientists unveiled the 'Peter Pan effect' in 1998. Most normal, healthy cells in the body divide up to 100 times before becoming senescent. The question that had long intrigued scientists was how they knew when to stop reproducing: what was the cellular clock? The answer – tick, tock – was that telomeres, the DNA strands on the end of every chromosome, became shorter and shorter. However, scientists at the University of Texas Southwestern Medical Center and biotech firm Geron showed that they could lengthen telomeres in normal human cells by adding the enzyme telomerase, present in reproductive and immortal cancer cells. The Texas scientists dubbed telomerase the 'cellular fountain of youth'.[22]

The elation was premature. The breakthrough was in tissue culture in the laboratory and in any case, cellular senescence is only one factor in ageing. The potential of the research into telomerase, which is present in most human tumors, may well lie in cancer therapy, both in diagnostics and in compounds that inhibit its activity. But the episode was a dramatic example of the far-reaching advances now under way in the medical battle against ageing.[23]

It is a battle that promises not just longer life but better life. For those worrying about what ageing will do to their brains, Dr Varmus of the NIH had this message: 'we are at the dawn of the golden age of neuroscience'. For those worrying about what ageing does to their bodies, he spoke of the promise of 'bioengineering techniques to fabricate replacement tissues and tissue mimetics'.[24]

Remember the incredible bionic man? He could look a lot less incredible in a decade's time.

From baby boom to baby bust

Rising longevity may now be contributing to the ageing of the West and Japan, but the root cause of the agequake is the startling shift to low fertility in the past three decades. Younger generations are no longer being replenished since the baby boom gave way to baby bust.

Unlike falling mortality, whose effects can work both ways, falling fertility makes populations unambiguously older. High birth rates make populations young. But when fertility declines, this rejuvenating effect is turned off and populations become older.

A gradual decline in fertility is why the average age of the US population rose from 16 to 30 between 1800 and 1950. The baby boom then caused this trend to reverse to 28 by 1970. The average age of Australians fell by three years between 1950 and 1970; that of Canadians dropped to 25.5 in 1965. Cue the Beach Boys and quintessential youth movies like *Easy Rider* and *The Graduate*. The ensuing baby bust, together with the impact of greater longevity, has since pushed the average age of both Americans and Canadians back to around 35.[25]

To get a grip on what is happening to fertility, demographers focus on the total fertility rate (TFR), a measure that allows timely comparison between populations of widely varying age structures. The TFR is the number of children a woman would have if she experienced the current age patterns of fertility through her childbearing years. Trends in this rate show just how much more extreme the baby boom in North America was compared with that in Europe. At the height of the upswing in the late 1950s, the fertility rate approached 4 births per woman. Similar highs were recorded in New Zealand and Australia. By contrast, the UK peaked at just under 3 and Denmark at 2.6. These rates contrast with the 2.1 replacement rate needed to stabilize populations in the long run.

Despite these contrasts, both the Old and the New World showed similar trends. The baby boom switched to bust with remarkable speed from the mid-1960s to the late 1970s. In the majority of European countries, the peak year was 1964. In Britain, the trough year was 1977

Figure 7 Mamma mia
Italy's total fertility rate, births per woman

when fertility fell below 1.7. In the US, the baby boom peaked some-what earlier, in 1957, and the trough came in 1976.

At first, this fertility switchback was seen as a temporary cyclical phenomenon. In 1979 the British government was projecting a return to replacement fertility by 1987. It didn't materialize. By the mid-1990s, the government was projecting a TFR of 1.8 for the foreseeable future.[26]

The decline in fertility has been deepest and most sustained where you would least expect it – in Italy, the land of hot-blooded Romeos and Juliets. Fertility fell below replacement in 1977: so far, so unsur-prising. It is what subsequently happened that is so unprecedented. The TFR continued to sink until it reached the astonishingly low level of 1.2 in the late 1990s (see Figure 7). Demographer Antonio Golini argues that in some regions, like Ferrara province, fertility is 'near a pos-sible absolute minimum'.[27]

An even more abrupt fall has occurred in Spain, where fertility was running at almost 3 for most of the 1970s. Since then, however, it has also plummeted to 1.2. The implications of such low fertility are scary. If current fertility and mortality rates are sustained, both populations will *inevitably* go into freefall in the absence of immigration. The decline will continue indefinitely unless fertility returns to replacement.[28]

Japan is currently experiencing the most rapid ageing in the world because of the unprecedented collapse in its fertility that occurred 40 years ago. After a brief postwar baby boom, the fertility rate halved within a decade to reach the replacement rate of just over 2 in 1957. It stayed around this level until 1973, after which it started to sink relentlessly again, reaching 1.4 in the mid-1990s. In 1995 the number of births was under half that of the late 1940s.

Could there be another fertility switchback?

Fertility is inherently the great unknown in demographic projections. The postwar baby boom came out of the blue, as did the ensuing baby bust. Could another fertility switchback surprise us again?

One thing is clear: demographic time is running out. With 20 years now elapsing between birth and work, the 2020s are upon us as far as future additions to the workforce are concerned. Furthermore, a rise in fertility would make the dependency crunch in the next two decades even worse: the working age population would have to support an increasing number of children as well as a rapidly rising elderly population.

In fact, demographic projections already factor in some recovery in fertility or a stablization in birth rates. For example, the UN's central case has Italian and German fertility rates returning to 1.5 by the 2020s. Japan's fertility is projected to reach 1.7 by then and Britain's is forecast to return to 1.9. The Organisation for Economic Co-operation and Development, the thinktank for richer countries, has based projections of rapid ageing among its members on the conservative assumption of a return to replacement fertility of 2.1 by 2030.[29]

So the real question – given the scale of ageing already anticipated in these projections – is whether fertility might recover by even more. To assess this question, we need to understand what has been driving the fertility switchback. There are essentially two broad explanations, one focusing on economic incentives, the other on cultural influences and attitudes. Both, however, point to the same conclusion: a second baby boom isn't even a blip on the screen.

The new home economics

Lessons in home economics used to prepare women for a life in the home bringing up children. The new home economics, by contrast, explains how women's move out of the home and into the labor market has caused fertility to fall.

The link between fertility and economic conditions goes back a long time. We tend to think that regulation of fertility has only been possible since the contraceptive pill, but there is ample evidence of effective birth control further back in the past in response to adverse economic conditions. One way was to restrict marriage, increasing the number of spinsters, an effective method when there were strong social sanctions against illegitimate births. The other was to use techniques like extended breastfeeding, which has a contraceptive effect, and *coitus interruptus*, referred to coyly as the art of 'threshing inside and winnowing outside'.[30]

There was little winnowing outside when North America was being settled and every hand was needed to break the virgin soil. Under these conditions, exceptionally high fertility rates were recorded. Widows with children, the wallflowers of the marriage market, became hot property. Adam Smith noted in 1776 that they were 'frequently courted as a sort of fortune. The value of the children is the greatest of all encouragements to marriage.'[31]

The same link between fertility and the economy was at work in the interwar years in countries like the US and the UK. This time, with the economy depressed and unemployment at record highs, the number of people who never married soared and the birth rate fell.

The puzzle posed by the postwar baby boom and bust is why fertility should have fallen while living standards have continued to rise.

The most influential explanation, formulated by Nobel prize winner Gary Becker, is that the cost of children has risen sharply. Because skills and expertise are so vital now, children remain dependent for much longer and parents have to invest much more in educating them. Even more importantly, women's entry into the labor force has raised the price tag on children. Women either lose earnings when they are looking after their family or have to pay for expensive childcare.[32]

These economic disincentives to having children make a sharp rebound in fertility improbable. The cost of having children continues to rise. The educational bill spirals upwards, as does the opportunity cost for mothers who leave the workplace, especially now that women's earnings are approaching men's. The new home economics suggest that children are continuing to price themselves out of the market.

Auf Wiedersehen, Kinder, Küche, Kirche

The very persistence of low fertility also suggests that we have moved into a new regime and highlights the importance of changed attitudes. Underlying the agequake is a *gender*quake. The majority of today's young women want to have children – that emerges from all surveys – but they also want careers. That means getting qualified to the hilt, which in turn means a delayed entry into the labor market, followed by a period of hectic activity to build up one's career potential.

The inevitable consequence is that children are postponed. Since the mid-1980s, for example, more European women have been having more children in their early thirties than in their early twenties – an unprecedented development. This delay in having children brings down fertility: there is a strong link between a woman's age at first birth and the average size of her family.[33]

The link works in two ways. First, the proportion of women who end up having no children at all has risen remorselessly. In the UK, about a fifth of women born in 1960 are expected to be childless, compared with a tenth of those born in 1945. Similar trends are affecting the rest of Europe, Japan and other highly developed parts of the Far East like Hong Kong and Singapore.[34]

Secondly, the women who do have children don't have enough to compensate for the increasing incidence of childlessness. The delay in first births occurs because women are juggling career and children. One way to resolve the dilemma is to have only one child; another is to stop at two. In parts of central and northern Italy, only children have become the norm.[35]

The genderquake is transforming attitudes towards women's place in society. There is no longer the overwhelming social pressure to conform to a template of maternity. With high divorce rates, women have naturally become more intent on ensuring their own careers.

This cultural revolution is not confined to the West. Television has disseminated the low-fertility lifestyle in the developing world. In Brazil, TV soap operas have created new role models for women, reducing the number of children they want. In Iran, the number of television sets per head of population rose threefold between 1986 and 1996, a period in which the fertility rate plunged unexpectedly.[36]

The continuing increase in women's education also suggests that the new regime of low fertility is here for good. The better educated you are, the lower on average your fertility is likely to be. A recent investigation in the US has shown that this relationship was unshaken and may even have strengthened between 1925 and 1990. Furthermore, girls are now outstripping boys at school. With better qualifications and a scarcity of young people, the effect will be to push up women's potential earnings still further, making it even more unlikely that they will forsake the chance to establish their independence.[37]

Sperm on the run

Many women put off having children, only to regret the ticking of the biological clock. The onward march of medical science might seem to offer the opportunity to silence that relentless ticking, but the world's first 60-year-old mother remains a medical curiosity rather than a portent for a different demographic future.

In-vitro fertilization (IVF) allows women to have children as late as their fifties, but there is an acute shortage of donor eggs. For those who argue that such techniques can halt fertility decline and thus ageing, it's time for a reality check. Fertility rates for women in their early forties may have risen in some countries, but such births contribute under 2 percent to total fertility across the age spectrum of childbearing in Germany and the UK and only around 1 percent in the US and Denmark.[38]

In the future there may be another problem: declining sperm counts. In 1992, Niels Skakkebaek of Copenhagen University documented a general trend in which sperm density had dropped by almost a half in 50 years. These findings were disputed but, in 1997, leading Californian epidemiologists confirmed them for Europe and the US. In addition, scientists at the Edinburgh Reproductive Biology Unit have shown that Scottish men born after 1970 have significantly lower counts than those born before 1959. Falling sperm counts, thought to be linked to environmental pollutants which mimic the effects of oestrogens and may also explain the rising incidence of testicular cancer, have not contributed to declining birth rates so far; although increasingly the finger of suspicion at infertility clinics points at the testicles rather than the ovaries. However, new research by Skakkebaek suggests that the threshold when falling sperm counts do materially affect fertility in the population at large may be double the level conventionally assumed: 40 million per milliliter rather than 20 million. On this basis, Dr Stewart Irvine, of the Edinburgh Unit, warns that 'if the trend continues it could materially affect fertility in Britain within thirty or so years' time'. Unpublished research findings suggest that Danish men may already be approaching this level.[39]

The new age of immigration

There is one possible antidote to the effects of these trends in both mortality and fertility: immigration. Immigrants are predominantly young and they compensate for population decline. Could they be the cavalry that will ride to the rescue of ageing and declining western populations?

Despite all the barriers that developed countries have erected against the free movement of people, a second age of immigration has begun. In the past 15 years, inflows into the US have hit postwar record levels. Net immigration, both legal and illegal, has been running at around 800,000 a year in the 1990s. Inflows into Germany after the Berlin Wall came down have been just as eyecatching. At its peak in 1992, net immigration was almost 800,000. Without this influx, Germany's population would actually have declined by 76,000.[40]

Short-run surges in immigration are hard to predict: no one could have anticipated the collapse of the Soviet Union, for example. However, the longer-term increase in immigration over the past 15 years should have come as less of a surprise. Long-run trends in international migration are strongly linked to demographic pressures. In a nutshell, emigration rises sharply when high birth rates lead to fast population growth. More precisely, it rises sharply with a delay of about 20 or so years, reflecting the fact that 20-year-olds are the most footloose. That's why an upsurge in emigration was quite predictable for the 1990s: the population explosion in the developing countries reached its climax in the late 1960s and early 1970s.[41]

The different population trajectories of the developed and the developing world have created low- and high-pressure zones. In the developed world, ageing populations produce an area of low pressure. In the developing world, the arrival of more and more young people on to the labor market creates a high-pressure zone. The inevitable result: people on the move, trying everywhere to break through the barriers of immigration controls.

In the Americas, the dividing line between the pressure zones is the Rio Grande. In Europe, the Mediterranean is the front line; by the year 2000, 15–24-year-olds will account for a fifth of Algeria's population, compared with a tenth of Italy's. To the East, the pressure gap may not be quite so extreme but is still a force to be reckoned with. Whereas birth rates collapsed in western Europe during the 1970s, they rose in eastern Europe because of pronatalist incentives introduced by Communist regimes. The consequence 20 years on is a mini bulge of young people in the East compared with the shortfall in the West.[42]

Immigration can only mitigate, not prevent ageing

A new era of immigration may have begun, but current inflows cannot prevent the agequake. The Organisation for Economic Co-operation and Development has mounted a major research project into the effects of ageing. A startling finding is that net migrant flows would have to rise to between five and ten times their present levels to neutralize the problems of ageing.[43]

This conclusion is spelt out in some stark numbers. The OECD calculated how many immigrants you would need to freeze the old age dependency ratio, the ratio of retirees to people of working age, at its 2010 level in 2020. Look at Figure 8. The US would need 66 *million* extra immigrants, 11 times more than net migration between 1985 and 1995. Japan would need over 20 million, even though net migration between 1985 and 1995 was actually negative: more people left than entered.[44]

A crucial point to grasp is that higher inflows would have to be sustained indefinitely. The new immigrants arriving in the 1990s will themselves age as inevitably as the existing population. So without a meaningful long-term recovery in the birth rate, they too will eventually become a burden. While immigrants do tend to have higher fertility initially, it tends to converge on the national average and thus only helps to a limited extent.

There is a further drawback to the idea of flinging open the doors to immigration as an antidote to ageing. New arrivals undoubtedly boost the number of people of working age, but they are generally less skilled and face language difficulties. The increase in the effective workforce – which takes into account 'human capital' – would therefore be much less. New arrivals from Mexico in the US earn less than half the earnings of native-born Americans, so on this calculation you

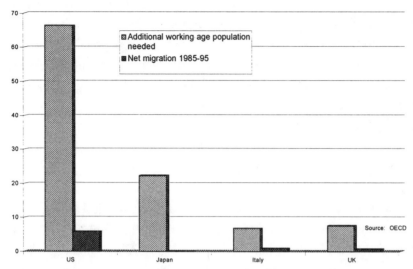

Figure 8 Thinking the unthinkable
The number of immigrants (in millions) needed to freeze old age dependency ratios in 2020 at their 2010 levels

would need two such immigrants to compensate for one 'missing' native-born endowed with all the stock of human capital needed in a modern economy.[45]

The American National Research Council (NRC) argues that immigrants will eventually help meet the bill for the US's ageing population. During their lives, immigrants will contribute an average of $80,000 in today's money to the public purse. But this view is not shared by everyone; opponents say that these benefits are a long way off. In the meantime, state governments have to make heavy investments in schooling and other welfare services to help new immigrants and their families.[46]

Mounting pressures to restrict immigration

Actual immigration flows will be determined by a battle between demographic and economic pressures and public hostility to immigration. This hostility is mounting throughout the West in response to the recent upsurge in immigration levels.

Two-thirds of people in Britain, Sweden and Spain want less immigration, as do over three-quarters of Germans. Far right German politicians capitalized on hostility to immigrants in a regional election in spring 1998: the Deutsche Volksunion party won 13 percent of the vote on an anti-foreigner campaign in the economically stricken eastern state of Saxony-Anhalt. Like Le Pen's Front National, the DVU polled heavily among disaffected young people.[47]

Compared with Japan and Europe, the US has been relatively hospitable to immigration in the past 15 years. Yet even here, patience is wearing thin. Opinion polls have shown increasing opposition to current levels of immigration: by the mid-1990s, two-thirds of Americans favored lower immigration. This compares to a third holding this view in the 1960s and almost half in the mid-1980s. Along the border with Mexico, a 'Tortilla Curtain' of steel walls and razor-wire barriers has been raised at key crossing points.[48]

What this suggests is that further increases in immigration flows are unlikely. If anything, the screws will be tightened to keep more immigrants out. Since the big influxes of the early 1990s, Europe has been trying to pull up the drawbridge. Immigration flows are substantially down – though not in the UK and the Irish Republic. In Germany, applications for asylum more than halved after changes to the law in 1993. Turkish hopes of entering the European Union, which would allow free movement of labor, were dashed yet again in 1998 at the instigation of German Chancellor Kohl.

The baseline projection of Eurostat, the EC's statistical office, is that net immigration will run at around 600,000 a year. Under its 'low' scenario, inflows run at 400,000 a year, which is still higher than in the early 1980s. Such is the intensity of opposition to immigration in Europe that the low scenario may turn out to be more realistic.

In the long run we are older

In the 1930s, the famous economist John Maynard Keynes struck a telling phrase – in the long run we are dead – to back up his call for urgent action to save the world from depression. I want to suggest another phrase: in the long run we are older. Global ageing will set the social and economic parameters of the near future. There are so many over-hyped exercises in futurology, particularly at the dawn of a new millennium, that many discount it altogether. This is a mistake when it comes to demographic trends, especially those as entrenched as the faultlines of the agequake.

The agequake won't erupt in earnest for 20 years. But its foreshocks will be felt long before that; indeed, they are already rippling through the world economy. In Part Two, I'm going to give you advance warning of what lies ahead over the next 10 or so years. The tremors will shake all aspects of your life, from prospects for the stock market to the value of your house, from the outlook for jobs to the future of your pension. Anticipating these changes will allow you to exploit them to the hilt.

Part Two

Tremors

3

Financial rollercoaster

SHAKESPEARE IDENTIFIED SEVEN AGES OF MAN, BUT IN FINANCIAL TERMS there are just three in adult life. In the first we are net borrowers, as we form households and start families. At this stage we are acquiring real assets – houses and durable goods – but incurring heavy financial debts. What little spare cash we have we tend to keep in banks or building societies so that we can call on it at short notice. Around 40, we move into our second age. The focus shifts to acquiring long-term financial assets, principally equities and bonds. Much of the acquisition occurs indirectly through pension funds. Our collective accumulation of assets in this period of our lives amounts to around half of total national wealth. Finally, in old age, a large portion of these savings is run down.[1]

What is happening now is that a record number of people are reaching the twin peaks, their forties and fifties, for this build-up of financial assets. With Bill Clinton leading the way, the first baby boomers turned 50 in 1996. In the 10 years to 2006, the number of 50-year-olds in the US will rise by half as much again to reach 38 million. Meanwhile, Americans born at the peak of the baby boom in the late 1950s are turning 40 at a rate of nine a minute.

The expanding number of 40- and 50-year-olds has to be set against what is happening to the population as a whole. For example, the boost to financial markets in the US in the late 1990s and early 2000s comes not just from ageing boomers but from the slowest growth of retirees since the war. The declining number of young people in western Europe should also push up overall savings, since on the lifecycle model they are net borrowers.

A simple way of capturing the overall effect of these age shifts is to work out how the number of people in the key years for accumulating financial wealth stacks up in relation to the adult population. I call this the 'twin peaks ratio': the number of 40- and 50-year-olds as a percentage of the adult population. Take a look at Figure 9, which shows how the American ratio has been moving since the early 1980s – and how this has tracked the shift of household wealth into equities. In 1986 it reached a postwar low point of around 28 percent, as the small generation born in the 1930s, by then in their fifties, were outnumbered by younger boomers. Since then, it has risen inexorably to 36 percent in 1998. The rise isn't over: it will continue until reaching a high point of 39 percent in 2006.

Here in a nutshell you have the demographic impulse for the long boom on Wall Street in the 1980s and 1990s. Furthermore, you can see how long this impetus will last. The number of 40- and 50-year-olds continues to grow in relation to the adult population until 2006, when

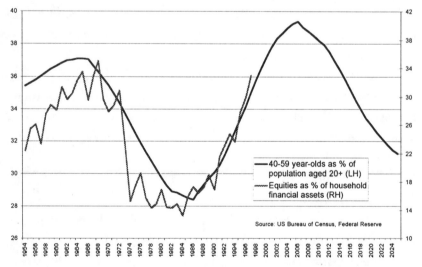

Figure 9 US twin peaks ratio and household equity exposure

it starts to decline as the first baby boomers turn 60. The ratio is also pushed down by a bounceback in the number of 20-year-olds as the 'echo boomers' – the children of baby boomers – leave their teens.

The British 'twin peaks ratio' rises in more subdued fashion than its American cousin but otherwise moves in tandem, turning up in 1987 and increasing throughout the 1990s. It also shows a good fit with the build-up of long-term financial assets in household wealth. As with the US, an important reason for the increase in the twin peaks ratio is the replacement in the 40–59 age group of the small age group born in the 1930s by the first postwar baby boomers. However, because the British baby boom topped out later than the US – in 1964 rather than in 1957 – the British twin peaks ratio reaches a maximum later, around 2012.

The 'twin peaks' era and the equity boom

These common patterns suggest that a demographic bulge has stoked a financial boom. There are a number of ways in which this has occurred. First, 40- and 50-year-olds are in the phase of their lives when they accumulate retirement funds in earnest, principally the long-term financial assets of stocks and bonds. Middle age is also the time in people's lives when they are most comfortable about holding riskier assets like shares. They can take a long view and so ride out the inevitable ups and downs of stock markets. They know that if equities do disappoint, they can make up for it by extra saving out of their working income.[2]

The 'twin peaks' era is a world away from the late 1960s and 1970s when the baby-boom generation first entered the economy. Young people are in a hurry to acquire cars and a home. As they barge their way into the economy, there is a battle for limited resources, argues Richard Hokenson, chief economist at American investment bank Donaldson, Lufkin & Jenrette. In the 1960s and 1970s that struggle was ultimately resolved through a surge in inflation, which was lethal for government bonds that pay a fixed income but also highly damaging for equities.[3]

By the 1980s, the youth shock was over and the transition to a more middle-aged economy was under way. Under these conditions, governments found it easier to deliver lower inflation. As inflationary fears receded, investors demanded less of a safety margin for buying bonds. The resulting boom in bond prices helped boost shares, which generally move in step with the bond market. The bond market has also benefited from the slowdown in the growth of the world's population after it reached a peak of about 2 percent a year in the late 1960s. The earlier acceleration in population increase contributed to the commodity price explosion of the 1970s as more and more young people entered the global economy. The subsequent deceleration has contributed to the commodity price declines of the past 15 years.

While the share price valuations put on corporate earnings have risen dramatically, those earnings, too, have increased fast. One reason for this profits recovery is again demographic. The growing number of workers in their most productive years has boosted corporate performance. The impetus to raise earnings has also been driven by the increased focus on shareholder value as ageing baby boomers increase their exposure to the equity market and pension funds flex their muscles.

An obvious retort to this demographic account of the equity boom is that the build-up in assets has occurred primarily through a valuation effect, through the very same run-up on Wall Street and in the City. In the US in particular, baby boomers haven't been saving like mad; they have let a roaring stock market fueled by over-easy credit do the hard work for them. By the same token, the increase in financial wealth could turn out to be as illusory as the Japanese equity bubble of the 1980s.

It is certainly true that the conventional measure of American personal savings has been in freefall in the 1990s. However, this misses the point on at least two counts. The first is technical, so skip it if you want to: the gist is that the fall in savings has been exaggerated precisely because of the stock market boom.

For technical junkies, the distortion has occurred because the stock market boom has magnified capital gains and taxes on them. Personal savings are defined as the difference between personal post-tax income and consumption. In the US, official statisticians don't count capital gains as income but do knock off capital gains taxes when calculating post-tax income. The effect of this illogical definition has become more pronounced in a bull market, since both capital gains and the taxes on them have soared. In 1997, mutual funds distributed capital gains of almost $200 billion, a twentyfold increase on 1990.[4]

Second and more significant, any economic model worth its salt expects savings to fall and consumption to increase as wealth rises. In the 1990s, the financial wealth of American households increased by trillions of dollars. Arguably, what is really surprising is that there wasn't more of a spending spree. In Britain, the personal savings ratio rose sharply from the late 1980s and then remained broadly stable, repeatedly confounding Treasury forecasts that it would fall as a result of increasing wealth.

More generally, the personal savings in any one country are only one ingredient in a big, global pool. The 1990s have seen concerted efforts to bring down government deficits in the West, as much as anything because of concerns about the future impact of an ageing population. In the US, the federal government's budget swung into surplus in 1998 for the first time since 1969. This was partly because of the huge increase in capital gains taxes, but it was also because of extra contributions being made to social security to shore up the pension system following reforms in 1983. Favorable trends in government finances have helped push down long-term interest rates, which has in turn bolstered stock markets.[5]

From counter-culture to equity culture

As any good cook knows, you need a touch of zest to make the perfect soufflé. That zest has been a generational love affair between baby boomers and shares that goes beyond the effects of age. In the 1960s boomers invented counter-culture; but in the 1990s they embraced equity culture. Counter-culture was by comparison a one-night stand: equity culture is here to stay, not just in the US but across the world.

This heady new love affair has made US mutual funds reach for the sky. Once they were dwarfed by bank assets. As recently as 1990 they were only a third of the size of the banking system. By the end of 1998, however, with assets of over $5 trillion mutual funds stood eye to eye with banks. This followed an astonishing growth spurt over two decades, with stock funds, which invest in equities, the star performers. In 1980 fewer than 5 million households owned mutual funds, but by 1997 their number had risen to over 37 million.[6]

So who were these investors transforming the American financial system? A survey in 1996 revealed that more than half of all mutual fund owners were baby boomers. Their average age was 44, their average household income $60,000 and two-fifths still had dependent children. Over four-fifths said they were saving through mutual funds for retirement.[7]

A key implication of this and other surveys was that even more members of the baby-boom generation would invest in mutual funds in future years. That's because ownership is heavily skewed towards wealthier households: almost three-quarters of those earning $75,000 or more in 1996 owned mutual funds, compared with just over a third of households on $35,000–50,000. So as boomers move into the prime earnings years of their late forties and early fifties, investment in mutual funds should continue to rise.[8]

The baby-boom generation has made a long journey from counter-culture to equity culture, but GenXers – those born between the mid-1960s and late 1970s – have signed up double quick to an equity cult. GenXers may be smaller in number than boomers, but they already have a higher proportion of their financial assets in mutual funds – 38 percent compared with boomers' 27 percent in 1996. A similar GenX enthusiasm for equities has been detected in the UK by market researcher Mintel.[9]

Much of the commitment to equity investment has come via tax-favored pension funds like the 401(k). That's the grabby name given by the American tax authorities to the fastest-growing form of retirement plan in the US, an employer-sponsored but individually controlled pension fund. According to domestic fund managers, you had to see the effect of Friday 401(k) paycheck deductions pouring into stocks on Monday to understand the power of the 1990s bull market. Assets in 401(k) plans more than doubled between 1990 and 1998, to reach a trillion dollars. By this point three-quarters of eligible workers were participating in such schemes.[10]

Whenever the government gives a tax break for savings, it is always an open question whether it stimulates extra saving or simply diverts existing saving into the new tax-favored channel. Leading American economists investigating this question say that 401(k)s haven't simply rearranged the savings furniture: they really have generated more saving. The same research also points to a powerful GenX effect. GenXers born in 1969 stand to collect over a third more than boomers born in 1959.[11]

The explosion of the American mutual funds industry and the rise of individually controlled pensions like the 401(k) mark the beginning of a global shareholder culture, says David Hale, chief economist at Zurich Insurance. He argues that the US equity boom of the 1990s had deeper sources than the fall in inflation and resurgent corporate profits. In his judgment, it was 'the first stage of a global financial revolution'. He predicts that the total world number of shareowners will grow tenfold, from fewer than 100 million when the cold war ended in 1989 to over a billion by the year 2010, as both industrial and developing countries introduce pension funds.[12]

Europe's turn

Europeans will be prominent in the spread of this equity culture. Most countries in mainland Europe have long stood aloof from the boisterous world of Anglo-Saxon share markets and equity ownership. Their stock markets have been stunted in relation to the size of their economies – but not for much longer.

Favorable demographics set the stage for a similar build-up of financial assets to the one seen in America. A similar bulge in the key age

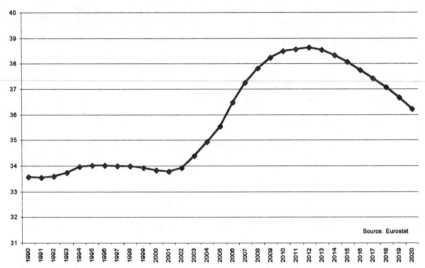

Figure 10 German twin peaks ratio 1990–2020
40–59-year-olds as percentage of adult population

bracket of 40- and 50-year-olds is on its way. The reason for the delay
compared with the US is the different demographic footprint of the
past. After an immediate surge in births after the war, fertility fell back
in many European countries until the mid-1950s when the real postwar
baby boom got under way, peaking in 1964, seven years after the US.[13]

Germany illustrates how distinct birth patterns long in the past
can lead to a quite different trajectory for the age structure of the
population. Unlike Britain and the US which experienced a baby bust
in the 1930s, Germany had a baby boom under Hitler. By contrast,
the late 1940s and early 1950s were a period of relatively low fertility.
The key decade for higher fertility was the 1960s. As a result, the ratio
of 40- and 50-year-olds to the adult population as a whole has been
broadly stable in the 1980s and 1990s. The big rise is scheduled for
the next 10 years as the generation born in the 1960s turns 40 (see
Figure 10).

Since European baby booms were weaker and shorter than those in
North America, the overall upswing in the key age group for acquiring
financial assets is not as large as in the US. But over the next decade,

the rise in the ratio of 40- and 50-year-olds to the adult population will just about match the second lap of the American increase. With a broadly similar pattern across mainland Europe, demographics will support stocks and shares in the first decade of the twenty-first century.

Embracing shareholder value

Europeans are also undergoing a generational sea change in attitudes towards share ownership. American equity culture has spread to Europe. As in the US, baby boomers have crossed the Rubicon. On the side they have left, their interests as workers were paramount. On the side they have reached, their interests as investors come first. Now that Europeans are asserting their rights as savers and investors as well as wage earners, they have served notice on economic systems that waste capital. Low returns are no longer tolerated.

This development has brought to a summary close a brief debate in the mid-1990s about the supposed superiority of 'stakeholder capitalism', a term borrowed from management consultants. Stakeholder economies were praised to the skies for the way in which they balanced the interests of employees and customers as well as shareholders. But by the time the role model of stakeholder capitalism was being urged on Britain, it was approaching its sell-by date in its German heartland. More telling than any debate was a Damascene conversion by German bosses. Led by Jürgen Schrempp of Daimler-Benz, they embraced the alien faith of shareholder value. When they saw the light, the phrase was heresy. But as equity culture began to spread in the European stock market boom of the late 1990s, shareholder value became the new credo.

Management consultants McKinsey estimate that the mutual fund market in Germany will increase fourfold between 1995 and 2005 to reach a total of DM1.5 trillion. With only a tenth of German household financial wealth in equities – compared with over a third in the US – the scope for further growth is self-evident. According to German fund managers like Dresdner Bank's DIT, the interest is most marked among people in their thirties and early forties, spurred by concerns about the viability of public pension schemes. Market research has shown that over half the population under 50 no longer believe that future governments will deliver on current promises.[14]

This generational shift could act like a turbo-charger for German financial markets still pygmy-like in relation to the size of the German economy. The potential arises from the gap between returns on equity made by German companies and Anglo-Saxon firms. With financial markets now believing that this gap will be closed, share prices have risen to what look like perilous valuations on historic measures. However, they may be warranted if a new era of shareholder value and corporate restructuring is dawning in mainland Europe.

Banquo's ghost turns up in Tokyo

Powerful demographic impulses – both actual and anticipated – thus contributed to the bull run on western stock markets in the 1990s. As boomers entered their forties and fifties, more and more of this key group have been building up their holdings of stocks and shares. This simple ageing effect has been reinforced by a generational shift – the much greater readiness of boomers and GenXers alike to invest in equities.

But throughout the 1990s there was a ghost at the feast: the Japanese stock market. In the 1980s, the benchmark Nikkei stock index rose like a rocket. By the end of the decade, Japanese equities were worth more than Wall Street and amounted to 41 percent of total world market capitalization. In 1990, the rocket fell to earth: the Nikkei dropped by over a third. By August 1992, the Tokyo stock market had fallen by more in real terms than the American stock market in 1932 after the crash of 1929. Six years later, the Nikkei index plunged even lower. In spring 1998, the UK stock market became more valuable than the Japanese, even though the British economy was less than half the size of Japan's.[15]

Yet when it comes to trying to build up financial assets, the Japanese are the sumo champions, not least because of their ageing population. Excess savings poured into government bonds in the 1990s, pushing yields to historic lows and creating a wild boom even as the stock market continued to sag. Excess savings also contributed to the economy's limp performance in the 1990s by consistently exceeding investment opportunities. All of which sounds a worrying warning: attempts by ageing populations to build up financial assets for their retirement could simply push economies into recession rather than stock markets into orbit.

For most of the 1990s, an outflow of Japanese savings helped sustain the US bond and stock markets. But in 1998, Japan started to export not just savings but recession. A further sharp decline in its economy undermined hopes of a quick recovery in South-East Asia. Japan's ailing economy, combined with the unwinding of financial speculation, threatened to throw the world into an economic tailspin, prompting talk about the onset of global depression.

The Japanese economic trauma is a salutary antidote to inveterate bulls who see stock markets traveling only upwards. History also puts us on our guard. The last great depression occurred in the 1930s during an earlier aborted run at an agequake, when western population growth plunged. Could we now be repeating the experience of the interwar years?

Japan in the 1990s certainly gave every sign of having returned unhappily to the future. Sorrows never come as single spies but in battalions; and so with Japan, afflicted by the dreaded 3Ds of the 1930s: debt, deflation and depression. Repeated attempts were made to kick-start the economy: package upon package of fiscal loosening (though many of these promised more than they delivered) and cuts in interest rates to wafer-thin levels. The economy stayed stuck in its 3D rut.

But underpinning the dreaded 3Ds was a fourth also prominent in the 1930s: adverse demographics. Throughout the 1990s, the kernel of the Japanese problem has been lack of investment opportunities to match the flow of savings. The Japanese have been saving prodigiously for their retirement. But because of past fertility declines, the working-age population is starting to decline. That means there are fewer investment opportunities, since there are fewer people to equip with capital.

It was precisely this analysis that Alvin Hansen made in his presidential address to the American Economic Association in 1938. We suffer from 'secular stagnation – sick recoveries which die in their infancy and depressions which feed on themselves', he declared, words with an eerie resonance for Japan's stuttering economy. Hansen highlighted the fall in the rate of population increase as the main cause, since it had reduced the demand for investment.[16]

Sixty years on, prominent economist Paul Krugman of MIT has been thinking along similar lines. His diagnosis of the Japanese disease resurrects an old Keynesian chestnut, the so-called liquidity trap, where the central bank loses power to stimulate the economy by lowering interest rates. Krugman believes that adverse demographics have ensnared Japan in the trap. Chillingly, he asks whether Japan may not be the forerunner for problems elsewhere: 'Europe faces Japan-style demographics; could a liquidity trap happen to EMU?'[17]

Dry run for the demographic downswing?

Japan is certainly showing the economic dangers that lie ahead as populations age. In *The Great Population Spike and After*, eminent economist Walt Rostow says that Hansen's earlier analysis, while premature, 'may well become a central preoccupation of the coming century'.[18]

The question is when and where. Within Europe, only Italy faces Japan-style demographics in the immediate future. Europe's labor force is likely to rise somewhat in the 2000s rather than drop sharply as in Japan. Indeed, employment could increase substantially if the big labor reserve of unemployed workers is drawn down and more women enter the workforce. The demographic crunch is a good 10 years away in Europe.

Japan's vulnerability to adverse demographics also lies in an economic and political system way past its sell-by date. Procrastination rules, partly because of the need to win consensus, partly because it worked in the past. Instead of closing down banks and writing off bad debt in a sudden-death financial reconstruction, the Japanese crossed their fingers and hoped for the best. This time, however, procrastination backfired: things got worse and worse. By contrast, the US faced a similar problem with the build-up of bad debts in savings and loans institutions in the 1980s, but lanced the boil by setting up the Resolution Trust Corporation, which swiftly disposed of assets to bring down debts to a manageable level.[19]

Belatedly in 1998, the Japanese embarked on measures that they should have taken years before to clean up the banking system. Yet the banks' chronic sickness reflected a deeper malaise in the postwar Japanese economic model. That model was designed to funnel savings into investment in industry. This worked while Japan was catching up with the West, but has since led to overinvestment on a prodigious scale, effectively wasting capital.

Japan has to change from a manufacturing economy to a service economy, from a producer economy to a consumer economy. It needs to save and invest less, but with higher returns. This requires the discipline of a more independent financial system and the injection of shareholder values into the economy. A model designed for a developing economy with a young and growing labor force must now be reshaped for a mature economy with an ageing population and declining labor force.

Hence the crucial importance of Japan's 'Big Bang' reforms to liberalize the financial system by 2001. Under this deregulation plan, foreign exchange controls have been abolished, barriers between different types of financial organizations are being lifted and restrictions removed on the investment of corporate pension fund money. These reforms may sound technical, but they could transform a system geared to channeling saving into investment in industry, however low the returns, with one that puts savers' interests first. Big Bang ultimately offers an escape route for Japan from the mire of economic stagnation.[20]

The boomer bubble

The prospects for Japanese shares may therefore be less blighted than the pessimists would have it. But there is another chilling lesson from the Japanese ordeal: the ease with which financial bubbles can first inflate and then collapse.

Baby boomers have zealously learnt one lesson of history, that equity investment pays off handsomely in the long run. But history also teaches us that share prices are manic depressives. They rise to unrealistic highs for long periods during a surge of investor euphoria, fueled by easy credit. When euphoria gives way to panic, the bubble is burst and share prices plunge. The stock market boom may have been primed by the middle-ageing of Western populations, but by the late 1990s it had gained a momentum all its own. It had become a boomer bubble, with valuations stretched beyond any but the most optimistic rationalization.

Investigation into the past performance of bonds and equities spells out the handsome pay-off from long-term investment in shares. The research focuses on total real returns – the inflation adjusted pretax return on your original investment, assuming that you reinvest income. On this basis, equities have won by a mile in Britain since 1918, with an annual total return of 8 percent, compared with 2 percent on gilts, the long-term securities issued by the government.[21]

The same holds true for the US over an even longer period. Jeremy Siegel, author of the influential *Stocks in the Long Run*, has shown that stocks made 7 percent a year between 1802 and 1997, double the real return on bonds. In the twentieth century, stocks' superior performance has been even more marked, with equities again returning 7 percent a year between 1926 and 1997 while bonds returned only 2 percent. Similar real rates of return of equity – between 7 and 8 percent – have been clocked up since the Second World War in several European countries.[22]

The first lesson from history is thus clear: equity investment reaps rich returns in the long run. On that score, boomers and GenXers are on firm ground. But history also teaches a second, less congenial lesson: that *below-average* returns have occurred for protracted periods in the past. For example, investors who piled into the British stock market at the end of 1936 had a big fat zero to show for their pains 16 years later in real return on their original capital. It was a similar story for anyone unlucky enough to put funds into the market at the end of 1968: 14 years later their investment had returned precisely nothing.

With valuations stretched way beyond trend levels in the big boom of the 1990s, the danger is that many investors have been beguiled into expecting quite unfeasible returns on the stock market. Investing in equities has paid off handsomely in the past because investors have been paid a premium for the risk they take in parking their money in stocks – the risk that values are much more likely to fall sharply in any one year than are alternative, safer assets like bonds. But if investors routinely expect that premium, then they may price it away. Either there will be a crash or prices will stagnate for years to come; one way or another, future returns must be more modest. In a letter to the *Wall Street Journal* in April 1998, Jeremy Siegel, a proselytizer of long-term equity investment, counseled caution: 'the greatest danger for the market today stems from unrealistic expectations of what stocks can earn. In no way can the high stock returns of the past five years or even the past 15 years persist.'[23]

The demographic fundamentals remain favorable

Bubbles burst, but the demographic building blocks for a subsequent return to robust equity markets in the first decade of the twenty-first century remain in place. Middle-age spread will come to the rescue as the bulge of 40- and 50-year-olds continues to swell in the US until 2006; or 2008 if you assume a retirement age of 62 (the date mentioned by baby boomers in surveys). In mainland Europe, the analogous bulge only really gets under way in the first years of the century and continues rising until around 2013/14.

A further reason for long-term confidence is that the 2000s will see a continuing sharp rise in the number of 50-year-olds in the US. By 2010 they will comprise a half of the 40–59 age group, up from around 40 percent in the 1990s. This matters because saving is particularly intense at this stage in people's lives. New research into the demographics of retirement saving pinpoints the importance of the last few years at work. These are 'remarkably important in determining wealth levels during retirement', according to a study by the Institute for Fiscal Studies based on new data from the British Retirement Survey. The research shows that people in their late fifties who stayed in work doubled their financial assets in just six years.[24]

However, baby boomers will have to do more hard saving in the years ahead. It is unrealistic to suppose that valuations can stretch indefinitely. The decline in personal savings rates in the US leads some to despair at the apparent recalcitrance of baby boomers in not digging into their pockets. You can take another view: that they are target savers. A study of American households showed that families were accumulating wealth in the early 1990s at double the rate of their active saving, thanks principally to gains in equities. This suggests that if the equity market delivers the goods, then households will reduce their savings rates. If, however, the stock market fails to perform in the 2000s, they will increase their savings rates. In a typical economic feedback, this will then help support share prices.[25]

Gentlemen prefer bonds

Before the great love affair with equities began in the postwar era, investors were bigamous, putting their money equally in stocks and bonds and often preferring the latter. The advantage of bonds over equities is that in the short term their prices move about less, making them less risky. The disadvantage is that they are vulnerable to inflation shocks because their interest payments and principal are fixed.

The postwar era of high inflation eroded investors' faith in bonds as surely as it eroded their value. But consider this: in the 10 years from 1987 to 1997, the total real return on gilts was 7 percent a year – only one percentage point lower than long-term equity return from 1918 and with much less risk on a short-term holding basis. Equities did better, returning 10.5 percent, but by a considerably smaller margin over gilts than in the past.

According to Barclays Capital's review of gilts and equities in January 1998, a rerating of bonds started at the beginning of the 1990s, as investors started to regain faith in governments' ability and willingness to keep down inflation. Looking forward over the next 10 years, they argued for a higher weighting of gilts, reflecting their belief that 'gilts will continue to be rerated relative to equities'. Over the period to 2007, Barclays Capital forecast that returns on equities would outstrip those on bonds by only two percentage points, far less than the six percentage point advantage recorded in the past.

In practice, much of this rerating occurred in 1998. Bondholders reaped big gains as prices (which move inversely to yields) moved sharply ahead. Further major gains in the decade ahead hinge on the outlook for inflation. The key question is whether we are moving from a low-inflation era to price stability or even deflation.

If we are moving to deflation, then the rerating of bonds will continue apace. As Japan slumped in the 1990s, the government bond market made spectacular gains – small wonder when long-term interest rates fell in late 1998 to historically unprecedented levels of little more than half a percent. If consumer prices are falling, that can still translate into a reasonable real return.

Once again, however, Japan looks to be an early warning of more distant dangers rather than a model for what is to come in the next decade. The underlying demographics in the West may point to a low-inflation era, but sustained deflation seems unlikely. One principal source of disinflation in the US and Europe in the late 1990s has been falling prices for manufactured goods, reflecting the huge overcapacity in East Asia. As this excess capacity is written off and investment plans are ditched, this source of low inflation should start to dry up.[26]

The other main source of disinflation has been falling commodity prices, which have been in long-term retreat since their highs at the start of the 1980s. This downphase has lasted so long now that many make the mistake of assuming that it will continue indefinitely. This seems unlikely: commodity price cycles are a constant of economic history. Walt Rostow believes a commodity price upswing is coming despite the deceleration in global population growth. In *The Great Population Spike and After*, he argues that the industrial progress of Asia and Latin America is 'likely to produce a phase of rising prices in foodstuffs and raw materials' in the early part of the twenty-first century.[27]

Looking further ahead, a thunder cloud does hang over bonds: the looming pressure on state pension systems which threatens to drive national debts up to levels not seen since wartime (see Chapter 8). The danger is that one way or another governments will default on their obligations, either explicitly, or implicitly through inflation; note that Paul Krugman's remedy for the Japanese demographic disease is a return to inflation.

Despite this risk, bonds should be part of any investor's portfolio, particularly as you get older. If you are in your forties or fifties, it is fine to know that equities deliver in the long run even if they have cratered in the short term. It is a different matter altogether as you move into your sixties, when you should start to reweight in favor of bonds. But unless you think that inflation is cracked for good, expect bonds to deliver solid rather than spectacular performance in the 2000s.

Invest overseas – think demographic

The collapse of financial markets in South-East Asia and elsewhere in the developing world has put emerging markets off screen for all but the most intrepid of investors. Looking ahead, however, a well-chosen portfolio of developing countries should outperform in the long term because of their potential for high economic growth. The Asian crisis could eventually prove a boon to foreign investors by instigating much-needed reforms to the financial sector that will make markets more transparent and less risky.

A natural reaction to the Asian crisis has been to dismiss all the previous talk of an economic miracle. This is as erroneous as the original hype. The Asian miracle was no mirage, the Asian tigers were no paper tigers. In the 15 years from 1980 they achieved average annual growth rates of 7.5 percent combined with modest inflation. Before the crisis broke in 1990, the last year in which real GDP growth in Thailand was significantly less than 5 percent was 1972. In Malaysia it was 1986, South Korea 1980 and Indonesia 1985. This achievement stands in stark contrast to the vast majority of developing countries.[28]

Received wisdom on the causes of this unparalleled record of super-growth highlights openness to trade, high rates of investment by foreign companies, and a commitment to education, particularly at primary levels. However, this leaves unexplained the heart of the East Asian growth miracle, the ability of societies to mobilize astonishingly high rates of investment and saving. Now two Harvard economists, Jeffrey Williamson and David Bloom, have come up with an answer. You guessed it: the economic miracle was founded on a demographic miracle.[29]

Think back to the pyramids and Chinese lanterns in Chapter 1. If you look at any country in sub-Saharan Africa, the age structure is a broadly based pyramid. The adult population has its work cut out just bringing up children. But when family size drops as sharply and quickly as it did in East Asia, the age pyramid swiftly turns into a Chinese lantern, with the highest possible proportion of working-aged people to the total population. And that is only half the story: resources that used to go into bringing up children became free for saving. It was only in the early 1970s, when the youth dependency ratio began to fall, that savings rates jumped in the first tigers like South Korea. Altogether, these favorable demographic trends are estimated to account for a third to a half of the East Asian growth miracle.

A day of reckoning will come when the Chinese lantern turns into an inverted pyramid and the swollen ranks of working-age people retire. However, this won't start until around 2015–20 for the first tigers. The implication of this analysis is that the crisis of the late 1990s has not snuffed out growth in South-East Asia.

Even so, radical measures are needed to restore rapid growth in the more mature tigers. In South Korea, for example, the big lift to higher output from increased numbers of working people is mainly over. A study by McKinsey argued that 'across-the-board reform' was needed to restore the country's prospects. If Korea continued to pump resources into manufacturing, neglecting the service sector, long-term annual growth of income per head would not exceed 3 percent. But if the service sector were deregulated, per capita GDP growth could return to 6 percent a year.[30]

By contrast, South Asia is poised to repeat the earlier miracle of South-East Asia as it passes through a similar demographic transition to a favorable age structure in the years ahead. Fast economic growth should translate into higher returns on two counts. First, big rises in output feed through to the bottom line. Second, there is far less capital per worker in developing countries than in the West, so the return on it should be higher.

In the past, these higher returns have often not materialized because of opaque and rigged markets. Investors have ended up with portfolios unduly weighted to risky property rather than high-quality exporting companies that have remained in family hands. Emerging markets have outperformed in some years but collapsed in other years. Even before the Asian crisis submerged emerging markets, long-run returns from investing in them were lower as well as much riskier than staying fully invested in the US.[31]

However, the very weaknesses of the Asian model are now being addressed. The crisis has highlighted the dangers of unbalanced economic development, where industry races ahead but finance remains unmodernized. The keynote of reform across South-East Asia is a restructuring of financial systems to make them more transparent and enhance the interests of investors, both domestic and foreign. Furthermore, the shift in the age structure of these economies to people in their forties and older should now promote this focus on shareholder value.

One way of exploiting the growth potential of developing countries is to back the big multinationals which can exploit these huge new markets. Like investing in emerging markets, this notion took a knock in 1998. Big global companies such as Coca-Cola, identified as firms that could capitalize on the potential of globalization, were marked sharply down. But an easing in overstretched valuations does not invalidate the original concept. Instead, it could open up buying opportunities for investors, not least since the Asian crisis has been an opportunity for those very companies to buy up assets and firms at bargain basement prices.

The alternative strategy is to invest directly in emerging markets. This is the approach advocated by Burton Malkiel, best known for his classic A *Random Walk down Wall Street*, and JP Mei in *Global Bargain Hunting*, a guide to investing in emerging markets published with unfortunate bad timing in 1998. While these authors accept that this is a riskier strategy, they claim that it should ultimately prove more remunerative. They warn, however, that you need a strong stomach and a long-term investing outlook to cope with the high volatility of emerging markets. For those who possess those qualities, 'commitments today are likely to prove extremely rewarding over the years to come'.[32]

Prospects for the 2000s

The agequake is already shaking up the financial markets. A driving force behind the great boom of the 1990s has been the demographic bulge of increasingly middle-aged boomers. But like past stock market booms, it got out of hand and turned into a boomer bubble, with valuations overstretched by all historical yardsticks.

Whatever their genesis, all financial bubbles are eventually pricked. However, demographics should still underpin financial markets in the 2000s. More and more people in the US and Europe are moving into the twin peak years of 40–60, when they seek to build up their financial wealth. Governments are no longer eating up spare savings by running big deficits; some are even running surpluses.

A critical point of support is the impending shift away from public pension systems that recycle contributions to pension payments to privately funded schemes. In the US, debate has moved on astonishingly fast to think the unthinkable: the partial privatization of the once untouchable social security retirement scheme. In western Europe, there is widespread acknowledgment that private pension funds will have to assume more of the burden in future.

Bottom line: whatever short-term reverses may occur, the demographic fundamentals should bolster equity and bond markets in the 2000s. Despite the collapse of emerging markets in 1997–8, they offer tempting prospects for the demographic investor. Japan's economic trauma is a demographic dry run for a more distant future. Middle-age spread will provide comfort room for both bond and stock markets in the 2000s.

4

The new property game

THE PROPERTY CRASHES OF THE 1990S HAVE SHATTERED A DREAM. FOR the first time in decades, you can no longer play and win Monopoly with your own house. The new demographics are creating a new property game, in which gains will vary much more than before, according to the type of home and its location.

Unlike equities and other financial investments, where older age groups set the pace, young people have historically held the golden key to the housing market. In Britain, the crucial period has been between 20 and 35; in most other countries, it is between 25 and 35. These are the years when you get married, have children and buy your first home.

The supply of houses is effectively fixed in the short to medium term: it takes a long time to effect a substantial increase in housing stock. Resistance to new development has intensified in the past two decades. So when the first-time buyer age group is rising as a proportion of the adult population, an irresistible force hits an immovable object. Something has to give – that something is prices. Equally, when the share of this crucial age group in the population is falling, the housing market will be much less buoyant.

Boom and bust in the UK property market

Received wisdom blames the UK property boom and bust of the 1980s and 1990s on Conservative economic mismanagement. Nigel Lawson, Chancellor between 1983 and 1989, gets the rap for overrelaxing monetary policy at a time when the government had deregulated mortgage lending. When the economy careered out of control, its reckless driver had to slam the brakes on with 15 percent interest rates, which spelt sudden death for the housing market. However, the hidden hand of demographics was also at the wheel.

In the UK, house purchasing has historically started much earlier than in other countries. In the 1970s and 1980s, a third of all first-time purchases were made by people under 25; the peak ages for house purchase were 23–25. Even in the early 1990s, over a quarter of first-time buyers were under 25. So for the UK it makes sense to look at 20–34-year-olds.[1]

Strong growth in this age group kept the housing market bubbling away in the 1980s. In the 10 years to 1988, the peak of the boom, the 23–25 age group increased by a quarter. As prices soared, panic broke out. Worried that they would never get a foothold on the housing ladder, young people brought purchases forward. The overall effect was to push up first-time purchases by 500,000 between 1983 and 1988. As a result, the housing market peaked about three years before the 20–34 age group reached its high in 1991 (see Figure 11).[2]

Then the house price bubble burst and boom gave way to bust. Nearly a million people had their homes repossessed between 1990 and 1995 and many more found themselves in negative equity, with mortgages exceeding the value of their houses. When the market picked up in 1996 and 1997, it was a patchy recovery, with transactions way down on the record levels of 1987 and 1988. While prices shot up in some parts of London, it took until the start of 1998 for house prices throughout the UK to regain the level of 10 years earlier. In real terms, adjusted for consumer price inflation, they were still substantially lower.[3]

The housing market has been buffeted from several directions in the 1990s. Mortgage tax relief has been whittled away. Households

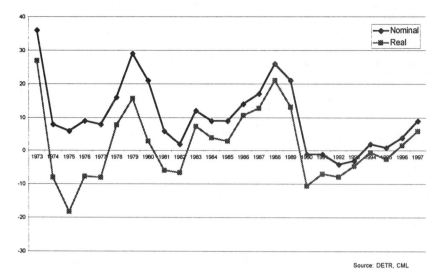

Source: DETR, CML

Figure 11 The boom–bust cycle in the UK housing market
Annual percent change in house prices

have been anxious to bring down the burden of mortgage debt, which became uncomfortably high in relation to the value of their homes when prices slumped in the early 1990s. However, a chill demographic wind has also been blowing. A reversal of earlier favorable population trends is a prime reason why the ensuing recovery has been so half-hearted.[4]

As Figure 12 shows, the baby bust of the 1970s is now working its way through to a sharp decline in the weight of 20–34-year-olds in the adult population. In particular, the number of 23–25-year-olds, so significant in the past, falls by 500,000 – a quarter – between 1995 and 2002. The demise of the first-time buyer removes a vital prop of the housing market, affecting its performance not just in the 1990s but in the first decade of the twenty-first century. Between 1998 and 2008, the ratio of 20–34-year-olds to the adult population falls by a seventh.[5]

A sophisticated statistical investigation of the boom and bust cycle in the British housing market in the *Economic Journal* corroborates the importance of shifts in and out of the first-time buyer age group. Research in Sweden, which experienced a similar boom–bust cycle, also highlights the importance of the changing weight of young adults

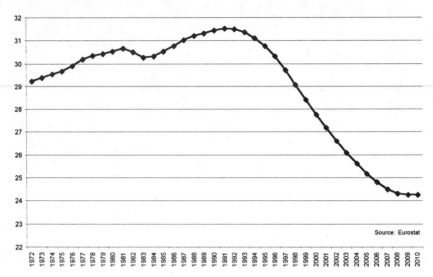

Figure 12 Rise and fall of the first-time buyers
20-34 year-olds as percentage of adult population, 1972–2010

in the population. The conclusion of John Muellbauer and Anthony Murphy in their study of the UK was that unfavorable demographic trends would dampen any upturn in the market after the 1990s slump. They also argued that this effect would be exacerbated by the increasing burden of debt young people are incurring in loans for higher education. No wonder the Halifax and other top building societies, traditional specialists in housing loans, converted to banks: they could see their prime borrowing customers were about to melt away.[6]

New age, new households
What makes the brows of building society chiefs furrow isn't necessarily a cue for ordinary homeowners to throw in the towel. Young people are vital customers for mortgage lenders, but they are not the only source of new households. And at the end of the day, it is new households that add to demand for homes, exhaust the existing stock of housing and push up prices in the private sector. Over the next decade and a half 20–34-year-olds may be a disappearing species, but the government still projects an extra 4.4 million households in England

between 1991 and 2016. That represents a much lower rate of increase compared with the 1980s, but it's still a big number, and one that has stirred up a hornet's nest of controversy as planners try to work out where they are to be housed.[7]

The burgeoning number of households at a time of sluggish population growth reflects a long-established trend in western countries as they age: the declining number of people living together. In Britain, the average size of household has fallen from 2.9 in 1971 to 2.4 in 1996. There is scope for it to fall still further: in Denmark, it is as low as 2.[8]

Four-fifths of the new households in England will consist of just one person, in itself a clear signal that the housing market of the twenty-first century will be very different from today's. A similar process is at work in the Netherlands, where almost all new households formed between 1996 and 2020 will be single-person ones, pushing up the national total by a fifth. In England, their number will jump by two-thirds between 1991 and 2016.[9]

Lower marriage rates mean that more and more people will be living by themselves. Over half the projected increase in the number of one-person households will consist of men and women who have never married. This increase will be particularly marked among 35–44-year-olds, with the number of single men and women in this category rising by over half a million by 2011. A further third will come from divorcees and separations.[10]

Contrary to what you might think, the great majority of the extra households will be owner-occupiers, says Alan Holmans, former chief housing economist at the Department of the Environment. He estimates that at least three-quarters of the new households formed between 1991 and 2011 will own their own home – a higher proportion than the two-thirds owner-occupier rate in the early 1990s. Of these privately purchased homes, the majority will be one-person households, as you would expect from the overall household projections.[11]

The continuing growth in households means that the alarmist talk about the demise of the housing market which surfaced in the dog days of the 1990s slump is off the mark. But house prices will no longer float effortlessly upwards on a rising demographic tide of young first-time buyers. Location, location, location is the mantra of all estate agents, but in tomorrow's housing market the watchword will be as much selection, selection, selection. Starter homes for young couples planning a family are no longer in demand; trendy lofts for affluent singles and divorcees are.

All the same, don't fall into the trap of assuming that most single people will want to live in town apartments. This is the dream of environmentalists, who favor urban cramming to building on greenfield sites, irrespective of people's actual desires or needs. It is an illusion to imagine that single people will obediently queue up for their places on 'brownfield' urban redevelopment. In the early 1990s, only a fifth of single owner-occupiers under the age of 60 lived in flats.[12]

With a higher proportion of future one-person households being younger there may be an increasing preference for city flats in the future. However, many will still plump for small houses with gardens in the country – and have the resources to make that choice stick. Many divorced men will also want homes large enough for their children to stay on weekend visits.[13]

The trade-up factor

In the new property game, trading up will be a much more potent force. This has already been a characteristic of the American housing recovery in the 1990s. A survey of homebuyers by the National Association of Realtors showed that 58 percent of home sales in 1997 were repeat buyers, mostly married couples. Buyers said that their need for more space and a larger home was a crucial reason for moving house.[14]

A similar trend is already affecting the British housing market. Figures from mortgage lenders show that trading up is fairly evenly distributed between 25–34 and 35–44-year-olds. The trend is for older age groups to become more significant in the trade-up market. Since 1982, the average age for repeat purchases in the housing market has risen from 36 to 39.[15]

The 35–44 age group is the one most likely to take the final step up the housing ladder. This is when the number of adults living as couples with dependent children peaks. It is the period in their lives when the demand for space – a larger home and a larger garden – is paramount. So if you want advance warning about shifts in the demand for big homes, this is the age group to monitor.[16]

Figure 13 shows what has been happening to the weight of 35–44-year-olds in the adult population. The ratio rose substantially in the mid-1980s, as the first wave of postwar baby boomers matured into their late thirties and early forties. The 1980s house price boom was thus also driven by the increasing number of people in their late thirties and early forties as well as the influx of first-time buyers. The share of the 35–44 age-group dropped in the mid-1990s, contributing in turn to the slump.

From 1995, the rollercoaster starts upwards again. Over the 10 years from 1995 to 2005 the ratio of those aged 35–44 to the adult population rises by a sixth, after which it begins a prolonged fall. But

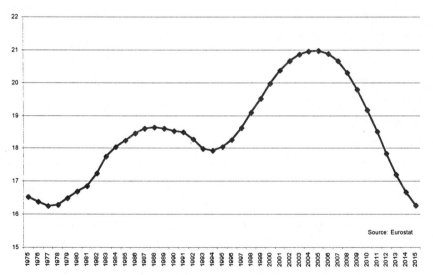

Source: Eurostat

Figure 13 *Demand for bigger homes to peak in the 2000s*
35–44-year-olds as a percentage of the UK's adult population, 1975–2015

don't leap to the conclusion that demand for large homes will imme-
diately suffer at this juncture. For one thing, there is also a growing
number of repeat purchases among 45–54-year-olds. For another, people want more and more space, not least because of the increasing
trend to working at home. This rises with age, as more people become
self-employed. Taking these influences into account, the final trade-up
market is likely to remain strong until at least 2010.

What this suggests is that there will be ample demographic support
for larger and more expensive homes in the first years of the twenty-
first century. The big gains will be made in quality homes in choice
locations as the better off among these boomer households bid up
prices.

Signs of this trend surfaced in the UK house market recovery of the
late 1990s. This was a remarkably patchy affair. The national picture
was one of stunted recovery, with average prices throughout the country only returning to their peak values of a decade earlier in early 1998.
But anyone living in up-market parts of London or the prosperous
commuter belt around the capital witnessed a very different story.
House prices in prime Central London almost doubled between 1992
and 1997, taking them well above their previous peak in 1989.[17]

According to property surveyors and estate agents FPD Savills, the
housing market in the late 1990s was increasingly polarized, with local
'hot spots' and 'black spots'. Hot spots were imposing period town-
houses, prestigious suburbs, fashionable new city-center locations, good
properties in picturesque nearby villages, and country houses. These
ranged from favored locations in London to the south-eastern suburbs
of Manchester; from the country house market around Bristol to the
city center of Leeds. Black spots were inner urban areas in economically
blighted regions. Hot spots and black spots could occur in the same
town. Prices soared between 1995 and 1997 in some select gentrifying
parts of Bristol, but sank like a stone on the other side of the city.[18]

A similar trend will occur through much of Europe, as the 35–44 age
group swells in response to the baby boom back in the 1960s. In
Germany there is a commensurate increase in the weight of this group

in the adult population between 1995 and 2005. As Nicola Düll of the IFO Institute in Munich points out, the big cohort born in the 1960s will reach the 'peak of their housing needs' in the 2000s.[19]

Empty nesters feathering new types of nest

Another trend to watch is the rise of the empty nesters, typically in their fifties. According to Harvard University's Joint Center for Housing Studies, the number of American couples without dependent children rose much faster in the 1990s than those still bringing up children. In the first decade of the twenty-first century, they will be the fastest-growing family type in the US with an increase of 5.5 million households. Meanwhile, married couples with dependent children will actually fall in number. Of course, many of the households without dependent children will still have adult children living with them. Even so, the number of empty nesters will rise sharply in the 2000s.[20]

The obvious prediction is that empty nesters will trade down to smaller, less valuable homes. This would undoubtedly knock the housing market. However, George Masnick, an American demographer who specializes in housing, says that 'empty nesters have been doing a lot of trading up'. Today's generation of empty nesters, he points out, demand more space than their predecessors who grew up in the depression years of the 1930s and had a less consumerist attitude to housing. The most successful buy trophy homes like the 'starter castles' of Aspen and Jackson Hole.

Today's empty nesters certainly seem to be looking for different kinds of homes in the US. Out with lots of bedrooms, but in with more bathrooms and luxurious amenities. Out with large gardens, but in with spacious patio houses in sought-after locations. However, predictions that empty nesters will repopulate city centers should be taken with a pinch of salt. Some may do so, but the housing specialists at Harvard say that most ageing baby boomers will remain in the suburbs or move even further away from the urban core.

In Britain, people over 55 are less likely to move than their American counterparts. In the early 1990s, owner-occupiers who did move tended to downsize, both in property value and in space. But members of the ensuing baby-boom generation may well behave more like their American counterparts. By the late 1990s, over-50s were starting to snap up expensive new apartments in the center of wealthy county towns like Winchester in the South of England.[21]

Second homes

The growing number of empty nesters will also boost the demand for holiday homes as the big family home is swapped for two smaller ones. American surveys show that vacation homes are typically owned by people in their mid-50s without dependent children. Demand for all second homes in the US grew by over 400,000 between 1995 and 1997 to reach 6 million. However, not all second homes are vacation homes: in the US, about half of them are used for recreational purposes. Sea, lakes, golf courses and mountains are the key draws.[22]

A further indicator to where people are buying holiday homes comes from timeshare statistics compiled by the American Resort Development Association. Timeshare has grown at a spectacular pace in the US – by 16 percent a year between 1992 and 1997. The average timeshare buyer is 49 years old, underlining the industry's growth prospects. In 1997, there were about 2 million owners in over 1000 resorts. Favored states were Florida and the Carolinas on the Eastern Seaboard, the Rocky Mountain states and California and Hawaii.[23]

A similar trend to greater ownership of second homes is also likely in Europe. Many will be bought in favored spots like the Dordogne, Tuscany and the Costa del Sol. In southern Spain, there are already more than 500,000 foreign-owned second homes, more than half of them British or German owned. Alan Holmans, former chief housing economist at the Department of Environment, forecasts a doubling in the number of owner-occupied second homes in England between 1991 and 2011. He attributes this increase to the growing number of people on large incomes. This trend has several sources, but one is the simple effect of ageing: as people get older their earnings become more widely dispersed.[24]

Immigrant power in the housing market

It could be the latest parlor game in California. You put your home on the market. Your realtor – estate agent – gets on the phone and tells you there's a possible buyer. Now for the quiz: what's his or her name? Smith comes top, as you might imagine, but second is Garcia. Indeed, no fewer than six of the top ten surnames of purchasers in 1998 were Hispanic. A further two were of Asian origin.[25]

In fact, the parlor game exaggerates the Hispanic influence: there is a greater clustering of surnames among Latinos and other new immigrant groups, as John Karevoll, the property analyst who did the database search, acknowledges. However, ethnic minorities – both first and second generation – now play a vital role in the Californian housing market. New immigration 'kept the housing market alive in the 1990s,' says Gerd-Ulf Krueger, economist at the Californian Association of Realtors. In 1998, a year when prices in several parts of the state reached an all-time high, 15 percent of buyers had been born outside the US. In Los Angeles County, the proportion is much higher.[26]

As ever, the Golden State is leading the way. In the mid-1990s, the American housing market took off. Between 1994 and 1997 the number of households owning their own home grew by well over 3 million, rivaling the previous three-year record set in the early 1970s when the first postwar baby boomers reached the age of 25.[27]

In part, the buoyant housing market was a delayed response to the long economic recovery that got under way in 1991. By the late 1990s, real earnings for ordinary Americans were increasing for the first time for a decade and the stock market was scaling new heights. But the new demographics were also at work. This was the first housing upswing to be propelled by minorities. Racial and ethnic minorities accounted for

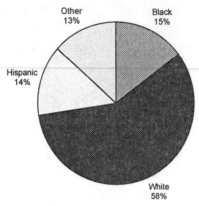

Source: Harvard Joint Center for Housing Studies

Figure 14 Minorities drive the US housing boom of the 1990s
Contribution to growth in homeownership 1994–97

42 percent of the increase in the number of owners – over two and a half times their existing share of the homeowner population. Because many also rent, their contribution to total household growth was even higher, at 68 percent.

The minority effect was still more marked among the new immigrant sections of the population. Hispanics and other ethnic groups, mainly Asian, accounted for less than a tenth of homeowners in 1997. But they contributed over a quarter to the growth in homeownership between 1994 and 1997 (see Figure 14). This increase was almost entirely driven by demographics. The Hispanic and other new ethnic minorities have been growing fast because of immigration. In addition, they are much younger than the rest of the population and so are more likely to be first-time buyers.

The powerful effects of high immigration have clearly offset the expected depressing effects of the baby bust of the late 1960s and 1970s working their way through to the housing market in the 1990s. New immigrants will continue to buoy up the American housing market in the 2000s, according to Harvard University's Joint Center for Housing Studies. It expects the number of households to increase by around a million a year, with new immigrants comprising a quarter of new households – about twice the share expected in England. With home-ownership rates among minorities still well below white households, the potential for continuing advances in the housing market is clear.

The immigrant effect is not confined to the US. In England, immigration accounts for over a tenth of new households formed in the 20 years to 2011. A historic switch in the Irish Republic from net emigration to net immigration helped fuel a runaway property boom there in the mid-1990s. According to a report commissioned by the Irish government, demographics were one of three principal impulses pushing Dublin house prices sky high. Independent experts canvassed by the consultants insisted on the significance of the demographic impetus behind the property boom.[28]

In and out places

Against a background of sluggish population growth and prospective decline in some countries, migration, both international and internal, will pack an ever bigger punch in the housing market. Across the developed world, some regions and towns will experience a hemorrhage of population while others will continue to grow strongly. The effect: national property markets will become much less uniform. More than ever, they will divide between in and out places.

One of the most striking features of immigration is the extent to which new arrivals cluster in a few favored locations. Nowhere is this tendency more apparent than in the US. Three-quarters of immigrants who arrived in the 1980s settled in just six states: California, New York, Texas, Florida, New Jersey and Illinois. In 1990, one-third of America's foreign-born population lived in one state, California, and a further 14 percent lived in New York State.[29]

The concentration of immigrants is even greater than you might suppose from these figures for states. About half the immigrants entering the US in the 1980s settled in just eight metropolitan areas, with Los Angeles, New York and Miami the three favorites. In 1990, almost half the population of Miami was foreign born and immigrants accounted for a third of Los Angeles' population. A similar clustering occurs in other host countries. In Canada, two-thirds of all immigrants have settled in just three cities, Toronto, Montreal and Vancouver. In the UK, planners expect to have to provide an extra half a million homes in the capital in the 20 years to 2011, mainly because of a new wave of immigrants who are expected to arrive almost exclusively in London.[30]

While immigration triggers offsetting flows of outmigration, such outflows do not generally cancel out the effects of immigration in boosting population growth in the host states. This is in part because of the higher fertility rates of new immigrants, who are generally in the prime years for childbearing. Between 1990 and 1996, over 400,000 people migrated out of Los Angeles. But over the same period, the Hispanic population of Los Angeles rose by a million and the number of Asians living there grew by 300,000. California and Texas, two of the major host states for immigration, will be top of the list for construction of new homes in the next 10 years.[31]

The pull of the South

For most states and cities in developed countries, domestic migration is much more important than immigration. In the US, for example, Nevada and Arizona are the states whose populations grew the fastest in the 1980s and 1990s. This growth has been primarily caused by inward migration from other states. Between 1992 and 1997, domestic migration into Nevada was 10 times greater than immigration into the state. In both states, domestic migration added many more people to the population than the natural increase, the excess of births over deaths.[32]

Individual states like Nevada in the West have been the fastest growing, but with many of the migrants coming from California, the West as a whole made no gains from internal migration between 1992 and 1997. The South remained the main magnet for footloose Americans. Meanwhile, there were hemorrhaging outflows from the Northeast.[33]

Such powerful flows inevitably work their way through to property markets. Between 1991 and 1997, house prices fell in real terms by 8 percent in the Northeast but rose by 5 percent in the South. This scissors movement is likely to continue, although the precise impact of demographic trends will be tempered by land-use policies. Where there are few planning restrictions, the supply of new homes adjusts to the shift in demand patterns. Where planning restrictions choke off extra supply, house prices can be expected to rise dramatically.[34]

A similar southward drift is projected to occur in England. According to official projections, households in the South West will increase at almost double the rate of those in the North over the next 20 years. Populations in some counties like Devon and Dorset in the South West would already be in decline but for inward migration. Once again, the impact is bound to be positive for house prices, while property values in northern regions losing population will come under pressure.[35]

New frontiers, new pioneers

As the settlers' wagons rolled westwards in America in the nineteenth century, the pioneers were overwhelmingly young men and women with families. But in the twenty-first century, a new breed of pioneers will explore new frontiers – older people migrating when they retire.

Although most older people stay put, more and more are choosing a change of air. As the number of 60-year-olds swells, there is the potential for a surge in retirement moves. Since 62 has become the *de facto* retirement age, this surge could start as early as 2008 in the US, reaching a peak around 2020. In the UK the increase will also start around 2010, but it will run in two stages, through to 2015 as the first postwar wave of baby boomers retires; with a second wind in the early 2020s as the second wave moves into retirement.

You might imagine that the areas favored by the new pioneers will rapidly turn into ageing ghettoes, devoid of economic dynamism. On the contrary: they are likely to be the most thriving regions and they will not age nearly as fast as you might think. Ironically, this fate is more likely to affect the states losing retirees.

The reason for this apparent paradox is that the regions attracting retirees are usually also those that are magnets for younger migrants. At the same time, the regions losing older people are also losing younger people. Since younger people remain more likely to migrate than older people – three to four times so in the US – this has an even greater potential to make exit regions age.[36]

Take Florida, the bellwether state for an ageing America. During the 1980s, Florida remained the big draw for older people on the move. However, the *ratio* of those aged 65 or more to the overall population of Florida actually rose by less than it did for the US as a whole. Meanwhile, many states in the Midwest saw the same ratio rise by much more than the national average. The reason: Florida was also attracting younger migrants, while the Midwest was losing them.[37]

These migration dynamics will continue into the twenty-first century. The American Bureau of the Census has identified eight states, almost all in the West, whose population aged 65 or more will double by 2020. Nevada is tipped to head the field, with Arizona and Utah not far behind. However, these states won't become the strongholds of the old that you might imagine. For one thing, six out of these eight states are currently younger than the US as a whole. For another, the retirees won't be the only people adding to their populations. They will contribute about a quarter of population growth in Nevada, Arizona and Utah in the 20 years to 2015, when Utah will still be younger than the US as a whole.[38]

The impact of retirement moves will be just as powerful in parts of Europe. According to a recent study of the new phenomenon of international retirement migration, older immigrants in southern Spain 'are if anything more venturesome than tourists or tourist developers in extending urban decentralization, taking up properties in areas of rural depopulation, and settling formerly uninhabited coastlines'. These European snowbirds turned settlers are predominantly better off, boosting the regions they move to. As in the US, the highest concentrations of older people are found in areas of domestic outmigration, typically inland.[39]

An increasing number of British people will follow these cross-border pioneers. Already almost a million British pensioners already live abroad. The great majority of these have moved to other English-speaking countries. Two-thirds live in Australia, Canada, the US and the Irish Republic. But retiring baby boomers are much more likely to move to southern Europe, some in search of sun and lower living costs, others in search of culture and lifestyle. Britons already represent over a quarter of the foreign European populations of Spain and Portugal and almost a fifth of those in Greece.[40]

The British will face competition. In the past they have vied with the Germans for who gets the sunbed by the pool: in the future, the competition will be for property. German projections indicate that the share of German pensions paid to people living abroad is expected to rise from 2 percent in the early 1990s to over 8 percent in 2040.[41]

The sun rises or sets over Sun Cities?

Think of retirement in the US and Sun City automatically springs to mind. Builder Del Webb created a major quoted company around the idea of special retirement communities in the Sun Belt. Starting with Sun City in Phoenix, Arizona in 1960, the Del Webb Corporation has built nearly 70,000 homes in what it describes as 'the active adult market'. People living in a Sun City have to be 55 or over and children under 18 can't reside there except on visits.

Looking ahead, the impending bulge of boomer retirees could therefore lead to an explosion of Sun Cities if they behave like their parents. But will they? Even today, only 6 percent of Americans over 70 live in such age-restricted communities. Baby boomers seem much less likely to plump for this lifestyle. Segregation by age could hardly have less appeal to a generation in denial about getting old. Del Webb believes however, that there will always be a niche who will be attracted to this kind of environment. A niche that will be a comfortable one when the baby-boomer retirement wave hits the shore.[42]

Many retiring baby boomers are likely to head off to what Jack Lessinger of Washington State University calls penturbia, village-like communities that combine rural location with urban lifestyle. In penturbia, he says, 'nature is only a glance away' – no matter where you live, work or shop. Lessinger argues that 'old-timers in search of a delightful and economical retirement are likely to be among the first arrivals in penturbia'. These communities settled by people of diverse ages will be as different from today's Sun Cities as chalk from cheese.[43]

Some American retirees are opting for an altogether different lifestyle, selling up and hitting the road in recreational vehicles (RVs). Some 3–4 million retirees are thought to spend part of the year in their RVs, with hundreds of thousands living exclusively in the vehicles until they settle for one location and turn the vehicle into a fixed mobile home. These pioneers of the road are likely to remain a small minority, but the trend is worth watching. If it catches on, the future property prospects in the main host regions will look less rosy.[44]

Special retirement communities are emerging by default in some *urbanizaciones*, purpose-built residential estates, on the Costa del Sol. However, they have never taken off in the UK and are unlikely to do so in the future. Where a new generation of retirees is likely to follow the US example is in plumping for the British equivalent of penturbia, small country villages and small towns. Census figures show that the fastest-growing areas are the most remote rural districts, while metropolitan districts continue to bleed population at a rate of 90,000 a year. As in the US, the lure of a better lifestyle in the countryside is the main reason for a move.[45]

The new rules of the property game

No one can predict the exact course of property in the years ahead. But one thing is clear: the old rules of the housing market no longer hold in the new demographic order.

In the old property game, house prices could be relied on to rise in the long run in real terms, in other words faster than consumer prices and in line with wage earnings. But this relationship, which has held for over a century, has taken place against a trend of rising population. As that trend comes to an end, we can expect major changes.[46]

So what are the rules in the new property game?

▼ You can't rely on a one-way demographic tide to float house values effortlessly upwards. The crash of the 1990s was not a one-off. Rather, it was a warning signal that you won't get rich in the new property market by investing in a starter home for a married couple.

▼ The very demographic pressures leading to the agequake – lower marriage rates, more divorces – are leading to some offsetting influences in the housing market, notably the growth in one-person households. The classic starter home may be in trouble, but the kinds of homes favored by single people, particularly those in their late thirties and early forties, should fare better.

▼ Baby boomers haven't gone away. They may no longer be first-time buyers but they remain a powerful force in the trade-up market. They want space – larger homes with bigger gardens for those under 50, with patios for empty nesters. Those who have made it want choice locations, reflecting the increasing inequality of income as people age and the goats are separated from the sheep.

▼ Watch the numbers. Immigration counts for more when the underlying rate of natural increase in existing populations is stagnant; so does domestic migration.

▼ Don't assume that the baby-boom generation will behave like their parents. An ageing society doesn't mean a world of Sun Cities. Watch how baby boomers behave now, where they are buying their holiday homes – the best indicator of where they will make that final retirement move – and the kind of property that empty nesters are plumping for.

5

The new business game

EVER SINCE THE SECOND WORLD WAR, COMPANIES HAVE TARGETED families headed by the under-45s. That's where the big numbers have been; that's where the big growth has been.

Not any longer. Take a look at Figure 15, showing what will happen to American families from 1995 to 2010. The fastest-growing group is aged 55–64, projected to increase by over two-thirds by 2010. Second to the finishing tape is the 45–54 age group, forecast to grow by over a third. By contrast, the number of households headed by 25–44-year-

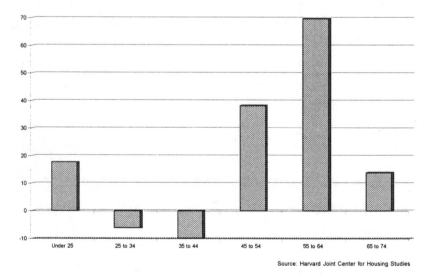

Source: Harvard Joint Center for Housing Studies

Figure 15 Percent change in US households, by age, 1995–2010

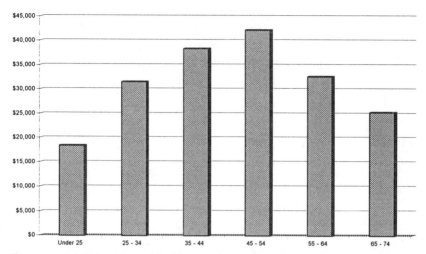

Figure 16 How household spending changes with age

olds shrinks by almost a tenth.[1]

Now take a look at how spending relates to age (Figure 16). Consumer expenditure steadily climbs to a peak in families headed by 45–54-year-olds. It then falls away for the 55–64 age group – but not enough to offset their advantage in sheer numbers as the baby boomers move into this age bracket. Broadly similar age profiles of expenditure occur throughout the West.[2]

Three conclusions follow. The first is that it is absurd to project a consumer-led economic boom in the next 10 years as the baby-boom generation reaches its peak spending power. American households headed by people aged 45–54 shell out on average only a tenth more than those headed by 35–44-year-olds. In the UK, the spending power of households in these two age brackets is broadly equivalent. In both countries, the big jump in spending per household occurs as people move into the 25–44 age brackets and set up families and homes. But in the 15 years to 2010, the number of such households *contracts* by about a tenth in the US.

The second conclusion is that companies producing goods and services predominantly for younger households will be hard pressed. Either they must look elsewhere in the emerging markets of Latin America and Asia, or they must batten down the hatches and consolidate with other firms to deal with the problem of saturated markets.

The third and most crucial conclusion is that the ageing of western populations will transform the composition of consumer demand. Younger households struggling to house and raise children have to concentrate on the basics. Spending on housing peaks among 35–44-year-olds in the UK. So does expenditure on household services, mainly because of the cost of childcare, and household goods, especially furniture.[3]

By contrast, older households have more discretionary spending power. New car ownership is highest in Britain among empty nesters, according to market researchers Mintel. People in their fifties and early sixties also splash out on their home as children leave; they are particularly big spenders on white goods and soft furnishings. But don't fall into the trap of classifying older adults as stay-at-homes. No longer tied to the house by young children, they're keen to use those new cars to get out and about. With more spare money at their disposal, households headed by 55–64-year-olds spend a quarter more than average in restaurants. Most importantly, older consumers are through with stocking up homes with essentials. They are keener on services than goods, preferring or requiring health treatments, financial provision and leisure experiences.[4]

Poppa's little helpers

It may be just one blue pill, but the 'Pfizer-riser' is more than a drug: it's a phenomenon in its own right, an expression of a generation's collective wish to retain the sexual vigor of its youth. For those who need Viagra, it represents the first genuine cure for impotence. For those who don't need it, it provides a rush of blood to recharge a flagging sex life. For Pfizer, it has been the fastest launch of any new drug in history. And for investors the biggest turn-on of all: a share price that more than doubled in less than a year.[5]

Viagra shows what can happen in business when a fundamental demographic shift coincides with advances in science and technology. The convergence of two such powerful trends makes the pharmaceuticals industry the front runner for explosive growth in the early twenty-first century.

The Viagra phenomenon also shows how woefully highly paid Wall Street and City analysts underestimated the potential of an entire industry, by ignoring the predictable consequences of the ageing of the baby-boom generation. Any analysis of ill-health shows its incidence rising sharply post fifty. Forty- and fifty-year-olds are also understandably keen to cling on to youthful well-being. Intriguingly, one survey finds that American men are more concerned than women about their physical appearance and sex drive as they get older, while women are more worried about the loss of mental sharpness and memory.[6]

Yet the pharmaceuticals sector was heavily downgraded in the early 1990s. Five years before Poppa's little helper hit the street, drugs firms were trading well below their historic values: Pfizer could be picked up for about a sixth of its 1998 price. Markets feared western governments were about to spoil the party by clamping down on high drugs prices. Even more extraordinary, it was not just the City and Wall Street that miscalculated the sector's potential but the industry itself. Some leading companies concluded that there was no longer a future in prescription drugs alone.

In the event, the scare story of the early 1990s turned out to be a non-event. The industry bounced back as governments realized that expensive pills are cheaper than beds for treating an ageing population. Viagra heralds a new era of 'lifestyle drugs', products designed to improve the quality of life for basically healthy people. The potential demand is enormous: this is where ageing baby boomers are certain to exert some of their spending muscle, however much private health plans and governments try to restrict outlays. American stockbroker PaineWebber calls this the 'new drug culture' – the concept of fixing things before as well as when they go wrong.[7]

Equally important, the revolution in expectations about health and well-being is matched by the most fundamental scientific revolution of our times. In a pathfinding project due to be completed by 2005, if not earlier, the mysteries of the human genome are being unraveled strand by strand. New DNA sequences are being added to the public database in Cambridge (UK) at the rate of one a minute. Scientific advances into the precise mechanisms of disease allow pharmaceuticals companies to identify exact points of intervention that they can design drugs to target. This is a world away from traditional pharmaceuticals R&D – the random testing of one chemical compound after another for possible therapeutic effects – which ran into a brick wall by the 1980s.

More than 100 US biotech companies were actively researching age-related disorders in 1998, according to BIO, the American Biotech Industry Organization. They form one of the industry's 'most significant areas of research' said BIO's president, Carl Feldbaum. Breakthroughs in biotechnology offer the tantalizing hope of keeping your looks without plastic surgery. Remember Geron, which attracted so much publicity in early 1998 for its discovery of the 'cellular fountain of youth'? The company believes that new insights into the role of telomeres in cell ageing may help keep skin young and elastic. Australia's national science research organization, CSIRO, reported in 1997 that cells regain their youthful appearance when treated with beta alistine'. Application of this substance, naturally present in human and animal tissues, increases the number of times that skin cells divide and helps prevent the cross-linking of collagen, which causes wrinkles. Products incorporating it are already on the market in Australia.[8]

Indeed, a whole new industry looks set to emerge as cosmetics and pharmaceuticals fuse in 'cosmeceuticals'. You see this already in claims made by cosmetics companies about the therapeutic nature of lotions that include alpha hydroxy acids derived from fruit and milk sugars. Cosmetics counters are already lined with products laced with Vitamin C. According to Victoria Ward of Gemini Consulting, cosmeceuticals represent a massive potential market driven by youth-conscious baby-boomers.[9]

But who will reap the harvest? Intriguingly, Ward argues that companies with a retail background will outplay the pharmaceuticals industry with its medical roots. One reason is that the American Food and Drugs Administration takes a stern line on the distinction between cosmetics and pharmaceuticals and does not recognize the term cosmeceuticals specifically. The FDA is currently investigating the effects of cosmetics containing alpha hydroxy acids, out of concern that their use may increase the long-term incidence of skin cancer.[10]

Another new industry set to emerge is 'nutraceuticals'. Using a broad definition of the term to include herbal extracts, minerals, vitamins and nutrients, market research company Freedonia Group estimates that world demand will grow by 8 percent a year to 2002, by which time the market will be worth $8 billion. However, the real excitement now is about the potential of developing a new array of food products that are scientifically designed to improve your health. The link between diet and health is well established: for example more helpings of fruit and vegetables reduce the risk of most kinds of cancer. The flavonoids in humble tea – certainly green tea – are also now thought to protect against heart disease as well as some cancers. The only trouble is that people too often don't want to eat them; while people are eating more fruit, consumption of greens has been falling in Britain.[11]

What remains unclear is the mechanisms that cause these beneficial effects. Initially the antioxidant properties of vegetables were the focus of attention, but nutritional scientists are also investigating other complex biologically active compounds present in plant foods. Ian Johnson of the Institute of Food Research in Norwich anticipates 'an eventual blurring of the boundaries between the pharmaceutical and the nutritional approaches to health care'. Once the precise active constituents can be isolated – something that could in principle be tailored to people's precise genetic make-up – it won't take long for food and consumer goods firms to add them to the food people want to eat as opposed to what they are supposed to eat. Unilever is one major company that is leading the way. In 1999, it is launching a new version of

Flora margarine with enhanced levels of plant sterols, which is designed to reduce blood cholesterol by 10 percent.[12]

With nutraceuticals, as with cosmeceuticals, it is unclear whether drugs firms will necessarily benefit. This unexpected conclusion highlights a more general point about the pharmaceuticals sector. The drugs industry as a whole may be the clearest winner of all from the agequake, but it uncomfortably resembles Hollywood. For every hit, there are a dozen flops; for every blockbuster like Viagra, dozens of drugs that never even pass go. According to Andersen Consulting, fewer than a tenth of drugs have turned into what it calls 'modest blockbusters' with annual sales of $350 million.[13]

Andersen argues that to keep pace with average industry growth of 10 percent a year, each of the top 10 companies must launch five of these box office hits a year. This requires hundreds of initial research investigations, most of which fall by the wayside. In an industry where no one company holds more than a small share of the global market, this development has led to a wave of mega-mergers. Towards the end of 1998, German company Hoechst and French firm Rhône-Poulenc merged their pharmaceuticals and agrochemicals divisions to form Aventis. Shortly afterwards Zeneca, the pharmaceuticals firm formed from the demerger of ICI, and Astra, the Swedish company owning Losec, the world's best-selling drug, announced another massive deal. At a stroke, the world league table of top drugs companies by sales was transformed, as the two companies vaulted into third and fourth position.[14]

Morgan Stanley analysts argue that pharmaceuticals are becoming 'a higher risk industry, more dependent on new products'. This conclusion holds true in spades for small biotech companies. Geron's share price gyrated in the week after the telomere story leaked to the press. The unhappy saga of British Biotech is a salutary example of the risks involved in investing in new biotech companies. For one brief, heady moment in 1996, the company was about to join the FTSE 100 on hopes for marimastat, an anticancer drug it was testing. Two years later, its share price had collapsed in an acrimonious row about an alleged failure to level with investors about the findings of drugs trials.[15]

Despite the risks with any individual company, the potential of the pharmaceuticals sector as a whole is enormous. The industry's dream is to extend the reach of physical well-being into late middle age and beyond. This dream was once the wishful thinking of futurologists, but it is now seen as an increasingly realistic vision.

Boomers are set to become the original bionic generation long before they become old. The bionic man was largely electronic, but it is cell biology allied with advanced material sciences that looks set to deliver the biotech body through 'tissue engineering'. In this technique, pioneered by doctors and scientists in Boston, Massachusetts, cells are isolated and grown in a shape-defining scaffold or matrix outside the body. The matrix is made of a polymer similar to that used in sutures, which dissolves in the body. In some instances, cell banks can be used without immune reactions; in others, patients have to provide seed cells to overcome this problem.

Tissue engineering offers the prospect of an array of replacement parts for the body. In a joint venture with Advanced Tissue Sciences, healthcare company Smith & Nephew already has a replacement skin substitute, Dermagraft, licensed for use to treat diabetic foot ulcers. 'Taking a ten year horizon, the technology will be available to deliver replacement parts for skin, cartilage, cornea, blood vessels and heart valves,' says Professor Alan Suggett, group director of R&D at Smith & Nephew. Actual products may take a further five years or so to become available.[16]

Woody Allen's spoof sci-fi film *Sleeper*, where an oppressive ruler is reconstituted from his nose, starts to look prophetic!

New masters of the universe

In the 1980s it was the takeover artists who walked tall on Wall Street, but in the 1990s it was the world's fund managers who became the new masters of the universe. Just how lucrative the business had become was highlighted in the brouhaha when fund manager Nicola Horlick lost her job at Deutsche Morgan Grenfell at the beginning of 1997. The case hit the headlines as she swept into Frankfurt with a media circus in tow to put her case to startled senior executives at the German parent bank. What captured the public's imagination was that this superwoman was so superpaid. Later the same year, American investment bank and stockbroker Merrill Lynch paid a cool £3 billion to snap up London fund manager MAM. Carol Galley, dubbed the City's 'ice maiden' because of her ice-cold calculation of financial advantage in takeover battles, benefited to the tune of £10 million, and Hugh Stevenson, MAM's chairman, received over £20 million. Merrill Lynch's reason for its largesse? It regards asset management as *the* growth industry within the financial services sector, a growth industry in its own right.[17]

Asset managers will continue to thrive as the private pension revolution spreads inexorably around the world. So, too, will the companies that service the fund management industry. The venerable State Street Corporation of Massachusetts has shown how lucrative combining the roles of fund manager and service provider can be. One of the US's top fund managers and a leading provider of services such as custody to institutional investors, it clocked up its twentieth successive year of double-digit earnings-per-share growth in 1997.[18]

State Street pinpoints four global trends that will keep asset managers busy: global ageing, the move towards funded private pension systems, expanded cross-border investment and increasingly complex investment strategies. Of these, it regards the impact of global ageing as the most powerful: 'a historic trend that is driving demand for retirement assets everywhere', says chief executive Marshall Carter.

Investment bank Goldman Sachs also believes that asset management has a great past and an even greater future. In 1998, analysts highlighted pretax margins of 30–35 percent for US publicly quoted asset managers, with those in private firms, astonishingly, even higher. Goldman Sachs emphasized the potential for global expansion, particularly in Europe and Japan: 'the global arena offers incredible growth opportunities to experienced companies'. The research paper argued that further consolidation in the sector was inevitable, both to cater for the US retail market and to capitalize on the opportunities of overseas expansion.[19]

Mergers and consolidation

While asset management is expanding fast, other parts of the financial services industry are having to cope with a decline in demand as the ageing baby-boom generation gives way to smaller successors. The counter-intuitive result: windfalls for millions of investors and borrowers in the UK when building societies turned themselves into public companies in the mid- to late 1990s. The bonanza occurred because the Halifax and other leading societies realized they could no longer rely on their staple business of lending for house purchase. With the vital 25–34 first-time buyer age group falling sharply, the field of building societies and banks was looking dangerously overcrowded.

The strategic implications are twofold: first, consolidation of the mature side of retail financial services; and second, the development of 'bankassurance', as banks link up with life insurance companies to use expensive bank branches to sell insurance products. On both counts, the Halifax, Alliance & Leicester and Woolwich believed that they could exploit these new opportunities more effectively as quoted companies than as building societies. Prices throughout the banking sector rocketed in 1997 as investors bet on the possibility of consolidations. Another demutualization took place in the insurance sector as the Norwich Union converted to a plc. Its share price subsequently soared because of its attraction as a potential takeover target for would-be bankassurers.

Where the UK led in conversions from mutual ownership, the US followed in early 1998 as Prudential Insurance of America announced that it was embarking on the biggest demutualization ever seen in the US. The Rock of Gibraltar – the Prudential's logo – had shaken in the agequake. The Prudential, like other US mutual life insurers, was squaring up to the awkward fact that people worry less now about dropping dead and more about outliving their savings. Like beached whales, American life insurers have been left stranded with sales of conventional life policies while mutual funds soared in popularity.[20]

In the US, a wave of mergers has occurred between major investment banks like Morgan Stanley and retail brokers like Dean Witter, as well as Travelers' purchase of securities house Salomon. According to Donald Marron, chief executive of PaineWebber, the growth of American household assets as baby boomers prepare for retirement was the driving force behind the merger activity. The merger mania reached new heights in 1998 when Citicorp linked up with Travelers in a $166 billion deal to create the world's largest financial services group, with 100 million customers in 100 different countries. The principal focus of this financial behemoth was the global consumer, with the merged group able to push a full array of insurance and investment products through Citibank branches around the world.[21]

In Japan, the combination of the fastest ageing population in the world and the deregulation of a moribund financial system has led to a flurry of new links and alliances with western financial groups. At the start of 1998, Merrill Lynch was quick to exploit the demise of Yamaichi Securities by purchasing 30 of the failed broker's outlets and taking on 2000 of its former employees. Around the same time, GE Capital launched a joint venture with life assurer Toho Mutual; the new company had the largest capitalization of any listed life assurance company. Michael Fraizer of GE Financial Assurance said that the decision had been reached because of the opportunity created by deregulation and demographics. Later in the year Travelers Group, while still in the process of merging with Citicorp, took a 25 percent stake in Nikko, Japan's third biggest stockbroker.[22]

Leisure generation

A hundred years ago, the economist Thorstein Veblen coined the phrase 'conspicuous consumption' in his famous *Theory of the Leisure Class*. He might have been describing the Great Gatsby. But now the leisure class has given way to the leisure generation.

Hard to believe it when you're stretched like a piece of elastic with work and bringing up children, but there is light at the end of the tunnel. By the time women hit fifty, only about a third of couples have dependent children living with them; as many have become empty-nesters – more if you include childless couples. Market researchers Mintel point out that the line when children leave home for good has become blurred, but even so there is a big difference between having grown-up children half-living at home and being fully responsible for dependants.[23]

Some baby boomers will retire early; more will continue to work but take things easier. Either way, as they reach their middle to late fifties they'll have more time on their hands. They'll also have a lot more money. Just as the leisure class plumped for conspicuous consumption, so the leisure generation will spend its money in ways affirming its status as people who've made it – and who deserved to make it. The successful pitch for baby boomers in their fifties? You *earned* the right to spend it your way.[24]

The thirst for leisure will make tourism a boom industry as the leisure generation looks for new ways of spending its time. In the UK, households headed by 50–64-year-olds spend almost a third more than all households on foreign holidays. The number of holidays taken by those over 55 increased by more than a third in the first half of the 1990s.[25]

One sector already benefiting is the cruise industry. In 1998, more than 40 new cruise ships were being built, increasing the effective size of the world fleet by over a third. One of them, P&O's *Grand Princess*, is a leviathan, 150 ft longer than an upended Canary Wharf tower. Aimed at the international market, the ship offers energetic passengers a choice of four swimming pools, a mini golf course and a sports court; and for the not so energetic, nine jacuzzis. The industry's £8 billion investment in ships followed a spectacular rise in the popularity of these holidays. In Europe, the number of passengers jumped by 17 percent a year between 1994 and 1997. Growth was even higher in the UK, Spain and Italy.[26]

Favorable demographics together with clever marketing are underpinning this explosion in cruise travel, which has even seen Disney jump in. The industry, once identified with a much older clientele, has succeeded in reaching out to the baby-boom generation as it turns 50. The average age of British passengers has fallen since 1993 by five years to 55. In the US, the average age of passengers is still lower at 48, as companies like Miami-based Carnival have introduced short trips that appeal to younger people. In the UK, the key innovation has been the introduction of the fly-cruise, which typically combines a week spent in a resort with a week on the water.[27]

Cruise holidays amount to a repackaging of the classic package holiday for middle-aged customers. In a report on 'The New Millennium American', stockbroker PaineWebber sees this as part of a general pattern in which stressed baby boomers are pulling back from high-energy holidays. With leisure time growing, middle-aged consumers are spending heavily on vacations. 'But they want leisure that comes easy: if it adds worry, energy or effort, it is not worth it.'[28]

One city already benefiting from the new leisure generation is Las Vegas. The 1990s brought an astonishing building boom as the US's fastest-growing city turned itself into a giant theme park. The $1.6 billion Bellagio Casino, recreating a scaled-down version of Italy's Lake Como in the unlikely setting of the Nevada desert, was just one of five major investments adding hotel rooms for the 30 million visitors who stream in every year. The city's population grew by over a third in the 1990s.[29]

With its gaudy, exhibitionist new hotels, one featuring a spotlight so bright it can be seen from the moon, Las Vegas is keen to promote a new image of itself as a tourist attraction and convention center. But the main lure remains gambling, with gaming revenue totaling a hefty $5 billion in 1997. Las Vegas is benefiting from the link between middle age and gambling as the number of middle-aged Americans swells. The average age of visitors, only a tenth of whom come with children, is 48. The *Grand Princess* for its part features the Atlantis Casino, the largest casino afloat.

In Britain, the National Lottery was thus launched into an ideal market. There has been understandable concern about the Lottery luring young people into gambling. But figures commissioned by the regulator OFLOT show that the fears are exaggerated: young adults are much less likely to play the lottery than older people. Participation and average stakes peak at exactly the same age as the visitors to Las Vegas, around 50.[30]

When they're not gambling their money away, fifty-somethings have another way to burn up that excess cash. Along with people carriers and four-wheel drives, sports cars have been the fastest-growing segment of the British market in the 1990s. Sales grew almost twofold between 1993 and 1997 – far faster than the overall market, which increased by a fifth. Industry sources suggest that empty nesters are prime customers. A new MG model launched in 1995 sells predominantly to people around 50 and young women. The average age of Porsche 911 owners is 48.[31]

Many other luxury services and goods, such as top-range jewelry, should also gain from the growing population of older, affluent consumers. When Thorstein Veblen wrote, conspicuous consumption was confined to a small group of robber barons in America's Wild West period of capitalism. A century later, conspicuous consumption of luxuries will spread across an entire generation.

Flat beer

There's nothing quite so unappetising as flat beer. Nothing, that is, except flat beer sales. In the US, for example, sales were actually down in volume in 1997 compared with 1990. There was a similar fall in the UK. The froth had gone out of beer sales because the core clientele of 20-year-old men was declining in delayed response to the baby bust of the 1970s.[32]

As we have seen, drugs and cosmetic companies, the financial services sector and leisure industries are the big winners from the agequake. But the brewers' difficulties show that the wheel of fortune isn't spinning in only one direction. Many industries no longer have demographics on their side. The companies hit hardest are those targeting

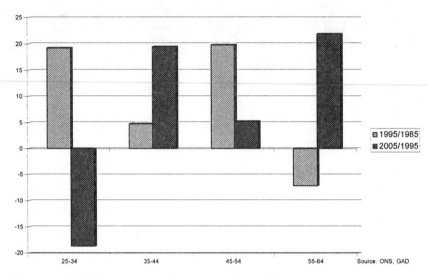

Figure 17 Consumers past, consumers future
Percent change in size of age-group in UK, 1985–95 and 1995–2005

young people in their twenties, who might just as well have joined the missing persons list. That doesn't turn these firms into automatic losers, but they will have to work a lot harder in the future (Figure 17).

One clear-sighted response to the new adverse demographics has come from Whitbread. Once principally a brewer and pub operator, it has reinvented itself as a leisure services company with a leading presence in restaurants through outlets such as Pizza Hut and Café Rouge. Through its budget Travel Inns, the company also runs the UK's second biggest hotel chain, and following its purchase of David Lloyd Leisure for £200 million in 1995, it operates a large chain of health and fitness clubs.[33]

The company devised its diversification strategy in the 1980s when it realized that the coming shortfall of young men, traditionally its key customers, combined with a trend towards lighter drinking were about to undermine its traditional pub business. Beer now accounts for only a third of turnover, and food comprises a third of sales in pubs. In 1995, Whitbread's chief executive said: 'young men drinking draught beer is no longer a core business for us'. Once a statement that would have been heresy and hara-kiri rolled into one, this was no more than a reality check: between 1990 and 1996 spending on beer in the UK fell by a tenth in real terms.

Whitbread expects the volume of beer sold in pubs and inns to contract further in the years to 2002. Only a shift to premium drinking in the form of specialist lagers will allow the value of this market to remain static in real terms. Not surprisingly, the company aims to rely in future still less on the contribution that beer makes to profits.

In contrast, the leisure market has good prospects for the company, with spending rising faster than overall consumer expenditure. In the immediate future, Whitbread is focusing on families with children in the fast-growing 35–44 age group by making its pubs more attractive to women and families. It calls this the 'three Fs' strategy of focusing on food, families and female drinkers. It is also targeting the even faster growing 55–64 age group through Beefeaters' Emerald Club. The strategy makes sense: there have been sharp increases in the number of people over 45 eating out in the 1990s, according to market researcher Mintel.[34]

Whitbread's move into health clubs is designed to capitalize on the desire of ageing baby boomers to keep fit and healthy. The potential for growth has been demonstrated in the US, where health club membership climbed by two-thirds in the 10 years to 1997 and older exercisers are 'in many ways reinventing the fitness movement', according to the Fitness Products Council.[35]

Diageo, the British food and drinks company formed from the merger of Guinness and Grand Metropolitan, has a different strategy to Whitbread's for dealing with the shifting age profile of the population. Diageo's forte comes from owning some of the world's top brands in spirits, like Johnnie Walker Scotch whisky and Smirnoff vodka. On the face of it, this should leave the company well placed as the West ages: consumption of spirits and liqueurs is half as high again in British households headed by 50–64-year-olds as it is for all households. In addition, Diageo can expect to benefit as older drinkers 'trade up' to premium brands that it controls. Set against this apparent potential, it seems unlikely that the baby-boom generation, brought up on wine, will be as heavy spirits drinkers as their parents. There is a strong underlying trend away from grain to the grape, although white spirits like vodka are faring better. Between 1990 and 1997, spending on spirits dropped in real terms by 15 percent in the UK, while wine purchases jumped by 27 percent.[36]

By contrast, demand for spirits has been more buoyant in emerging markets, particularly in Asia, where international labels command cachet. Diageo, controlling a clutch of the most sought-after brands, stands to benefit from growing demand in these markets. The strategy took a knock in 1998 with the Asian crisis, but leaves the company with a sound demographic strategy in the long term.

Pass on the Big Mac?

With consumers willing to fork out more and more on eating out, you would think that the good times would continue to roll for the burger industry born and bred alongside the baby-boom generation. The McDonald brothers started it all in 1948 and the Big Mac was invented in 1968. So 1998 should have been both a thirtieth and a fiftieth birthday to remember, celebrating an American icon in the shape of the Golden Arches. Instead, McDonald's suffered bruising attacks in the press, reflecting a traumatic midlife crisis as profits stagnated in its key US market.[37]

Americans had fallen out of love with the burger giant. Business mistakes apart, generational shifts were responsible, as baby boomers increasingly looked for a more sophisticated choice of food. McDonald's responded in 1996 with its Deluxe line supposed to appeal to adults with a spicier, more 'grown-up' taste, but this Mcflopped, 'failing miserably' according to one Wall Street analyst. The company's 1997 annual report read like a *mea culpa*, with the then chief executive Michael Quinlan admitting that it had been 'a disappointing year – our financial performance wasn't what we wanted and our stock price lagged the market'.[38]

The company's problem is that the burger market is no longer synonymous with fast food. There has been 'a sustained trend to adult sandwiches', according to Ralph Rush of Technomic, a market research company specializing in the food industry. As a result, the burger business has been growing more slowly than the overall quick-service sector through the 1990s. 'McDonald's has lost some of its relevance to American culture', reported *Business Week* in early 1998.[39]

In a nutshell, the US has grown up and McDonald's hasn't. It's not that Americans have lost their appetite for eating out: the reverse is true. Almost as much is now spent on food eaten outside the home as at home – compared with a third when the Big Mac was launched. The trend seems inexorable, as more and more women work and value for time matters more than value for money. However, Americans are evidently looking for a more diverse range of eating experiences than you can get at McDonald's.[40]

One way out of the impasse is through further international diversification. Half of McDonald's sales and 60 percent of its profits already come from overseas: the company operates in over 100 countries. The potential for further growth in the fast-food market is spelt out by market research company Euromonitor. European spending on fast food per head of population is a small fraction of the American level. The potential is still greater in emerging markets. 'This is where McDonald's future lies 15 to 20 years out,' says Stacy Jamar, who follows the company at investment bank Salomon Smith Barney.[41]

In the more immediate future, McDonald's also has to find ways of regenerating demand in the US market, which still accounts for over two-thirds of global food sales. Under Jack Greenberg, who replaced Quinlan as chief executive in 1998, the company is using new technology in its kitchens to make to order a much greater variety of fast-food products. Early signs are that this is paying off. John Grace, executive director of consultancy firm Interbrand, says 'the company has finally understood that the brand stood for a value – rekindling the kid in each of us – and for experiences, not for fries and burgers'. The question for the future is whether customers in an older America agree.

Denim blues

Levi Strauss's agonies in the 1990s show how rapidly the leader of the pack can turn also-ran, when the demographic rollercoaster changes direction. After sales actually dropped in 1997, the company announced it was axing 11 plants employing one in three of its manufacturing workers in North America. The closures were forced by a sharp decline in the company's share of the key men's jeans market from almost half in 1990 to a quarter. Levi Strauss had been slow to cotton on to what young consumers wanted. It was caught napping by a sudden switch in fashion to ultra baggy styles exploited by rival manufacturers, including private-label producers.[42]

Less than a year later, Levi Strauss announced that more factories would have to be shut down, mainly in Europe. It blamed this latest set of closures on the declining European youth population, the traditional core consumer target for denim jeans, as well as changing fashion and fiercer competition. In the US market, where the number of teenagers is rising thanks to the 'echo baby boom', the company now accepts that it took its eye off the key youth market. By failing to come out with new styles in the early 1990s, Levis came to be identified by teenagers as the jeans their parents wore – always a turn-off. In this way the continuing success of Levis with the now ageing baby-boom generation had backfired.

Levi Strauss has introduced sweeping changes to retrieve its hold on the youth market. A new, if uncomfortable sounding, product line – 'Hard Jeans' – was launched in 1998. A new advertising campaign sought to reconnect with young people with one-liner 'truths' such as 'Best Friends' Moms are Usually Sexy' and 'Teachers Make Great Pets.' Which only goes to show how difficult it is to sound hip if you're seen as middle-aged. John Grace of Interbrand says: 'The company still needs to redefine the brand to make it relevant for modern Americans.' The company argues that its brand values remain as relevant as before but that it needs to reconnect them with a new generation of consumers.[43]

Sports shoe manufacturer Nike has also found the going unexpectedly harder because of shifting demographics. In less than two decades the company with the swoosh logo swooshed from revenues of $8 million when it went public to over $9 billion. Nike 'just did it' by appealing to the swelling ranks of keep-fit boomers and fashion-conscious younger age groups, for whom a pair of sneakers was a must-purchase.

But in 1998 the company started running on empty: revenues declined in the spring and it recorded a net loss of $68 million. While it had been hit hard by a sharp fall in demand in Asia, a more serious problem lay at home. Like Levi Strauss, Nike had been hit by a sudden switch in fashion among young people, in this instance away from sneakers towards 'brown' shoes. Nike may ostensibly be a sporting goods company but it is really in the fashion industry; a study by US market researchers NPD found that more than half of athletic footwear purchases are for casual use only.[44]

At least both companies can look forward to considerable growth in the number of young people in the US as the echo-boom generation replaces the baby-bust Generation X. The task is to find a way of appealing to the new entrants to the marketplace without alienating existing customers. In Europe, fashion industries face the problem of declining numbers of 15–24-year-olds. Without a strong following demographic wind, this will leave fashion companies more and more vulnerable to the shifting tastes of young people.

The retail dilemma

Walk through any big supermarket or department store, look at the shoppers and you can see what dry statistics confirm. The big spenders on food, clothing, footwear and household goods are households headed by people aged 35–54, shopping not just for themselves but for their families. The number of these households is growing strongly as the postwar baby boom swells the middle of the age profile. But not far behind them in high-street spending power is the 25–34 age group.

This key group of consumers is contracting sharply in the UK between 1995 and 2005 as the delayed effect of the baby bust works through. The growing number of 55–64-year-olds offers only partial compensation, because in absolute terms their increase to 2005 is more than outweighed by the decrease in 25–34-year-olds.[45]

The shift in demographics benefits retailers once out of favor, like upmarket department stores. The best of these are popular with the older age groups who are currently expanding fast. But many of the retailers which thrived in the 1980s are facing a real challenge. Tried and trusted formulae that worked well before have been found wanting in the 1990s. For example, the declining number of 20-year-olds has hit specialist start-up furniture chains like MFI and cheaper jewelry chains like H. Samuel, according to Clive Vaughan, research manager at retail consultants Verdict.

Ultimately, however, all major retailers face a problem of saturated national markets. The new demographic conditions mark an end to buoyant consumer growth, says Richard Hokenson, chief economist and demographic expert at Wall Street investment bank Donaldson, Lufkin & Jenrette. Mainstream economic models, which made a poor job of predicting consumers' behavior in the 1980s and early 1990s, link consumption primarily to income and wealth. Hokenson insists on the importance of demographics. He argues that the weight of first-time buyers in the population acts like an accelerator or brake on the underlying trend of consumer spending growth. When 25–34-year-olds are increasing in importance, as in the 1980s, consumer spending growth takes off. When they are declining in importance, consumer spending growth tails off.[46]

This certainly fits the pattern in the UK, where consumer spending in the recovery grew by only 2.5 percent a year from 1991 and 1997, half the rate chalked up in the earlier economic cycle between 1982 and 1988. In 1997, there was some overheated talk about an overheating economy as consumers took to the high street and spent their windfalls from the demutualization of building societies. In the event, the wild boom ended up at half the astonishing 7.5 percent increase in 1988. In the US, consumer spending also grew more slowly until 1997 compared with the 1980s.[47]

Add to this the shift in composition of consumer spending from goods to services as middle-aged households become the fastest-growing demographic age bracket, and you have the measure of the challenge facing retailers. As Hokenson points out, it is no coincidence that most of the US retail bankruptcies in the 1990s have been in the Northeast, the American region with the lowest birth rate.

In Europe, even more unfavorable demographics mean that demand for the stock-in-trade of big retail chains is now growing only sluggishly. Consumer spending in the big four markets of Germany, Britain, France and Italy is forecast by Corporate Intelligence on Retailing to increase at an annual rate of little more than 2 percent in the 10 years to 2005. The organization warns that 'the fastest spending growth in future will not be in shops selling food and consumer goods, but on the provision of services of various types – like leisure, transport, health – increasingly directly sold into the home'. In Denmark, for example, spending on health, leisure and education will grow at over double the rate for food, drink and housing.[48]

Significantly, the main exception to this dull outlook is the Irish Republic with its more youthful population, which explains why British retailers have been expanding there. Tesco, for example, spent over £600 million acquiring a presence across Ireland in 1997. In more mature European markets, the days when you could grow fast by carving up small stores are largely over. This is a much more unforgiving environment where a stumble can catch out even revered names like UK-based retailer Marks & Spencer, which disappointed shoppers with its lines and investors with its results in 1998.

One response from retailers has been to diversify into the more profitable area of financial services, exploiting their brand name with consumers. Marks & Spencer led the way in the 1980s and more recently other retailers such as supermarket Sainsbury's have rushed on to the field. Another trend is to expand abroad. Cross-border moves by retailers in Europe doubled between 1990 and 1997 compared with the whole of the 1980s, according to a report from the Oxford Institute of Retail Management and commercial property specialist Jones Lang Wootton. The expansion was led by the UK and Germany.[49]

Underlying these moves is accelerating integration in the European single market. This is widely expected to create the opportunity for rationalization, although in practice much consolidation could take place on a national basis. Germany's Metro, Europe's biggest retail group that runs a big cash-and-carry operation, believes a major shake-out lies ahead. In 1998, it announced a major corporate reorganization designed to strengthen its position in a consolidating market. Not long after, the world's biggest retailer, the American discounter Wal-Mart, significantly increased its presence in Germany when it acquired 74 German stores.[50]

An alternative strategy is to exploit the potential growth of less developed markets. This explains why there has been an explosion of moves into Central and Eastern Europe. A third of all cross-border moves between 1995 and 1997 were in the Czech Republic, Hungary and Poland. Tesco is opening 14 hypermarkets in the region as part of a strategy of operating large stores in emerging markets. In 1998, the British food retailer exploited the new opportunities for inward investors arising from the Asian crisis by acquiring Lotus, a chain of hypermarkets in Thailand. As the company pointed out, two-thirds of the Thai population is under the age of 30. Tesco is currently investing some £300 million a year outside the UK.[51]

Whatever the strategic logic of retailers spreading their wings overseas, earlier international moves are littered with the corpses of failed aspirations. A foray by Tesco into the French market proved short-lived. Swish Paris department store Galéries Lafayette was unable to export its formula to Manhattan, and natural cosmetics retailer Body Shop's outlets in the US have lost money. Nor have moves by American firms in the opposite direction necessarily worked out. Toys 'R' Us, a pioneer of the retailing 'category killer' concept, appeared to have real potential for global expansion. Yet in 1998, beset by fierce competition from discounters in the US, it announced the closure of 50 of its overseas stores, mainly in Europe.[52]

Retailers are caught between a rock and a hard place. If they stay at home, they risk a dog-eat-dog battle in saturated markets, forcing returns down. But retail brands, however well established they may be in the home market, don't transfer readily across frontiers. 'Retailers find it more difficult to operate across international boundaries than manufacturers or the service sector,' cautions the Oxford Institute of Retail Management.

US broker Morgan Stanley Dean Witter also strikes a sceptical note about the scope for retailers to make a fist of international strategies in its 1998 edition of *The Competitive Edge*, a hit list of companies possessing a distinct global advantage. Its retail analysts cited 'investors' scepticism that such a decision may represent the acknowledgment of domestic saturation'. Retailers singled out for their global potential were those with a distinctive brand franchise, like The Gap, Hermès, Tiffany and Gucci. The broker's overall conclusion, however, was that 'retail may remain largely a domestically based industry'.[53]

No automatic winners and losers

The new business game plays into the hands of some sectors while putting others at a disadvantage. In general, it intensifies the longstanding shift from manufacturing to services, as consumer spending moves away from goods. It favors industries catering for older age groups, while putting those targeted at younger age groups at a disadvantage.

But don't leap to the conclusion that you can work out winners and losers among companies simply from their placing in the demographic handicaps. This is naive reasoning. As we saw with pharmaceuticals, a sector that cannot fail as populations age, individual corporate success is akin to Hollywood even among the largest firms. Small biotech companies are notoriously risky. Hence the trend towards mergers among the big firms to reduce risk and spread R&D costs. In another demographically blessed sector, asset management, consolidation is also now required in order to exploit opportunities outside the US.

In some of the sectors now toiling under a demographic disadvantage, it is possible for individual companies to break out of the laager on to more favorable ground. This has clearly inspired moves by retailers to exploit their undoubted brand strengths by offering financial services. Conglomerates have won a bad name over the years as exercises in empire building, leading to dilution of management effort and expertise. The financial markets generally now prefer the alternative formula of 'sticking to your knitting'. The challenge for retailers diversifying into financial services is to prove that conglomerate service providers can be more successful than conglomerate manufacturers.

The industries best able to overcome adverse demographics in the West will be those that can globalize most effectively. That is why consumer goods industries with strong brands should be able to ride the shockwave of the agequake. By contrast, most retailers face an uphill struggle in going global because their brand identity is anchored in domestic markets and is difficult to leverage internationally.

Demographic shifts offer some sectors heightened growth potential, others the challenge of saturated markets. But how companies respond will be the key to their future. Before you invest your hard-earned money in a particular company or decide to work for it, watch how it is tackling the agequake.

6

Cultural revolution

'I REALLY WOULD LIKE TO BE A ROCK STAR,' QUIPPED DOUGLAS ADAMS, author of that favorite boomer text *The Hitch-Hiker's Guide to the Galaxy*. 'I feel I'm nearly old enough.'[1]

A throwaway remark, maybe, but a one-liner that should be framed on the office walls of anyone involved in marketing and communications, not least the ultimate marketing and communications business of politics. As we progress through life, our demand for products and services passes through predictable stages – buying houses when we get married or start living together, splashing out on luxury treats when we become empty nesters. There is therefore a temptation to assume that our values and attitudes change in like fashion as we pass through these life stages.

An understandable temptation, but one to resist. Some lifecycle effects certainly occur: people become more politically engaged as they get older and drop postures of youthful revolt when they become parents and have wealth to conserve. Midlife crises sometimes occur as we reappraise our goals and aspirations. However, as Douglas Adams implied, we often cling to the core cultural and social values imprinted in our adolescence and early twenties. Furthermore, most people of all ages move with the times, so that the shifting tides and currents of public opinion and social attitudes affect all generations.[2]

Resetting the clock

There's nothing revolutionaries like better than reinventing time. Julius Caesar destroyed the Roman Republic and introduced the Julian calendar – hence July. His successor, Augustus Caesar, established the empire and grabbed another summer month. Christians introduced a new chronology – as did Muhammad. The French Revolution introduced a new calendar, though it didn't last for long. Now the cultural revolution induced by the agequake is resetting the very metric of age. Middle age is redubbed mid-youth, old age is renamed third age. Meanwhile, any self-respecting American child rejects 'teen' by the age of 16, often earlier.

The reluctance of ageing boomers to accept the label of middle age can be put down to vanity (or panic), but it also makes objective sense. This is a generation in better shape than its predecessors and it knows it. Baby boomers can expect to live longer than their parents and in better health. The concept of middle age, together with the unflattering connotations that it carries, is bound to change as lifespans lengthen. If you can expect to live 35 years or more when you hit 40, middle age needs to be redefined. One reason that the death of Princess Diana at the age of 36 seemed so tragic is that we no longer expect people in their thirties to die. When her will was published, legal sources disclosed that the divorce settlement had been based on the assumption that she would live a further 50 years.[3]

Marian Salzman, who scans lifestyle trends for Brand Futures Group in New York, says that 'mid-youth now runs until the onset of menopause with 36 marking the absolute age of power and those aged 42 and above still regarded as "hot", bringing to relationships experience, enthusiasm and – thanks to new fertility tricks – even the prospect of children'. You can expect even these boundaries to stretch as more and more baby boomers turn 50. With hormone replacement therapy (HRT) now widely used, even the menopause no longer represents the limit to mid-youth. And HRT is not the only trick open to this generation of Dorian Gray wannabes. When Dustin Hoffman played *The Graduate* in 1967, he was told to get into plastics. Smart career move for a graduate today: become a plastic surgeon.[4]

Americans never do things by half-measures and that applies in scalpels to plastic surgery statistics. If you want to know who was cut, where and why, surf the net to the National Clearing House for Plastic Surgery Statistics. In 1997, over 120,000 women had breast implants, almost four times as many as in 1992; a third were aged 35 to 50. Not surprisingly, face lifts are most popular with those in their fifties and early sixties. The most common cosmetic procedure is liposuction, with a giant sucking sound as flab rather than jobs heads south. Half those syphoning away the fat are between 35 and 50.[5]

In the past cosmetic surgery was done by men on women. Now men are queuing up to defy the march of age. In 1997 they accounted for one in seven liposuctions and almost a tenth of face lifts in the US. This does not simply prove what women have long suspected, that men have always been closet peacocks. According to Dr Lynch, president of the American Society of Plastic and Reconstructive Surgeons, 'more men are viewing cosmetic surgery as a viable way of looking and feeling younger. Looking younger to compete in the workplace is one of the most common reasons I hear from men seeking cosmetic surgery.'

As boomers strive to remain Peter Pans, a similar redefinition of age is occurring further down the line. If you're an ageing surfer on the Internet, the site to visit is Third Age. Again, it's easy to scoff at the concept as an embarrassed euphemism, but I back the third-agers. Once, old age was nothing much to look forward to: a short, dismal time between retirement and death. But now retirees can expect to live 15 or more years, the vast majority of which will be enjoyed in relatively good health. Many retired people are also better off than younger people struggling to bring up children.[6]

According to one major investigation, the third age – defined as those over 50 – is 'an entirely new phenomenon ... a period of increasing freedom from the structures of work and of a family with dependent children'. The Carnegie Inquiry, held in the early 1990s, argued that 'a whole range of outdated attitudes and policies stand in the way of third-agers participating in society in ways which can be profitable and enjoyable for them and valuable for society'. It suggested that future third-agers will be 'adaptable, flexible and emphasizing the value of individual achievement'.[7]

But as middle age turns to middle youth and old age to third age, something equally strange is happening down the line: fewer and fewer young people admit to being teenagers. According to Peter Zollo of Teenage Research Unlimited, the term is now only accepted by Americans aged 12 to 15; it is rejected by Americans over 15. This, he believes, is why the newly launched and highly successful *Teen Magazine* has a younger age skew than that of *Seventeen* and *YM*. 'When products are launched with the word "Teen" as part of their brand name, they seem to more attract tweens and young teens – those approximately aged 10 to 14 or even 15.' At the same time, media giants like Disney worry that the period of childhood – and thus receptiveness to the icons of Disneydom like Mickey Mouse – is contracting as children grow up so much more quickly. As one Disney executive admitted to me, a major challenge is how to deal with this continuing 'skewing down' of the upper age of childhood. Similar concerns are expressed in the toy industry, which has also been hit by this age compression.

The upshot? As in the financial lifecycle we met in Chapter 3, Shakespeare's seven ages collapse into three. But the dividing lines are very different: 40 is no longer a key boundary. Instead, the three social and cultural ages comprise childhood and early teens, extended youth, and old age starting somewhere in our sixties, or maybe even later in our seventies. Even here the elastic may be stretching further: is Robert Redford, aged 60 when *The Horse Whisperer* was released, objectively, let alone subjectively, old? Or what about David Bellamy, leading an Alpine botany nature trail aged 65?[8]

Generational faultlines

The redefinition of age bears a strong resemblance to the redefinition of class in western societies. For the swelling ranks of youth, read the burgeoning ranks of the middle class as it gobbles up most of the working and upper classes. But as we reject the labels of middle and old age, plumping for the ideal of endless youth, something equally odd is occurring: generational divisions are coming to the fore.

Generational labeling increasingly permeates modern culture and is faithfully reflected in the mirror of the media. Pick up any newspaper, watch television or tune into a radio station and you will find a growing number of references to generations. The popularity of generational Internet sites shows that this is more than a media fad. Click on Tripod, one of the most visited domains, and you are in GenX territory. Third Age bills itself as 'the Web for Grown Ups'. Visitors to the Internet Herald, another GenX site, are likely to encounter a hostile tirade against baby boomers for their new obsession with retirement saving.

According to one survey, a third of Americans believe that they belong to a generation. The US is a more rootless society than European countries – but Japan, that most structured of nations, also highlights specific generations. People born before 1912 are called the Meiji generation; those born between 1913 and 1926 the Taisho generation; between 1927 and 1944 are the Prewar Showa generation. After the baby boomers – 1945–58 – come the Shinjinrui (literally new human race!) – 1959 to 1970 – followed by the echo baby boomers. This identification with generation makes sense in a society of lifetime employment with a pecking order identified by seniority and age.[9]

For many people, the term generation is no more than shorthand for a particular age group at any one time. But the idea of belonging to a generation means more than a coded reference to a particular age. A generation is formed when its outlook bears the continuing imprint of conditions and events in its formative years. Significantly, the classic postwar statement on the molding of generations came in 1965 when the first American baby boomers were becoming young adults. In his presidential address to the American Sociological Association, Norman Ryder argued that 'in an epoch of change, each person is dominated by his birth date'. He likened the arrival of each new cohort – people born in the same period and ageing together – and the attrition and eventual extinction of older cohorts to a process of 'demographic metabolism ... the society whose members were immortal would resemble a stagnant pond'.[10]

Because of its sheer size, the baby-boom generation, born between 1946 and 1964, forged a common identity and pioneered social change. What is more, it has stuck by and large to the cultural attitudes formed in its early youth. British baby boomers have remained faithful to the permissive society, with two-thirds believing that premarital sex was 'not wrong at all', compared with just over a third of those born in the late 1930s. They are also more secular minded: half of those born in the early 1960s say they do not belong to any religion compared with under a third of those born in the 1930s.[11]

As older generations are replaced by younger ones, overall attitudes shift. Roger Jowell and Alison Park, who monitor British social attitudes, depict this process – common to both the US and the UK – as a cascade, with each cohort's attitudes displacing the previous one's as it moves up the age hierarchy. 'Young people with permissive attitudes do not turn into middle-aged prudes – no, not even once they have children of their own. So, as older more censorious generations die out, society as a whole becomes more permissive by means of cohort replacement.'

But the shift isn't always towards more permissiveness. GenXers, born between the mid-1960s and late 1970s, seem to have swung back towards more conservative attitudes. A comparison in the 1990s of Britons born in 1958 and 1970 found that twenty-something GenXers scored higher than thirty-something baby boomers on concepts such as 'marriage should be for life' and 'stiffer sentences for criminals'; and lower on favoring redistribution from wealthy to needy. The one exception to this shift towards conservatism was that they supported sexual equality even more than the baby boomers. This may explain why the younger cohort strongly backed the Labour Party, which had itself adopted many of these more conservative ideas under Tony Blair, such as 'tough on crime, tough on the causes of crime'.[12]

A similar generational backlash seems to have occurred in the US over sexual permissiveness, according to Norval Glenn, a sociologist at the University of Texas. In a striking inversion of what you would expect, young adults have become more restrictive in their attitudes to sexual behavior than those who are middle aged and older. With a doubling in the divorce rate between 1966 and 1976, the roots of this shift are not difficult to find. A study of GenXers aged 22 or more in 1995 found that the long-term effects of discord in the home were 'pervasive and consistently detrimental'. The backlash explains why young people have turned out to be more unforgiving about President Clinton's sexual escapades than older generations. One poll in 1998 found that over half of young adults backed impeachment if Mr Clinton committed perjury about his relations with Monica Lewinsky compared with a third of older Americans.[13]

Generations at war?

Class consciousness gave birth to class warfare. So it is not surprising that the idea of generational conflict has surfaced as generational identity becomes more salient. Baby boomers are pitched against GenXers, senior citizens against both – or so the story goes.

What are they fighting about? Money, of course – the money spent by government. To keep tabs on who's footing the bill, a new type of accounting has been invented. Generational accounting aims to work out, in today's money, who will shoulder the tax burden for government spending, present and future. Calculations along these lines indicate a game of passing the generational buck. Future Americans, for example, are now expected to face a tax burden half as high again as those born today. Generational imbalances in many other countries like Germany and Japan are even higher.[14]

Such findings, which require heroic assumptions, are hotly disputed. They only tell you about the position as it stands looking forward, making no allowance for previous taxes paid by older people, nor for the sacrifices so many made in the Second World War. The calculations necessarily assume no change in policies. The results are highly sensitive to assumptions about the underlying growth of the economy and the choice of discount rate used to convert all the sums into today's money.[15]

Despite these shortcomings, generational accounts do dramatize the yawning gap in government budgets around the world that will open up in the twenty-first century as people live longer and the birth rate falls. The rising bill has not been a deliberate act of policy; it has occurred primarily because the agequake has shattered former assumptions about longevity and continuing population growth. Nonetheless, the figures certainly give ammunition to those who want to stir up generational conflict. GenXer Robert George, assistant to Newt Gingrich, then Speaker of the US House of Representatives, wrote in 1997 that 'a new Cold War exists. This one is generational. It has the most spoiled and self-indulgent generation in history on the one side and their dissed and deprived successors on the other.'[16]

That's just the battlelines for GenXers vs baby boomers, even though it's today's retirees who have supposedly walked off with the generational swag in the form of over-generous state pensions. In Germany there is talk about the 'treaty between the generations' breaking down. In New Zealand, historian David Thomson has documented a fundamental switch in resources from young to old starting around the 1970s. In his book *Selfish Generations?* he warns: 'we have created and are now worsening the conditions for deep, hurtful and destructive generational conflict'.[17]

Despite such forebodings, I find this talk of generational warfare vastly overblown. In Florida, seniors call for crime-busting programs while younger people want extra spending on education. But even in this prototype state for an ageing America, political polarization on generational lines is much less marked than you might expect. In *Young v. Old*, an examination of generational divisions and politics in Florida, Susan MacManus concludes that 'mostly, the generations differ in the intensity, rather than the direction, of their opinions'.[18]

There may be tensions between generations, but there are also powerful family bonds. Bumper stickers may famously declare 'I'm spending my kids' inheritance', but there's another message in the actual figures for family gifts. According to estimates for the mid-1980s, American parents were giving their grown-up children $33 billion a year while grandparents chipped in a further $5 billion. Add other forms of transfers like payments into trusts and the annual flow came to around $60 billion. This financial support was admittedly among the well-to-do, but a social survey of different generations in Albany, New York State, found altruism rather than self-interest. The researchers found that 'on a broad range of policy and family issues, people's attitudes do not reflect their current generational self-interest'. For the time being at any rate, generational markers are essentially cultural: they are not a new set of war paint.[19]

Mellow, mellow?

The lasting effect of some generational values, mainly cultural, does not mean that we don't change as we get older. In 1998, the British television program *42-Up* revisited the lives of some 42-year-olds who had been filmed for this series every seven years since the age of 7. The initial aim of program makers Granada had been to illustrate the impact of class on people's lives; but 35 years on, what stood out as much was the effect of age.

Baby boomers in their forties and early fifties may retain distinct attitudes formed in their early youth. But equally, they are different people, by dint of their age and experience. For one thing, most have become parents; for another, most are established in their careers. Perhaps most importantly, they start to feel the first intimations of mortality: time no longer stretches ahead in an endless vista. For all the advances in health and well-being, the gradient of ill-health still starts to rise after fifty. While some soar in their careers, the majority find the road ahead increasingly blocked with no alternative route available.[20]

For some this is the time when the dreaded mid-life crisis strikes. However, if stress is any indication of this much debated phenomenon, the peak period is in your late thirties and early forties. Indeed, social researchers who have been following a panel of 10,000 individuals in the UK through the 1990s have found that stress levels fall markedly after the age of 50 and stay low for the next 20 or 30 years. 'Contrary to earlier suppositions it seems that this is a particularly satisfying period of married life', write demographers David Coleman and John Salt. By contrast, younger baby boomers often face multiple stresses. These are particularly acute for those trying to combine work with bringing up children and caring for parents. In the US, the average caregiver is a married woman in her mid-forties who works full time with more than one child of 18 or under living at home – no wonder she feels like the filling in a sandwich.[21]

Theodore Roszak made a name for himself with his account of the counter-culture in the 1960s. He now argues that ageing baby boomers will reject shallow consumerism for deeper values. The tilt towards longevity will lead to a sea change in attitudes, away from out-and-out competition and 'the frenzied pursuit of marketing novelties and technological turnover' to the more enduring values of wisdom and compassion. Society will no longer be grounded on the survival of the fittest but survival of the gentlest, as the cult of youth gives way to the power of the 'New People'.[22]

And we'll all live happily ever after. The need to coin yet another euphemism to describe older people, now the 'New People', signposts the uphill struggle that Roszak faces in arguing his case. He himself tellingly documents 'the senior follies' – the flight from age through longevity potions and recourse to the cosmetic surgeon's scalpel. The idea that we will reach utopia through ageing is very American, but like all utopias is wishful thinking.

Pollsters have asked Americans for almost three decades questions that probe the kind of values Roszak is upholding. For example, do people deal fairly with you or try to take advantage of you? Or do people try to be helpful or are they looking out for themselves? Most young people start by being cynical but become more trusting: however, the change has occurred by the time they reach their mid-thirties. A similar finding is reached by social researchers who have been tracking a panel of British households in the 1990s: 'it is only young people, still living in their parental homes, who appear to be rather self-centred', they report. So by this reckoning the great sea change in values should already have happened. Many claims have been made for the impact of the baby-boom generation – but social redemption as they age is a claim too far.[23]

Rainbow societies

A more realistic look into the future focuses less on a tilt towards the values of older people and more on a greater diversity of values and attitudes. The agequake is causing society to splinter in many other ways than along the new generational faultlines. The very forces that drive ageing are splitting the social spectrum. The result: rainbow societies.

Once upon a time, marketers and advertisers could happily focus on the traditional family as the principal type of household. At the start of the 1980s, married couples with dependent children accounted for a third of all households, but by 1996 that share had shrunk to less than a quarter – lower than that of single households (Figure 18).

As we saw in Chapter 4, there will be no let-up in this trend over the next two decades. Indeed, the absolute number of households occupied by married couples is expected to decline. By around 2005, fewer than half of adults will be married – down from 66 percent of men in 1981. One of the key drivers of ageing – the reduction in fertility as more people choose to remain single – is thus contributing to greater

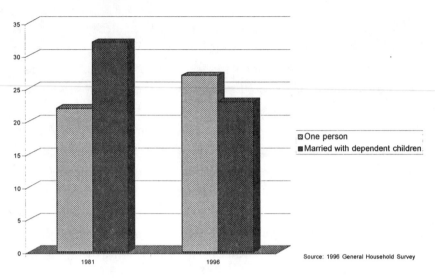

Figure 18 Eclipse of the traditional family
Household type as percentage of all households

social diversity. A further driver of ageing – the increased divorce rate which makes children more risky for women – is creating another color in the rainbow society: the increasing prevalence of stepfamilies. Almost a tenth of British families now contain one or more stepchildren. An ageing society is much less homogenous than a high-fertility society.[24]

The one limited antidote to ageing – immigration – is also contributing to the rainbow society. Net immigration accounted for a third of total population growth in the UK between 1983 and 1993. Already, ethnic minorities comprise 3.2 million or 6 percent of the British population. Continued immigration and the younger age profile of minorities – for example, about 40 percent of those stemming from Bangladesh and Pakistan are under 15 – will ensure that ethnic minorities will increase both in absolute and in relative size. In 1992, demographers David Coleman and John Salt projected that the ethnic minority population would stabilize at 4.5 million, assuming an end to immigration within 15 years. However, the government now assumes that net immigration into the UK will continue at an annual rate of 65,000 over the next 20 years.[25]

In practice, much of the increase will be concentrated in a few urban centers, primarily in London. The 1991 Census showed that a fifth of Londoners were members of ethnic minorities. Projections made by the London Research Centre show this increasing to 27 percent by 2006. The diversity of London's population is even more marked when you include all the white people born outside the UK, who comprise some 10 percent.[26]

Similar trends are at work throughout the West. Nowhere is this more apparent than in the US, which is returning to its nineteenth-century role as the world's melting pot. Then, the nationalities mixed in the blender were the different 'races' of Europe. Now, with net annual inflows in the 1990s approaching a million, the flavors being added are more exotic: a touch of Latino here, a dollop of Asiatic there to add to the plain vanilla of continuing European immigration.

Although gross inflows of immigrants, both legal and illegal, in the 1990s have come close to the peak of 1.3 million reached in 1907 and 1913, they have been much smaller in relation to the American population, which has grown more than threefold since the start of the twentieth century. But when you look at the contribution that immigration is making to population *growth*, the story changes. In the 1990s, immigration will account for 37 percent of the increase in the number of Americans; between 1900 and 1910 it accounted for 28 percent. Indeed, if net immigration continues at its current levels, these new Americans will account for *two-thirds* of the increase in the population over the next 50 years.[27]

The result: the US is about to become even more of a melting pot in the second age of immigration than it was in the first. Then the existing population was having lots of children; now no longer. Taking into account likely intermarriage rates, the National Research Council forecasts that if immigration continues at its current rate, non-Hispanic whites will only comprise a half of the US population by 2050. Those of Asian extraction will rise from 3 to 8 percent of the population, while Hispanics will jump from under a tenth to a quarter (see Figure 19). In practice, there is bound to be a blurring of these ethnic

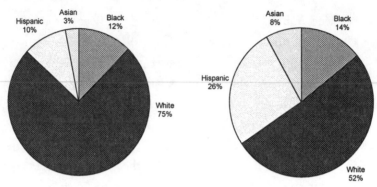

Figure 19 A *new American demographic landscape*
The US population by racial/ethnic group, 1995 and 2050
Source: NRC The New Americans

boundaries, as more and more Americans have multiple ancestry – like Tiger Woods, the US golf champion who is a quarter Thai, a quarter Chinese, a quarter black, an eighth white and an eighth American-Indian.[28]

In Europe, the contribution of immigration to population increase is even greater than in the US. Across the whole of the EU, net migration has outweighed natural increase, the excess of births over deaths of resident populations, since the end of the 1980s. By the mid-1990s, the proportion of foreign-born to the total population was almost as high in the Netherlands as in the US, at around a tenth.[29]

Rock on

A redefinition of age, the emergence of generational faultlines and the creation of rainbow societies: these are the sweeping social changes under way because of the agequake. They add up to a cultural revolution rewriting the rules of the marketing game – though not in the direction that most would expect.

You might suppose, for example, that the way to target the burgeoning numbers of people in their forties and fifties is to appeal to their age. Wrong: explicit age labeling in advertising will remain taboo. Whether they are middle aged or middle youthed, 40- and 50-year-olds don't want to be categorized by their age.

That still leaves the marketers and advertisers with a real dilemma: how to target older age groups without alienating them. One approach, drawing on the generational model, is to appeal to distinct generational experiences. Hence the nostalgia craze that hit the US in 1998. *Business Week* reported that 'these days nostalgia marketing is everywhere, from almost forgotten brands such as Burma Shave to jingles that borrow from classic rock'.[30]

And the revival of the love bug. Thirty years after the summer of love, VW brought out a revamped model of the bug where so many boomers legendarily lost their virginity. With sloans like '0–60? Yes' and 'Less Flower. More Power', the generational pitch of the campaign – for which the advertisers won an international award – was an instant hit. It was an example of 'not attacking an age-group in an obvious way but subliminally', comments Garel Rees, director of the Centre for Automotive Research at Cardiff University.[31]

VW was careful not to target boomers alone but to broaden the appeal to GenXers. The approach made sense on three grounds. First, why limit your market for a product like a car? Second, over-specific targeting takes you back to age labeling – still taboo. Third and perhaps most important, younger people tend to be more experimental – even if this means retro chic in the shape of revamped Beetles.

So don't expect a deluge of gray advertising just because western populations are ageing, not least since the average age of the population will only be moving into the early forties. Some companies are dipping their toes into the market – for example, a soft drink campaign for Lilt starring 58- and 60-year-old Blanche and Hazel. More typical will be minor adjustments: for example, Kellogg's Special K abandoned thin models in its US 'reshape your attitude' campaign starting in early 1998, in a concession to the ageing of the baby-boom generation. For the most part, however, youth will continue to dominate marketing strategies.[32]

Television plays an important role here. Because older people are such heavy viewers, schedulers and advertisers can take them for granted. In-your-face youth shows like British channel BBC2's *Reportage* found ironically that their audience included large numbers of pensioners. By contrast, young people are much lighter viewers and therefore have scarcity value. In the US, advertisers pay a premium to reach younger viewers because adults aged 18–49 watch 40 percent less TV than do older people. So if you target younger age groups you'll pick up the older audience at the same time – and enlighten them on what presents to buy for their grandchildren. One American record company found that the largest consumers of rap and techno music were those aged 55 and over.[33]

What this meant in 1998 was a plethora of *Ally McBeal* shows as networks and advertisers sought to hit the new G-spot: upmarket women in their twenties and early thirties. As columnist Maureen Dowd wrote in the *New York Times*, US television is 'now desperate to capture the same audience of 18–34-year-old women who turned Ally into such a fad – smart, urban working women who shop and have intimate relationships with American Express'. She quoted the blunt dismissal of older American women by Dick Wolf, the show's executive producer: 'Women don't want to see older women that they can't relate to. They want to see people that are from their generation who are doing things that are important.'[34]

As usual, if you play hard to get, it only incites the chase. With young people's adult tastes still unformed, there's everything to play for. As veteran marketer Sir George Bull, former head of drinks firm Diageo and now chairman of Sainsbury's, told me: 'Choices are forged in people's twenties and thirties by and large – you do need to get them pretty young. They're the real new emerging markets.' With both the broadcasters and the advertisers still using youth to sell products, expect youth culture to remain entrenched even as society ages. It's no coincidence that television programs made in and inspired by still youthful Australia have global appeal where British programs have failed despite both countries sharing the common advantage of the English language.[35]

The rise of generational marketing?

The American VW Beetle campaign can be interpreted as an example of generational marketing – an appeal to emotions and attitudes held with particular conviction by particular generations. US sociologist Glenn Firebaugh, though a sceptic about some of the larger claims made about generational differences, highlights differences in musical taste as one of the clear dividers. With boomers confessing to information overload as they struggle to keep up with the non-stop high-tech revolution, it comes as no surprise to find companies like Intel and Microsoft using classic rock tracks to promote their high-tech products.[36]

In their book *Rocking the Ages*, J. Walker Smith and Ann Clurman claim that generational values are now as important, if not more, in determining consumer decisions than the usual demographic suspects of income, education and gender. The authors, who hail from market research group Yankelovich, say that their generational model has allowed them to make early prediction of new market trends.[37]

According to Yankelovich, today's generation of retirees – 'matures' – were brought up in the Depression and war years, so they were taught the values of frugality and duty. They are conformist where boomers are individualist, materialist where boomers hanker after experiences. Boomers were brought up in an era when the economy boomed and everything seemed possible; they have had to adjust their horizon to the growth slowdown of the 1970s and 1980s that capped those vaulting expectations. GenXers, by contrast, have much more diverse values. They are more entrepreneurial while more financially conservative; unlike boomers who express themselves through work, GenXers want a life outside work.

The bottom line that results from such divergent values? Each successive generation will respond differently to the marketplace as they pass through the lifecycle. 'Boomers will look nothing like Matures when they reach retirement; Xers today look nothing like the Boomers of twenty or thirty years ago. Same life stages, different consumers.'

Although nostalgia marketing has shown its worth and appeal in the US, I find the Yankelovich conclusions overstated. For one thing, the notion has hardly caught fire outside the US. In an international survey in 1997 conducted through focus groups with 45–54-year-olds, Research International painted a similar picture of early baby boomers as a generation that has done well but is now beset by worries about job and financial security. Nevertheless, the UK was the only European country where baby boomers, like Americans, responded to explicit generationally targeted messages. At the other extreme, individualism ruled in France and Italy, where boomers were resistant to being sorted into generations.[38]

The greater resistance of European cultures to new generational demarcation lines makes sense. For one thing, the postwar baby booms weren't nearly as intense or as long as those in North America. For another, European societies are more rooted in class and place. In any one year about a sixth of Americans move – a far higher proportion than stick-in-the-mud Europeans. Generational faultlines are starting to surface in Europe, but they will be less pronounced than in the US.[39]

A more important weakness in the idea of generational marketing to older age groups is that it presupposes that they retain fixed mindsets throughout their lives. This is only partially true. Baby boomers may retain certain core attitudes, but like all generations they will respond to the overall tide of social and cultural change. Reporting a survey of research into attitude change across cohorts, Stephen Cutler of Vermont University concludes that 'there is no evidence that older cohorts are rigid, set in their ways and incapable of change … If public opinion at large was shifting, change characterized the older cohorts as well.'[40]

Just as baby boomers once set that tide in motion, so now they will respond to new currents set by the emerging generation. A classic study of the parents of boomer high school graduates in the 1960s and early 1970s showed they were much more flexible than the researchers anticipated, changing their views along with their children. If that was true, then how much more so with baby boomers. After all, they share with their own children much higher educational levels. Revealingly, too, they are much happier about sharing their home with grown-up children than were their parents.[41]

There may be a limited place for generational marketing to older age groups by hitting emotional hotspots that they associate with their salad days, but you can only milk nostalgia so far. A central lesson of generational research is that while older generations do remain faithful to some key opinions, they also move with the times. Those times are set by younger generations. As ever, it will be the new generations that will make waves – which older ones, including boomers, will have to ride. In the US, the generation to watch is the echo boom, whose first members are now turning 20.

Unlike their parents, echo boomers have been brought up not in a world of black and white – communism vs capitalism – but one of relativism. They have been brought up in a world where the remote has liberated viewers from the dictates of TV channel controllers. Through the Internet they can surf to wherever they want. Having grown up with the computer, they are at home and at ease with it in a way that still eludes many of their parents. They have also been brought up in an era of unparalleled sexual explicitness because of the need to target health messages about AIDS.

Already this 'freestyle generation' is making waves with its taste for retro, hiphop and techno music. Marketers have found that 'reverse marketing' – messages that deprecate the product – is often more effective than the traditional in-your-face approach. Hollywood swiftly dropped plans to schedule films aimed at thirty-somethings to target the more lucrative market of the teen echo boomers. Echo boomers won't pack the same force as their parents – they may be the same absolute size but proportionately they are smaller – but they will dictate the cultural fashions of tomorrow.[42]

Marketing to rainbow societies

As societies fragment in the agequake, rainbow marketing will come to the fore: marketing for a multicultural world. The challenge for marketers will be how to reach out to ever more diverse populations.

Narrow focus is not the way forward: minorities wish to enjoy dual identities, not be confined to their minority quarters. What this means is that brands will become even more important. Fragmentation, in society and in the media, makes it progressively more difficult to build new brands and drives up the value of established ones. But the era when they could be sold by identifying with social stereotypes has gone. Marketing to rainbow societies requires messages that draw on universal images and stories.

Quite apart from the growing numbers of ethnic minorities, there is another reason that they will become the apples of marketers' eyes: their youthfulness. Minorities may still only consist of a quarter of US citizens, but they add up to a third of those under 18. That makes them a crucial component of the markets of tomorrow. Indeed, they pack an even bigger punch than a simple body count might suggest. Marian Salzman of Brand Futures says that her best prediction was that white teenagers want to be black. Sir George Bull accepts that 'it's increasingly important to appeal to ethnic groups'. As long as ethnic minorities remain the trend setters, marketers and advertisers will have to keep their ear to the street.[43]

The street, not least because of the tendency of ethnic groups to concentrate in just a few major metropolises; what demographer William Frey calls 'minority magnet metros'. As he points out, 'the largest blocks of hispanic and Asian consumer groups, voters, and multi-lingual Americans are highly clustered in only a few metro areas'. So even though the drift away from the cities can be expected to continue, the cutting edge of youth culture will remain the big city, particularly the melting pots of Los Angeles and New York, where hiphop represents a musical melding of diverse cultures.[44]

Arguably, the term melting pot is now misleading. Modern communications make the experience of immigration very different from what it was earlier in the twentieth century. Air travel makes it possible, if not to commute, certainly to make frequent return visits. In New York, today's immigrants can talk directly to their families via special videophone parlors. The net result is that they retain more of a dual identity than previous arrivals. According to an editorial in the *New York Times*, New York now 'stands at the center of a new transnational immigrant culture'.[45]

Perhaps most important of all in the US is the spread of Hispanic values. John Grace of Interbrand says they 'are already infiltrating American culture in hundreds of ways'. Jennifer Lopez is the first of a new generation of Latino film stars, Latin dance is taking the floor in clubs and Mexican food loading the tables in restaurants. A sign of the times was McDonald's decision in 1998 to take a stake in a chain of fast-food restaurants serving Mexican-style food.[46]

The impact of Hispanic culture will be all the stronger because unlike earlier waves of immigrants, today's Latinos have a homeland on their doorstep. Until the recent change of heart in California about bilingual education, their children have been educated in Spanish. Hispanic TV channels complete the picture. As a result, Hispanic culture will become increasingly influential. To see the future, take a trip to Los Angeles where the Latino share of the population will reach 46 percent in 2000 and 51 percent in 2010. Already the buying power of Latinos in the US is larger than Mexico's economy.[47]

The big bulge in young Latin Americans will intensify the reach of Hispanic culture in all its varieties. In Brazil, there is already a similar bulge of young adults to the one that transformed US society in the late 1960s and early 1970s. In Mexico, there will be a big increase in the next decade. With this demographic following wind, the fusion of Hispanic and American cultures is set to become a dominant global force.

Breaking waves

The social and cultural changes brought about by the agequake will be full of surprises. One is that the very concept of age – and youth – will become ever more plastic, and not only because of plastic surgeons. Youth culture will not give way to middle-age culture. Instead, adult youth will stretch forward to encompass people in their forties and fifties. At the same time, it will stretch back to include young teenagers, who are growing up much earlier than previous generations because of the all-pervasive reach of the mass media.

Yet even as everyone worships at the altar of youth, generational differences are likely to become more salient. Generational faultlines are usurping the old class divide. Politicians, never slow to latch on to a popular mood, increasingly use the language of generational renewal. Tony Blair, for one, attributes his landslide election victory in 1997 to a generational change. Germany's new Chancellor, Gerhard Schröder, used a similar rhetoric in his election campaign. Class warfare will not give way to generational warfare, as some fear, but there will be a growing sense of generational identity.[48]

Societies will fragment in other ways under the pressure of the agequake. The very forces driving ageing – low fertility and lengthening lifespans – are contributing to social fragmentation by creating more single households. Immigration, the sole compensating force against ageing, makes ethnic minorities ever more important. California, the bellwether of America, will become a 'majority minority' state as early as 2001, official demographers revealed at the end of 1998.

These changes add up to a cultural revolution that will affect everyone who wants to communicate to these new constituencies, whether in the marketplace, the workplace or on the election trail. An ageing society is socially and culturally much more complex and diverse than a youthful one. Companies that cotton on to this demographic effect will snatch a vital advantage over those who don't. The Chinese cultural revolution was supposed to be permanent; it wasn't. The cultural revolution generated by the agequake will have more staying power.

7

Work makeover

NOWHERE WILL THE AGEQUAKE STRIKE HARDER THAN IN THE WORKPLACE. Yet nowhere seems less prepared for the challenge. Companies can no longer rely on a bubbling spring of new, young recruits. That spring is drying up to a trickle. The existing pool of workers is ageing rapidly.

Across the western world, workers are growing older. The process is gradual but inexorable. Take the European Union. In 1995, 40- and 50-year-olds constituted 45 percent of the prime working-age population (defined as 20–59). But by 2015, they will comprise 55 percent.[1]

Not everyone in the working-age population works or wants to work. To estimate what's happening to labor forces, you need to take into account activity rates, the proportions of adults at given ages who participate in the labor force. The International Labour Office (ILO) has done this in global projections for the economically active population, which includes both employed and unemployed, up to 2010. Over the next 10 years, these show a variety of ageing trends in the developed world: youth deficits, shrinking middles and bulging older age groups.[2]

Italy faces the most acute youth deficit. Between 2000 and 2010, the number of 20–34-year-olds in the labor force will drop by a quarter. Indeed, the only age group in the workforce projected to show any substantial growth at all is 40-year-olds – but not on sufficient scale to make up for the drastic decline in the number of younger Italian workers.

The US may be suffering from an epidemic of obesity but the American labor force will shrink in the middle. The 35–44 age group is set to fall sharply between 2000 and 2010. The baby-boom echo and immigration mean that the US does not face youth deficits. Even so, the bulging portion of the labor force will consist of people over 50.

These trends are already under way. They lie behind one of the most striking trends of the 1990s: the continuing waves of corporate downsizing and management delayering, notably in the US. A ragbag of reasons has been advanced to explain this phenomenon, ranging from the recessions at the start of the 1990s, the pressure from Wall Street for quick-buck returns, to the impact of globalization in enhancing competition. However, the more fundamental effect of the age shift is often strangely overlooked. Companies found themselves top heavy as the baby boom bulged into middle age and the baby bust brought down the number of new recruits. The upshot: too many middle-ranking chiefs chasing too few Indians.

One way of capturing the demographic impetus for delayering is to calculate the ratio of people in their late forties in the labor force to those in their late twenties. Typically, the older age group will be managing the younger recruits in companies, so you would expect there to be fewer of them.

In the past, you could generally rely on the underlying age structure of the population to deliver the desired ratio of fewer managers to workers. But this no longer holds true under the new demographic dispensation. Because the American baby boom was earlier than the European one, the change has already largely occurred in the US (see Figure 20). As recently as 1990, there were two people in the American workforce aged 45–49 for every three aged 25–29. But already by 2000, there are more American workers in their late forties than in their late twenties.

A similar shift lies ahead for many European countries. Falling numbers of young Germans have pushed the ratio up in the 1990s even

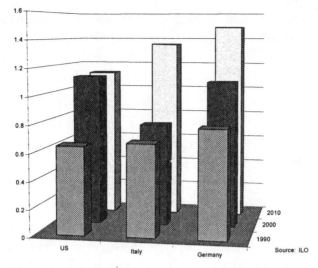

Figure 20 The age shift at work
Ratio of 45–49 to 25–29-year-old workers in three Western countries

before the delayed effects of the baby boom are felt. By 2010, there will be almost three German workers aged 45–49 for every two in their late twenties. Pressure for delayering in German companies will thus be intense in the first decade of the twenty-first century. The age shift will be even more pronounced in Italy in the 2000s. In the UK, too, 45–49-year-old workers will exceed 25–29-year-olds by a quarter in 2010.

Man overboard

Adjusting to the age shift will involve a root-and-branch rethink of the way we organize work, both in the private and the public sector. The exodus of older men from the workforce shows the power of the forces sustaining the status quo. From hard-nosed private company bosses to supposedly enlightened employers in the public sector, the easy option has been to keep the workforce young by discarding older workers.

In Britain, less than a tenth of men aged 65 or over and only half of those in their early sixties are still in the labor force. Even more extraordinary is what has been happening to 50-year-olds, the vast majority of whom worked in the past. By 1995, a sixth of them had quit the labor force.[3]

Yet in many European countries still fewer older men now work. In 1997, only 48 percent of 55–64-year-old men in the EU still had jobs, compared with 59 percent in the UK and 66 percent in the US. In France and Finland, even more men have been thrown overboard: only about a third of 55–64-year-olds are employed.[4]

Japan is often seen as an exception to this trend, but this is only partially true. The lifetime employment model in major companies has a cut-off point at 55, precisely to keep workforces young. With mandatory retirement at this age, albeit with a lump sum, most older workers are forced to carry on working elsewhere at much lower wages. Even so, the proportion of Japanese men over 65 who are in the labor force has been falling since 1970.[5]

Ageism at work

In most advanced countries, participation rates of older women have remained broadly stable, so is the high departure rate of older men another defeat in the sex wars? No: the same tendency is at work with women. It has simply been disguised by the strong upward trend in overall female participation in the labor market, as the employment rates of successive generations of women rise.[6]

Neither are older people leaving the labor market because they work in declining industries. Older workers tend to be under-represented in the fast-growing finance and business services sector and over-represented in the declining agriculture sector. Overall, however, there is little support for the notion that young workers are employed in growing sectors and older workers in declining sectors.[7]

That leaves ageism as the villain. Older people are favorite targets of redundancy programs, which have a more devastating impact on them than younger people because they then find it so much more difficult to find work again. Recruitment consultants admit that they screen out people over 50 because that's what their clients brief them to do. As Howard Davies, then deputy governor of the Bank of England, told an employers' conference in 1997: 'each time there is a downturn the older workforce tends to be shaken out and when the upturn comes they don't get back in'.[8]

Age discrimination is certainly prevalent in Britain. Manifest in the dispatch with which older workers get the chop, it also takes the form of negative attitudes to older employees at work and age exclusions in job adverts. A survey of 2000 employees in the mid-1990s found that four out of five workers over 50 thought they'd been turned down for a job because of their age.[9]

Explicit age limits in advertisements are no longer so prevalent thanks to pressure from organizations like the Institute for Personnel and Development. According to a survey published in 1998 by the *Equal Opportunities Review*, there was a sharp reduction in the proportion of advertisements using numerical age limits between 1993 and 1998. However, some ads resorted to coded language – 'young, dynamic environment' or 'young, fast-moving entrepreneurial company' – to deter older workers. Examples cited of age-exclusionary advertisements included top companies like Vodafone and PepsiCo.

Revealingly, the adverts with explicit age exclusions for executives, drawn from a survey of recruitment in the *Sunday Times*, show that you're only really safe from age discrimination in your thirties (see Figure 21). The ideal age is 35: after that you'd better watch out. For secretarial and clerical positions, drawn from a survey of London 'free' magazines, the ideal age is even younger at around 25.

Ageism is tied in with corporate control, which is why it sets in well before 50 in most firms. Over half of managers use age informally in recruitment and selection, according to a survey for the UK Institute of Management. Employing disproportionately large numbers of older workers challenges the hierarchical structure of companies and the idea of a career path leading ever upwards. It also creates a problem on a personal basis for younger managers. As one respondent to the survey said: 'most

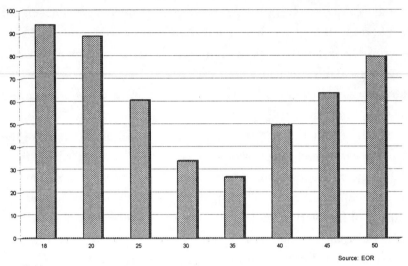

Figure 21 Over the hill at 40
Percentage of people, by age, excluded from jobs stating an age preference

people do not want their staff to be older than they are'. Another com-
mented: 'there is a natural tendency for managers to appoint staff
younger than themselves'. How much easier to avail yourself of the latest
influx of enthusiastic young recruits; that way you keep the whip hand.[10]

The self-employed are their own bosses. The result: far fewer of
them quit the labor market early. In the UK and Germany, the self-
employed are three times as likely to work in their early sixties than
male workers in general.[11]

How governments collaborate in ageism

Employers have been able to dispense with older people because governments have colluded in the practice, picking up the tab through
higher benefits or earlier pensions. Such measures are not sustainable
in the long term: they overload the public finances, contributing to
persistent deficits and spiraling public debt. But if offered a choice,
most politicians will always plump for the easy short-term rather than

the hard long-term option, whatever their rhetoric. Indeed, govern-ment employers have often been among the worst offenders.

Since the early 1970s, many European governments have actively collaborated with employers in using early retirement as a means of reducing unemployment. This economically illiterate policy is based on the 'lump of labor' fallacy, that there is a fixed number of jobs to be shared out, even though jobs have grown in line with the working-age population over the past century. Predictably, it has done nothing to help alleviate the European jobs crisis, which is rooted in labor market rigidities and sky-high employment costs. Ironically, those costs have been pushed up by the burden of financing the retired, including the very people who've been laid off in the first place.

One of the main ways governments have colluded with employers is by rigging the benefits system to bring down the official unemploy-ment figures. This distortion helps explain why so many individuals attribute their withdrawal from the labor force to poor health. At the start of the 1990s, over half of men and 40 percent of women aged 55–64 in Austria were receiving invalidity benefit. Such shock-horror figures tell you more about the perverse incentives of the social secu-rity system than they do about the health of older Austrians.[12]

Dial 999 – for pensions

The easiest way to get rid of unwanted older workers is to retire them early on substantial pensions. Few can resist the bait. Wherever state pensions allow early retirement, the opportunity is gratefully snapped up. The behavior of East German workers after unification highlighted the perverse incentives of an over-generous pension system. With jobs being decimated and pensions 60 percent higher than they had been under the Communists, there was a mass bolt for the door of early retirement. In just two years, the labor force in eastern Germany shrank from 66 to 41 percent of the working-age population. Despite subsequent reforms, the pension system remains biased in favor of early retirement.[13]

In the UK, the meager state pension is still tightly linked to the official retirement age, which is why early retirement on the state has come indirectly via other social security benefits like those for incapacity. However, it's another matter altogether for those who work for the state and are members of official secondary pension schemes. Welcome to an Alice in Wonderland world, where you'll soon be dialing 999 for pensions rather than for the fire brigade.

Fireman Sam is becoming Pensioner Sam: more than 70 percent of firefighters retire early. In London, over a fifth of the entire bill for fire brigades goes on pensions; there are actually more pensioners than firefighters on the books. Tony Ritchie, leader of the London Fire and Civil Defence Authority, warns that 'if we carry on the same way all we will do is pay pensions'.[14]

As for council workers, the cost of early retirement between 1990 and 1995 came to an astonishing £6 billion, enough to clear the entire capital repairs backlog for schools in England and Wales. According to a hard-hitting report from the Audit Commission, the watchdog of local government, three-quarters of council employees retiring in 1995 left early, at an average age of 54.[15]

Once again, ill health is the ostensible reason for this cascade of early retirement among council employees. But it is hard to believe that working for a council is so much more unhealthy than other jobs. Certainly not such that they are almost four times as likely to retire on grounds of ill health as employees of retailer Sainsbury's – and thirteen times more likely than those working at Kodak.

Perverse incentives and implicit taxes

The lure of early retirement is not confined to public-sector workers. A survey of private schemes in 1997 found that over 70 percent of retirements were before 60 – many well before then. At Imperial Tobacco, four-fifths of those retiring were in their early fifties. According to the UK's Institute for Fiscal Studies, private occupational pensions have been an important reason for the falling proportion of older men who work. Companies have used pension fund surpluses to fund early retirement on generous terms to employees they are easing out. A quarter of people receiving a pension from their former employer in 1995 were under the state pension age. In the US, similar incentives in private pensions have also contributed to the rising tide of early retirement.[16]

Incentives in pension schemes and state benefits to retire early amount to an implicit tax on older workers. If, for example, you work an extra year and your benefits do not increase, then your entire contributions are, in effect, taxed away while you lose a year of benefits. Calculations along these lines reveal that workers in their late fifties and early sixties face punitive tax rates in some countries. In 1995, the overall implicit tax rate on work in Italy was 79 percent; in the Netherlands 57 percent; and in Denmark and France it was about 50 percent.[17]

That suggests that even those who take early retirement are in effect being pushed. And yet the cost of early retirement is daunting. An estimate for the UK in 1998 put the cost of 'institutionalized ageism' at £26 billion in lost output. According to the World Bank, it is already lopping off 2 to 4 percent of GDP among advanced countries and 1 percent in developing economies. This lost production would cover more than half of total pension spending in many countries.[18]

The cost of paying out pensions and not receiving contributions means that governments have been running bigger budget deficits and therefore raising the national debt. This is the exactly the reverse of what they should be doing: repaying debt to reduce the burden on future generations. This will exacerbate the impact of future ageing in the twenty-first century.

Live longer, work longer

Not before time, governments have woken up to the social costs of early retirement. Already, official retirement ages are being pushed back. In Britain, women's retirement age will rise from 60 to match men's at 65: the change takes effect between 2010 and 2020. In the US, the retirement age will gradually rise from 65 to 67, starting in 2003 with an increase of two months.

The reason for introducing such reforms is transparent: it reduces the cost of pensions by cutting the number of years they have to be paid. Because the changes are scheduled for the medium term, no one screams blue murder when they are announced. For example, the UK Treasury will gain £6 billion a year once women's pension ages are fully equalized with men's.[19]

These measures are just the beginning. Governments often use the Paris-based Organisation for Economic Co-operation and Development, an intergovernmental thinktank for the leading industrial countries, as a stalking horse. Just as they always blame recessions on international events while taking all the plaudits for booms, so they prefer to introduce unpopular reforms in concert. For much of the 1990s, the OECD has been breaking the ground for its member governments with a major research effort into global ageing.

In 1998, it unveiled a policy wishlist inspired by this research. *Maintaining Prosperity in an Ageing World* is advance warning of the behind-the-scenes intentions of western governments. Significantly, the report highlighted the importance of staunching the hemorrhage of early retirement. If this continued, said the OECD, it could cut future living standards as much as demographic ageing itself would. Early retirement has a greater effect than increased longevity because it both increases the number of retired people and reduces the number of productive workers.[20]

The OECD called for an end to the perverse financial incentives implicit in pension schemes, taxation systems and social programs that encourage early retirement and deter workers from staying on. As if this were not enough, it has calculated that the effective age of retirement (the actual rather than the official one) would have to increase to 70 to cope with the fiscal burden of ageing populations – dashing boomers' hopes of retiring at the same age as their parents, let alone earlier. Such an increase is highly unlikely, but it gives a measure of the problem as the effective age of retirement heads in the opposite direction.

Don't say you haven't been warned. Employers and employees alike should brace themselves for a battery of measures designed to stem early retirement. One inevitable change is a formal banning of age discrimination; although rooting out such prejudice involves a change in social attitudes as well as formal legislation. The US has outlawed discrimination on the grounds of age since 1967, as has Canada since 1978 and New Zealand since 1992. In the UK, the Labour government backtracked on a reform pledge in opposition because of worries that it would expose the New Deal program for young people to legal challenge. Age discrimination will nonetheless be banned eventually. In 1996, the Law Society's Employment Law Committee concluded that legislation would be both workable and effective.[21]

A restructuring of pensions is also on its way to encourage later rather than earlier retirement. Governments everywhere will seek to restore the link between spending more years at work and getting higher pensions. This basic principle of actuarial fairness is flouted in both state pensions and private schemes. In western Europe, the imperative is to reform state pensions; in the US and the UK, to reform private schemes.

An end to ageism at work?

Companies face a major challenge. Their favorite strategies for keeping their workforces young are running into the demographic buffers. Governments are signaling that they are no longer going to pick up the social bill for offloaded older workers and there is a limit to pushing the cost of early retirement on to company pension funds. Quite apart from these considerations, there is a demographic imperative at work. Since the major source of workers is now older, why cut off your nose to spite your face?

In the past, employers often had good reason to slough off older staff. Age–earnings profiles show that workers in the developed world generally hit peak earnings at around 50 (see Figure 22). In Britain, they peak even earlier. The standard interpretation of this pattern is that individual productivity generally declines in one's fifties. It is easy to see why this might be the case with manual workers, who are no longer in their physical prime. However, this can also occur with non-

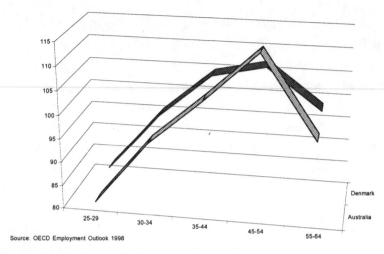

Source: OECD Employment Outlook 1998

Figure 22 Earnings fall away past 50
Earnings for age-groups as percentage of average for 25–64-year-olds

manual workers, as the skills and expertise they have acquired through education and at work become less relevant to a fast-changing economy. Employers say this is a key reason for their reluctance to employ and recruit older workers. Retraining could overcome this problem, but companies then worry that they cannot recoup the cost with older people who are not expected to stay as long as younger employees.[22]

The two unquestionable advantages that older workers do possess are greater experience and authority. They have been around; they have seen it all. No one doubts Alan Greenspan's credentials to head the most important economic post in the world as chairman of the US Federal Reserve, even though he is in his seventies. When Greenspan said in late 1998 he had never experienced similar economic conditions in almost 50 years, that judgment commanded respect. Greenspan is not alone. An international survey by the UK's Cranfield School of Management found that the most effective leaders were older senior managers who were 'more able to take a balanced view on issues before reaching a decision'. They also proved better at motivating colleagues and subordinates and at managing relationships outside their organizations.[23]

The trouble is that these advantages can only benefit a chosen few. We can't all be senior managers. Ironically, the niche for such leadership skills turns out to depend on the very hierarchical organizations that are bound to exclude all but a tiny minority of older people from exercising them.

Employers' ageism towards the majority of older workers is thus less irrational than it may seem. From an employer's perspective, older workers expect higher pay but don't cut the mustard. They are less willing to move jobs and more likely to be absent from work through sickness. Employees' willingness to leave work in their fifties, particularly when offered tempting pension carrots, also makes more sense. The returns from working start to fall at the very time when the desire to enjoy more leisure is rising.[24]

However, you can interpret the decline in earnings in people's fifties in a different and more optimistic light. Instead of reflecting age-related productivity, it may reflect generational differences in education and training. The generation born in the 1930s and early 1940s did not enjoy the same educational opportunities as postwar children. So as a group they have found it more difficult to adapt as older adults to the new skills requirements of a rapidly changing economy. The better-educated baby-boom generation should be able to meet this challenge more effectively.

By the same token, employers will not have good reason to discard the over-fifties in future. The OECD estimates that half all workers aged 45 to 64 in the developed world had less than upper secondary education in 1995. By 2025 this should drop to a quarter. It argues that 'this educational upgrading should provide the basis for workers to acquire skills throughout their working life and thus enter their older age relatively well equipped'.[25]

Governments are hoping that employers will respond positively to the coming bulge in older workers. There are some signs that their hopes will be answered. In the UK, a number of companies have created the Employers' Forum on Age to press the case against ageism and the case for employing a workforce of all ages. Dominic Cadbury, chairman of UK drinks and confectionery firm Cadbury Schweppes, asks: 'Why have so many businesses allowed so many valuable people to retire early when their knowledge is virtually irreplaceable?' Employers in France, where early retirement has become a way of life, have expressed similar regrets about the loss of 'corporate memory'.[26]

Leopards don't change their spots

Despite these brave hopes, I suspect that older people will continue to have a rough time in the workplace, certainly in sustaining a traditional career. On paper, ageing baby boomers may have roughly the same qualifications or length of time in education as successor generations. But the skills and qualifications of today's new entrants to the work-force are often much more relevant.

The central problem for older workers is that the use-by date on their expertise is closing in all the time. In the past, skills and know-ledge retained their value for quite long periods. Now they depreciate almost as quickly as computer equipment in many lines of business. Meanwhile, the returns on new investment in 'human capital' – the latest MBA, the latest hotshot computer technology graduate, the rocket scientist recruited by the City – are far higher than the returns on old investments – the degrees of yesteryear. Half the graduates recruited in 1998 started on salaries of £15–18,000 and the top 15 per-cent of them earned more than £20,000, according to the Association of Graduate Recruiters. Starting salaries for graduates rose much more sharply than economy-wide earnings.[27]

This may be a case of life imitating modern art. Judging by the val-uations put on their work, the first generation of modern American artists like Mark Rothko and Willem de Kooning peaked in their early fifties. By contrast, the second generation – artists like Jasper Johns – produced their most successful work well before the age of 40. David Galenson, a labor market economist at Chicago University, believes the valuations reflect a shift in the art market away from technical excel-lence and towards innovation.[28]

New recruits are rather like greenfield sites – capable of much more efficient production to meet today's industrial needs – while older workers are more like long-established plants, difficult to adapt to new working practices. New entrants to the workforce are inherently more adaptable than long-established workers, who have built up an investment in skills specific to a particular employer or profession. Managers identify lack of flexibility and problems with new technology as two principal disadvantages of older workers.[29]

As companies strive to make themselves more flexible, more responsive to the quicksilver of changing consumer demands, these are formidable incentives to recruit younger rather than older workers. Even without these incentives, big companies won't change their spots. If they are to mimic the emerging age profile of the working-age population, they too will have to invert the traditional hierarchical pyramid. But this runs counter to the most deeply ingrained instincts of any large firm, cutting out promotion and career incentives.

With all the talk of flatter organizations, it's easy to forget how intensely hierarchical big companies remain; and the extent to which these hierarchies remain anchored in age as well as ability. 'Managers have cut off points by which age people are supposed to have achieved certain levels in their careers,' comments Carl Gilleard of the Association of Graduate Recruiters. If you don't make it to a given level at a given age, you're seen as incompetent or lacking the necessary drive. Delayering may have stripped out many middle-management jobs, but it's given even greater authority to those higher up the scale. For example, a study by McKinsey of quality management around the world in the car component industry highlighted the move to lean organization in successful companies. However, the main effect of this streamlining was to widen the reach of control for those at the top.[30]

Consultancy firms are themselves notoriously ageist, hiring legions of junior consultants to service senior partners and then winnowing them out after a few years with a ruthless 'up or you're out' policy. Neither they nor the companies they serve are going to break with this practice: they will remain hierarchical creatures.[31]

What this suggests is that firms will not respond to the demographic shift in the workplace by employing older workers directly.

Instead, they will seek to draw on the talent in the marketplace through subcontracting. Firms facing a surplus of middle-aged staff, who would become discontented with the lack of opportunities, will encourage them to leave – but with a difference. Unlike the indiscriminate downsizing of the past few years, they will actively seek to build links with workers whom they know and value.

'Stick to your knitting' has been a corporate refrain of the 1990s. The days are gone when giant conglomerate companies acted like mini economies in their own right. Within the more focused firms favored by the City and Wall Street, managements have sought to whittle down their key activities to those where they are clearly adding value and to buy in all the remainder. The demographic imperatives of an ageing workforce will give a new impetus to this trend.

Small businesses will flourish as never before in this new corporate landscape where large companies sit at the hub of a network of bespoke, specialist suppliers. Many of the suppliers will be staffed by older workers who have left the big firms. Expect a continuing surge in management buyouts as large companies continue to spin off divisions and functions that aren't central to their operations.

For many firms, this will still not be enough to crack the problem of an ageing workforce. That will require new ways to sustain incentives where promotion opportunities are limited. More than ever, companies will link pay to performance, in order to align the interests of workers whose careers have run their course with those of the firm. Stock options will become the norm rather than the exception.

The talent trawl

Many companies will still seek to keep their workforces younger than the population at large. This will have two principal effects. First, there will be a talent hunt for younger workers in the West. In particular, companies will seek to employ more women in countries where female labor force participation rates are still low in the younger age brackets.

Second, multinationals will seek to draw on the younger workforces of developing countries, giving a further impulse to globalization.

The age shift is already affecting big employers in the UK, not least the National Health Service and schools. Both the medical and the teaching professions have reported acute shortages of young recruits. More than anything else, this will help rectify the problem of poor pay in the public sector as government is forced to pay better wages to attract new recruits.

The talent trawl for graduates will be unremitting. Once the top professional and financial services firms could skim the cream, but now they face fierce competition from all corners of industry and commerce. Microsoft relentlessly targets the brightest rising stars in the computer industry. The only companies that will thrive in the knowledge economy are those which recognize that people are the ultimate scarce resource.[32]

While some companies fight it out for the pick of the graduate crop, others will seek to employ more women. This is often seen as a hidden reserve, particularly in Mediterranean countries. In Italy only a third of adult women are in the labor force compared with half in Denmark. However, it won't be easy to find the younger women whom employers will ideally want to recruit. In Denmark participation rates of women in the labor force virtually match those of men in their thirties and in the US and UK the gap has been steadily closing. While there is undoubtedly scope to employ more women under 40 in Italy, the striking incidence of lower employment is among older Italian women.[33]

Another reason not to exaggerate the potential of this hidden labor reserve is the prevalence of part-time working among women, which accounts for a fifth of employment in the US and almost a third in the EU. Even so, you can expect employers to bend over backwards to recruit more women in the younger age groups. Here is an opportunity for enlightened firms to steal a march on their competitors by offering flexible working hours and childcare facilities that will entice women to work for them.[34]

If you can't find them at home, then the obvious answer is to recruit from abroad. Already McKinsey's 600-strong London office employs people of 46 nationalities and looks increasingly to India and Eastern Europe for recruits. High-tech firms in California's Silicon Valley have been clamoring Congress to relax immigration controls on highly qualified professional and technical workers. In 1998 the annual limit was doubled from 65,000 to reach 115,000 by 2001. The 1998 cap had already been exhausted halfway through the year.[35]

Finally, multinationals will use their global muscle to move the work to where the young workers are – in developing countries. The explosion of foreign direct investment (FDI) by companies in developing countries has many causes. But the World Bank argues that in a long-term perspective, FDI is, in effect, a substitute for migration: moving the capital to the workers rather than the workers to the capital.[36]

Avoiding the boomer jam

Sometimes there's safety in numbers, but not always. It would be nice to think that companies will adapt to an ageing workforce by becoming less ageist, but you would be naive to bet your career on it. Baby boomers are creating a jam for themselves, clogging up the middle ranks of big companies. In the US this jam has already affected the first wave of boomers. In Europe, with its later baby boom concentrated in the 1960s, the pile-up will occur in the 2000s. With the 'up or you're out' mentality of so many companies, today's 30- and 40-year-olds have got to prepare for the worst. They can't take for granted that economic pressures will put an end to ageism in the workplace.

To survive in this harsher climate, the baby-boom generation will have to raise its game. The time is past when you could expect to live all your life off the knowledge you acquired at school and college. Middle-aged workers are caught in a two-way squeeze between the need to prepare for working longer and the ever-decreasing half-life of knowledge. The only answer is to upgrade your skills and complement them with new ones. Lifelong learning is one of those slogans more honored in rhetoric than in practice. But if baby boomers are to stay in the workplace longer, then they will have to pay more than lip service to it.

They also need to be realistic about the employment marketplace of the future. To reiterate, one place where the jobs won't be as they get older – but for the chosen few – is big companies. On past form, they will be doing everything in their power to retain the classic pyramidal structure of command and control. The 30-year-olds who are currently so employable for big companies will find the tables turned as they enter their forties.

By contrast, small businesses, which are inherently much less hierarchical, will provide many more employment opportunities. These will be the firms that will benefit from the trends towards outsourcing. Revealingly, that same survey of British executives which showed how extensively companies use age to sort people out found that managers in small and medium-sized enterprises were more positive about the future recruitment of older workers. Better still: set up your own firm. Despite the risks, it will pay as never before to be entrepreneurial in your own right to avoid the boomer jam.[37]

Turning from types of company to kinds of activity, manufacturing will continue its longstanding decline as an employer. This is the sector of the economy where productivity gains are fastest thanks to automation and where competition is fiercest because of foreign competition. For employment opportunities in developed countries, this is a sector to avoid – though there will of course be many opportunities to manage and advise the ever-expanding foreign subsidiaries of Western-based manufacturing companies.

The area to work for is services. Its share of employment has grown throughout the twentieth century to reach some three-quarters of the US labor force. Within this vast and varied array of activities, the ones to target are those that will prosper from the shifts in demand generated by ageing. Healthcare, financial services and the leisure industry are three sectors with bright prospects.

Adult education and training should be another growth industry. There will be an explosion in retraining and relearning in the next 15 years to rekit ageing workers with the new skills they need. Here is an opportunity for educational entrepreneurs – to cater for adults in their prime working years, when they are run off their feet both at work and at home. The requirement is for concise learning packages that address people's exact needs in as timely a fashion as possible.

Increasingly, such packages will be provided over the Internet so that people can learn where and when they want to rather than having to turn up at some college at a fixed point only convenient to the educators. Already some prestigious universities are starting to dip their toe in the water. Oxford University started two courses related to computing at the start of 1999. Stanford University has launched a master's degree program in electric engineering that can be conducted entirely over the Internet.[38]

Preparing for the work makeover

In an ideal world, mounting demographic pressures would banish ageism in the labor market. Age walls in the workplace would be torn down. As we grew older, the great majority of us would continue to work, although many of us would wind down our full-time engagement and work increasingly part-time or as freelances.

But formidable obstacles stand in the way of a genuinely non-ageist labor market. Big companies remain inherently hierarchical. Many will prefer to solve their problems by going overseas. To date, experiments with gradual or partial retirement have foundered wherever they have been tried.[39]

A work makeover is coming, but it will accelerate the demise of the lifetime career with one employer. As the old corporate dinosaurs contract, they will become hubs at the center of a dense network of sub-contractors and freelance talent. This will prove a testing environment for ageing baby boomers. If you have entrepreneurial flair, you should deploy it: the labor market will be one where it is easier to provide work for yourself than to rely on employers. For most of us, the imperative will be to keep our working skills and expertise as well honed as possible, so that we remain employable on our own terms.

8

Pensions crunch

THE DOWNSWING OF THE DEMOGRAPHIC ROLLERCOASTER WILL OPEN UP a cavernous gap between contributions and payments in most state pension systems in the West. Something has to give. Either contributions will have to rise drastically or pensions will have to be cut drastically. If contributions rise, that will impose an intolerable burden on tomorrow's workers. But if payments are cut, that amounts to a default on pension pledges to tomorrow's retirees.

Throughout the developed world, governments are wrestling with this dilemma. Pension reform has moved to the top of the policy pile. The temptation is leave it to the politicians. The precise workings of pensions are forbiddingly abstruse and actual payments a long way off for most working people. Don't fall for the temptation. It's vital to keep tracks of what politicians are plotting. On past form, you can be sure that they will obfuscate their true intentions towards a vital part of your wealth.

You may not think of pensions as a form of wealth, but they are. In 1995, the rights built up in the UK's modest state pensions were worth three-quarters of the value of owner-occupied property; and all pension rights, public and private, were worth nearly double. In America, expected retirement payments from social security are equivalent to two-fifths of the total assets of households headed by 50-year-olds. By the retirement age of 65 these rights are worth some $160,000 for the average household. In countries where public pensions are more lavish, they form an even more important share of wealth holdings. So reforms will affect your pocket as much as any gyrations in house or share prices.[1]

Another reason to get to grips with pension reform arises from its potential impact on financial markets. Many countries rely on 'pay-as-you-go' arrangements in which working people fork out for today's pensioners in the increasingly forlorn hope that tomorrow's workers will pay for theirs. The system is already starting to buckle under the burden of lavish commitments to a rising number of retirees. A move towards funded schemes offers a possible escape route from the pensions dilemma by offering higher returns on contributions than pay-as-you-go schemes can deliver in the future.

Already, leading financial groups are circling over the rotting carcasses of state pension systems, hoping for rich pickings from the ultimate privatization. Reforms in Europe and the US that create new funded schemes could divert a huge stream of funds into stock markets, driving up share prices in the process. That's why the future of pensions is so important not just for tomorrow's society but for today's financial markets.

Pyramid scams

You might think that state pensions, purportedly embodying cast-iron obligations, have nothing in common with the flimsy promises of Charles Ponzi, the Boston swindler of the 1920s; but you'd be wrong. The trick he played was to set up a pyramid scheme whose extravagant payouts to early investors actually came from capital raised from subsequent investors.[2]

That is precisely what state pensions are: gigantic 'Ponzi schemes', doomed to implode as they mature in the new demographic order. Established when workers greatly outnumbered beneficiaries, pay-as-you-go pensions allowed previous generations of politicians to win

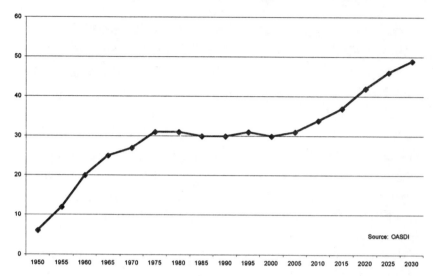

Figure 23 The American pensions timebomb
Beneficiaries as percentage of contributors

plaudits and votes on the cheap by transferring money to relatively few old people who had contributed next to nothing. Ida May Fuller, the first American to receive a regular social security pension, paid $25 in but got $23,000 out. Lucky Ida (who lived to be 100): the rest of us won't be so fortunate. The number of pensioners has grown enormously, they are living longer and the number of contributors is falling. As the age pyramid flips in the twenty-first century, so the pensions pyramid will flip too, bringing the swindle out in the open (see Figure 23).[3]

The fraudulent nature of state pensions is less surprising when you consider the motives of their founder, Otto von Bismarck. Germany's Iron Chancellor made no bones about why he wanted to introduce public pensions a century ago: 'Anyone with the prospect of a pension in old age or infirmity is happier and more *tractable* ... Whether or not this is State Socialism, it is *necessary*. It is said that it would cost perhaps 200 million marks: 300 million would not deter me. Contentment of the impecunious and disinherited would not be dearly purchased for such a sum. They must be *made* to understand that the State gives as well as demands.'[4]

The poor dears: how Otto worried about them. In this engagingly double-edged rhetoric, two of the principal themes of state pensions are encapsulated: the money-no-object purchase of political support and the desire to create dependency on the state. In a final fraudulent twist, Bismarck took the precaution of ensuring that the pensionable age was set at 70, well above the average life expectancy of contributors, so that the state would not have to fork out that much in any case. For his part, Lloyd George, architect of the UK's first old-age pension, fought the 1911 election campaign on the something-for-nothing slogan of 'nine pence for four pence'. He, too, made sure that the pensionable age was 70.[5]

War and inflation in the first half of the twentieth century made a mockery of these pledges in many countries, not least in Germany. However, the baby boom and strong economic growth after 1945 made the postwar era the heyday for public pensions. Nobel prize winner Paul Samuelson, that great popularizer of economics in the US, celebrated their fraudulent foundations in 1967. He wrote in a *Newsweek* editorial: 'The beauty of social insurance is that it is actuarially unsound. Everyone who reaches retirement age is given benefit privileges that far exceed anything he has paid in … How is this possible? … Always there are more youths than old folks in a growing population. More important, with real incomes growing at some three percent a year, the taxable base upon which benefits rest in any period is much greater than the taxes paid historically by the generation now retired … A growing nation is the greatest Ponzi game ever contrived.'[6]

But in the three decades since Samuelson wrote, the two foundations of successful pay-as-you-go systems – rising numbers of workers and increasing productivity – have been progressively undermined. Population growth tapered off, as fertility rates reached postwar lows in the US in the late 1970s. A sharp deceleration in productivity growth meant that real income growth fell back sharply. The effect has been to slash the effective return on pay-as-you-go contributions. With similar trends at work across the developed world, state pensions are no longer the greatest Ponzi game in town.[7]

Some argue that the problem with state pensions lies less with economic and demographic trends and more with unsustainable promises. You don't necessarily need an ageing population to set up a Ponzi-style welfare state, points out Richard Disney, author of *Can We Afford to Grow Old?* Witness the mess that Italy and many other countries have contrived for themselves. Brazil's acute difficulties in 1998 and early 1999 arose from a skyhigh budget deficit of around 8 percent of national income, of which two-thirds came from the deficit on a pension system riddled with abuses.[8]

But the US has not bungled its pension system and yet contribution rates have spiraled upwards to try to balance the books. In 1945, there were over 40 workers for every retiree. Each employee paid no more than $30 a year, a sum matched by the employer. By 1998, there were only three workers for every retiree. Not surprisingly, they were paying a lot more even taking inflation into account – over $4000 a year, with the employer coughing up a similar amount. Even with this increase, social security was actuarially broke.[9]

Most state schemes are not just actuarially broke but politically bankrupt. In the past decade, there has been a corrosive loss of trust in state pensions, testified in numerous opinion surveys in Europe and the US. Trustees of the American public pension scheme admitted in 1997 that there had been 'an alarming erosion of public confidence in the Social Security system over the past few years, particularly among younger generations'. Voters have become aware that the pensions game is played in counterfeit currency, likely to be devalued at any stage. Their suspicions are amply justified. State pensions suffer from that most intractable and malign form of risk: political risk.[10]

The pensions triangle

The pensions world divides into three parts: think of it as a triangle. At one point stands the European model, at another the diametrically different template pioneered by Chile. At the apex stands the Anglo-

Saxon approach, which mixes elements of both the European and Chilean models. The overall thrust of reform is away from the European approach towards the other two systems.

The pensions terrain in most countries in the European Union is lush savannah: generous but lacking in diversity. Private pension provision is modest. In Germany, company pensions amount to less than 5 percent of total retirement income. However, the main pay-as-you-go schemes offer much more generous benefits than in the UK or the US, with German pensioners receiving around 70 percent of average net income before retirement. Benefits are even more lavish in Italy and France.[11]

The need for reform is most acute in Europe. Somehow or other the strain of an ever-increasing burden of benefits in relation to contributions must be reduced. In Germany, contribution rates from workers and employers are already extremely high – a fifth of relevant income – and yet the public pension budget is heavily in deficit, requiring substantial tax subsidies. Even that deficit understates the financial burden, since civil servants' pensions are financed by general taxation.[12]

The Chilean template turns the European model on its head. Pay-as-you-go transfers between the generations have been replaced by a fully privatized model in which individuals build up their own nest eggs in equities and bonds. If you could start with a clean slate, this model is better suited to the new demographic order than an exclusive pay-as-you-go system. When labor forces are stagnating or declining in size, returns on contributions that are invested should exceed the effective returns on those into pay-as-you-go schemes. The danger, however, is that extravagant marketing costs will reduce returns, which may also prove volatile and ultimately susceptible to the demographic downturn. And in practice, developed countries cannot start with a clean slate.[13]

The Anglo-Saxon pensions model stands halfway between these stark alternatives. A universal state pay-as-you-go pension is complemented by extensive private pensions. The UK exemplifies this approach. A particularly stingy basic state pension means that only half of all income received by British pensioners comes from the state in the form of pensions and other benefits. In other countries which follow

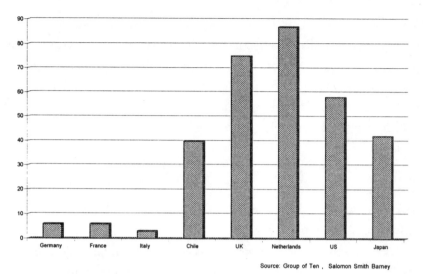

Source: Group of Ten , Salomon Smith Barney

Figure 24 Mind the gap
Pension fund assets as a percentage of GDP in 1996

the Anglo-Saxon model like the US and Japan, social security pensions are considerably more generous.[14]

The distinction between the different models is captured in the scale of pension fund assets in relation to the economy. The value of pension fund assets in countries like Germany, France and Italy is puny compared with those organizing their pensions along Anglo-Saxon lines (see Figure 24). Despite the relative immaturity of Chile's funded pension system, it had already built up pension assets worth 40 percent of GDP by 1996. In the more mature private funds of the UK and Netherlands, assets are much higher. No wonder fund management groups look at the foothills of the European model, compare them with the Anglo-Saxon mountains and *salivate*.[15]

Don't read their lips

The need to cut pensions to the new demographic cloth is pressing, but in most countries politicians have ducked the tough decisions needed.

The main exception is the UK, where stealthily introduced reforms have proved brutally effective in slashing pensions. Elsewhere, pension promises remain over-generous and ultimately unaffordable. Take a long, cool look at the reform attempts so far: if they don't convince you that state pensions should carry a wealth warning as prominent as the health warning on cigarette packets, nothing will.

In the US, the jointly run retirement and disability funds have stumbled from one crisis to another. In 1983, contributions were hiked to ensure solvency for the next 75 years. But within 15 years the reform had come unstuck. Projections in 1998 showed that the system would only deliver three-quarters of promised benefits by 2032.[16]

A key reason for the deterioration is a little-known but highly revealing Congressional fix just before the mid-term elections in 1994. Contributions to finance old-age pensions were raided to cover a shortfall in the notionally separate disability fund, which was about to go broke. The public didn't notice at the time, but there is a direct link between that surreptitious Congressional fix and the renewed sense of crisis in the late 1990s about the future of social security.[17]

In the UK, similar covert tactics were deployed by the Conservative government of the 1980s to bring about a radical restructuring of state pensions. Here, however, the aim was not to cover up the need for reform as in the US, but to axe future benefits. In 1980, the basic state pension was indexed to prices rather than wages. The change seemed innocuous but effectively froze the real value of the pension. Pensioners for whom it was the main source of retirement income no longer shared in the country's growing prosperity. By the time the Tories were kicked out of office in 1997, the change was saving the Treasury £8–9 billion a year, the equivalent of 3p on the basic rate of income tax.[18]

Next the Conservatives turned their attention to the state earnings related pensions scheme, Serps. The costs of this secondary pay-as-you-go scheme, established in 1978, had been greatly underestimated, not least because, astonishingly, the original forecasts for spending stopped short at 2008, the very time when the swollen baby-boom generation would start to retire! Alarmed by the potential impact on the public accounts, the Conservatives swung the ax on future benefits on two occasions. Their second bite of the cherry was in 1995, but was so cunningly technical – they altered the indexation methods – that only a handful of pension-spotters noticed them. Altogether, their cuts together with the growing number of people opting out of the scheme slashed spending on future benefits to less than a *third* of the original plan.[19]

One reason the Conservatives laid siege to Serps was to increase the appeal of personal pensions, designed to allow individuals to build up their own personally controlled nest eggs. The initiative backfired badly. Personal pensions were the wrong product for people on low incomes because administrative and marketing costs were too high in relation to the level of contributions. In addition, many personal pensions were wrongly sold to people who were already members of company schemes that offered better value because the employer also made substantial contributions. The personal pensions bandwagon of the 1980s became the misselling saga of the 1990s, with an ever-escalating number of claims against the insurance companies that were primarily responsible. By the end of 1998, the cost of misselling was estimated at £8–11 billion. Inevitably, other policyholders rather than shareholders became the fall-guys, footing the lion's share of the bill.[20]

The overall effect of these changes was to emaciate the main state pension, emasculate Serps benefits and undermine faith in private pensions. But the underhand methods were undeniably effective for the public finances. Alone among major western countries, the UK's pensions books broadly balance both now and in the future.[21]

In Europe, by contrast, restructuring has been far less drastic. Changes have been most sweeping in Italy, where politicians have hacked away at pensions no fewer than three times in the 1990s. However, the reforms have essentially tackled the absurd excesses of the system – fully indexed pensions of up to 80 percent of final salary and retirement in people's early fifties – rather than the demographic timebomb. The changes will only be phased in over a long period – by 2035! – and still leave benefits at an unaffordable level of 15 percent of GDP – three times as high as in the UK.[22]

Yet the need for reform in most European states is far more pressing than in the US and the UK because benefits are so much more generous and the future imbalance of retirees and working people so much more acute. The agequake will ultimately strike Germany, Italy, Switzerland and Austria more violently than even Japan. The pivotal old age dependency ratio – the number of retirees in relation to working people – will rise far more than in the US and the UK.[23]

Seldom have reforms been more unsatisfactory. In the US, the social security system remains in place but requires yet another bout of restructuring to restore long-term viability. In Britain, the threat is of a return to poverty in old age for the many who have no private pension. In continental Europe, state pensions remain largely intact but impose an unsustainable burden on future generations of workers. As politicians have sought to dodge the central trade-off in reform – higher contributions or lower benefits – public pensions have come to look dodgy themselves. It's always a good idea *not* to read politicians' lips, but nowhere more so than with pensions.

The oversold Chilean model

No wonder more and more people have been looking for a way to avoid the pensions crunch. The result has been a mass trek to Santiago to find out how Chile's radical new model of funded state pensions works. The Chilean approach formed the template for the British Conservative government's plan to replace the basic state pension wholesale with a funded scheme before the 1997 election. But the model, like pensions in Chile, has been over-marketed and over-sold.

If state pensions were established by an Iron Chancellor, modern funded pensions were founded under an Iron General, Chile's Augusto Pinochet. Introduced in 1981, the system differs fundamentally from the classic postwar state pension under which each working generation pays for its elderly. By contrast, funded schemes create individual nest eggs, explicitly owned by their contributors, who can choose between different fund managers. Compulsory contributions are set at a tenth of gross wages and the state provides a residual safety benefit, funded by general taxation.[24]

At first sight the concept seems highly attractive, addressing the central political weakness in pay-as-you-go, that you can't rely on the next generation to honor its dues. The Chilean model also offers the alluring prospect of more bangs for your buck: higher returns on contributions than you can get from pay-as-you-go schemes in the new demographic order of the twenty-first century. The reform coincided with a surge in the national savings rate and growth. Not surprisingly, José Piñera, the minister who masterminded Chilean pension reform, sees cause and effect at work.[25]

Imitation is the sincerest form of flattery. By that token, the Chilean model has been a raging success. In the 1990s it spread like wildfire across Latin America. By 1998, similar funded schemes had been introduced in Peru, Colombia, Argentina, Uruguay, Bolivia, Mexico and El Salvador. By the year 2000, over $200 billion of Latin American pension fund assets is expected to be under private management, according to US investment bank Salomon Smith Barney, rising to $980 billion in 2015. The popularity of the Chilean model reflects the bankruptcy of pension systems throughout Latin America. In Peru, public investment managers pulled off the remarkable feat of *cutting* the real value of state-controlled pension funds by over a third every year in the 1980s. Given track records like this, you can see why any alternative was seized with open arms.[26]

But the Chilean model is not all milk and honey. One of its most serious drawbacks is high administration costs, amounting to 10 percent of contributions in 1994. Much of this cost arises from pointless, promiscuous switching by contributors between the various pension providers. This drives up sales and marketing budgets, which accounted for half of all costs in 1996 and 1997. When the Mexican scheme was launched in 1997, the new fund managers hired a total sales force of 50,000. Pensions aren't sexy, so the firms employed girls in miniskirts to parade up and down the streets wearing their company's logos. Luis Rubio, director of the Centre for Development

Research, wrote in the Mexico City daily *Reforma*: 'Now that we are being bombarded with publicity, it's worth noting that we are in danger of being fleeced by the new institutions, in the same way that our state pensions have been plundered.'[27]

Competition and marketing go hand in hand, but such heavy costs inevitably reduce net returns in the long run, just as has happened with British personal pensions. The gross returns on investments in Chile's funded pensions have been excellent at over 10 percent, but the net yield for contributors has been significantly lower. Those chest-thumping claims about the invigorating effect of the new funded system on the economy also fail to cut the mustard. One IMF study showed that pension reform did not push up savings, but that it had boosted economic growth by spurring the development of financial markets. A study at the Chilean Central Bank was more positive, but calculated that the reform contributed less than a third of the increase in the savings rate and a quarter of the increase in the growth rate.[28]

Yet given the dire starting point in Latin America, almost any reform was bound to be for the better. An added advantage for countries at this stage of development has been the powerful stimulus given to the development of financial markets by pension privatization. Furthermore, Latin American countries remain relatively young. When Chile introduced the reform, only 6 percent of its population was aged 65 and over. Such favorable demographics have minimized the trauma inherent in introducing such sweeping changes.

For governments in the West, by contrast, the appeal of throwing out pay-as-you-go and replacing it wholesale with the Chilean model is not so obvious as in Latin America. With more highly developed financial systems, the gains from unleashing funded pension power are more limited. The demographics are also more unfavorable, since so many more people are already retired and drawing benefits – almost a fifth of the British population are of pensionable age – or in their middle years, with legitimate expectations about benefits based on their contributions to support the current generation of pensioners. With the pension crunch still years away, the political temptation to postpone is enormous.[29]

The US grasps the third rail

Despite these difficulties, the need for a move away from pay-as-you-go to partial funding is as real as ever. Otherwise, state pensions will simply cave in under the strains of the agequake. In a telling irony, the most lively and informed debate has not been in Europe, where the pension dilemma is most acute, but in the US, where the problems are more manageable. Europe faces a migraine, the US a headache; yet it's the Americans who've been energetically sorting through the medicine cabinet to find a cure.

One reason for the superior debate in the US is that the finances of state pensions are so much more transparent. In Britain, your money is shuffled around behind closed doors in Whitehall, with ministers advised by the Government Actuary, one of those shadowy figures like the Official Solicitor who pops up at awkward moments for the government but is otherwise firmly kept in the backroom. The general public hasn't a clue about whether pensions are in balance with contributions. In contrast, US Trust Funds have to report regularly on the financial health of retirement and disability and healthcare schemes, opening up the secret world of state pensions.

Since large-scale reforms in 1983, OASDI, short for Old-Age, Survivors and Disability Insurance and popularly called social security, has been running a big surplus to reduce the future strain of boomer retirees after 2010. This surplus is notional: it simply means that the US government has been borrowing less and the net public debt is lower by that amount. The much vaunted move of the federal budget into surplus in 1998 would not have occurred without the social security surplus.

However, even with this accumulated Trust Fund surplus – worth $655 billion at the beginning of 1998 – the long-term outlook for social security deteriorated sharply in the 1990s. By 1998, the long-range gap between benefits and contributions had risen to over 2 percent of taxable payroll. Bringing it back into balance would entail contribution rates immediately jumping by almost a fifth. The longer such an increase were postponed, the bigger it would eventually have to be: leave it too late and contributions would have to jump by two-fifths.[30]

The endemic problems of the social security funds in the 1990s contrasted with the astonishing ascent of the US stock market. This gave the privatizers a tremendous fillip. The state retirement system has long been regarded as a 'third rail' for reformers – lethal to anyone who touches it. But when President Clinton mounted a roadshow into social security reform in 1998, the privatizers were in the saddle and partial privatization had become a serious option.

This followed earlier calls from an Advisory Council on Social Security to divert some employee contributions into the stock market. Under one of its three reform proposals, almost half of total employer and employee contributions would go into individually owned 'personal security accounts'. This diversion of funds into the stock market would create a gap in the money needed to pay existing retirees. This gap would require additional contributions of 1.5 percent over 75 years.[31]

No free lunch

One eminent economist has argued that the long-term returns from equities have been so consistently good that they can be relied on to overcome the transition cost at minimal cost; and eventually deliver the same level of benefit at much lower cost. Martin Feldstein, former adviser to President Reagan, claims that the same social security benefits could be delivered in the long run with a contribution rate of just 2 percent instead of the current 12.4 percent, provided that this money was invested in the financial markets.[32]

During the transition period, extra contributions would not rise above 1.5 percent, and total payments would drop below current rates within 20 years. Just how credible is this offer of a free lunch? Not very. The extra investment induced by the reform would drive down returns from the unrealistically high rates assumed by Feldstein. If returns were as good as he hopes, the government would be tempted to tax some of the profit away. Another problem is administrative costs, which would eat into returns. These needn't scale the ridiculous heights of the Chilean system, but they could still be quite high in comparison with the costs of running the current pay-as-you-go scheme. Other top economists say that 'the popular argument that Social Security privatization would provide higher returns for all current and future workers is misleading': one way or another, they will have to pick up the bill for the largesse showered on the early lottery winners like Ida May Fuller.[33]

There are further worries about the complete privatization of US social security. The key risk is that you strip out social insurance completely, leaving everyone dependent on the fickle whims of financial markets. Equity returns have declined by more than 10 percent over one year eight times in the last 70 years; on three occasions the drop over a year or two was more than 35 percent. Another problem, pointed out by British economist David Miles, is that you bank heavily on returns from physical capital. By contrast, a pay-as-you-go scheme gives you more exposure to 'human capital' – economists' jargon for the skills and knowhow created through education and training – which is becoming more and more important in advanced economies.[34]

Any move to funded schemes in the US is therefore likely to be a top-up to the core, basic pay-as-you-go system rather than a comprehensive switch. This makes sense. By reducing the overwhelming pressure on pay-as-you-go state pensions, you reduce the risk that a future generation of workers will renege on them. One way or another, states have to provide safety nets for people in retirement so they may as well do so explicitly – although with lower benefits than those currently provided by US social security. At the same time, you don't put all your money on the uncertain future returns of the stock market. But whatever the wrinkles of reform, something that was unthinkable at the start of the 1990s was firmly on the public agenda by the end of the decade: partial funding of compulsory contributions.

Move over Darling: Britain tightens its embrace of private funding

Britain, too, is moving to enhance the role of partial funding, although on a voluntary basis. This decision follows a no-holds-barred battle in government over the future of pensions that saw bloodletting at the social security department. Top minister Harriet Harman was sacked and her deputy, Frank Field, designated the welfare reform minister and a keen advocate of the compulsory principle, resigned in Tony Blair's first cabinet reshuffle in mid-1998.

Alistair Darling, the new Social Security Secretary who had won his spurs at Britain's notoriously cheeseparing Treasury, ended the long suspense over the government's intentions in the closing days of 1998. The Green Paper, *Partnership in Pensions*, presented itself as a radically distinctive reform. But stripped of rhetorical flourishes, it fitted into the lineage of many of the key changes introduced by the Conservatives. Indeed, it went further than the Tories dared by pensioning off Serps, that unhappy orphan of earlier, more grandiose aspirations for state pension provision introduced by a previous Labour government.

Compulsory contributions to secondary private pensions, along the lines introduced by Australia in 1992, were rejected. Instead, the government's reform focused on a drive to encourage the take-up of funded secondary provision via 'stakeholder pensions' aimed at around five million people on moderate incomes, typically those earning between £9000 and £18,500 a year. These will be cheaper, simpler and more flexible than personal pensions, but contributions will be limited to an annual ceiling of £3600. Despite the new label, they amount to a refurbished version of personal pensions: income from them will depend wholly on returns from the stock market. In another resemblance, the big carrot for these moderate earners to join stakeholder pensions will be generous rebates from mandatory National Insurance contributions. The big stick will be an effective freeze on benefits if they stay in the public system. The new state second pension that will replace Serps is designed to deliver flat-rate benefits to low earners.[35]

Another proposal full square in the Conservative reform tradition is the decision to keep the basic pension anchored to prices. This ensures that the main item of pension spending will gradually wither on the vine. Since 1979, the basic pension has already fallen from 20 percent of average male earnings to 16 percent. It is set to decline to just 11 percent by 2020. This steady erosion of value shows again how it is the decisions that aren't spun to capture the headlines that matter most for pensions. It keeps up the pressure on middle to high earners to beef up their private pension savings, as the basic pension becomes nothing more than a safety net – placed on the ground.

Unlike earlier Conservative reforms, *Partnership in Pensions* sets out to be more generous to poorer pensioners, both current and future. Although the basic pension will become more derisory than ever, the government is now offering a more generous minimum income guarantee to retirees of around a fifth of average earnings. Under the Secondary State Pension, very low earners will do much better than under Serps, and carers will also be credited with rights for the first time.

Despite these concessions to Labour's redistributive tradition, the overall effect and intent of the reforms are to shift pension provision still further away from the state to the private sector, while leaving a large portion of future pensioners dependent on means-tested benefits, so reducing the incentives to save for low earners. The eventual £5 billion cost of the more generous arrangements for low earners is small change set against the £30 billion cost of uprating the basic state pension in line with earnings. The government's projections show that private pensions will account for 60 percent of all pension income by 2050, compared with 40 percent today. No wonder the reforms received a warm welcome from the fund management and insurance industry.

European Titanics: full steam ahead

Fundamental reform is far more urgent in most other countries in the European Union, but governments have shied away from confronting the issue. This political cowardice threatens the ruin of the public finances. Unless additional funded pensions are introduced to relieve the burden of unaffordably generous pay-as-you-go pensions, European countries are so many *Titanics* surging full steam ahead towards their date with demographic destiny. What makes the political inaction inexcusable is that the icebergs have been visible for years.

The reluctance to grasp the nettle simply raises the stakes for the future. Suppose that Germany sticks with its lavish public pensions. The International Monetary Fund calculates that it would then have to raise contributions as a proportion of current GDP by a third. If, on the other hand, the government puts off the evil hour, contribution rates will eventually have to nearly double to maintain the same level of benefits.[36]

But even a rise of a third is quite unthinkable. VAT had to be raised rather than pension contributions in 1998 to meet the imbalance in German retirement funding. The battle over this increase was such that then Chancellor Helmut Kohl accepted that 'we have arrived at the limit of what is possible'. Horst Seehofer, the federal health minister, warned young people that their 'living standard in old age is no longer secured through the pension insurance. You must make your own provision through private life or pension insurance or other capital assets.'[37]

Kurt Biedenkopf, Saxony's minister-president, warns that continued tinkering is leading to 'a pension political nightmare'. Together with Meinhard Miegel, head of a leading thinktank, he calculates that someone entering the system in 1995 and starting to draw a pension in 2040 will get only four-fifths of their contributions back under existing arrangements. By contrast, someone starting to draw a pension in 1995 receives a real return of over 4 percent a year. The system is even on the point of becoming unconstitutional, they claim.[38]

Klaus Friedrich, general manager and chief economist of Dresdner Bank, believes that a move to a partially funded system is imperative. But time for reform is running out: 'The question is whether we will have missed the demographic window?' The unfortunate answer is yes, according to two German pensions experts at the University of Mannheim. Axel Börsch-Supan and Reinhold Schnabel are gloomy about the prospects for reform. 'Major changes such as a transition from the current pay-as-you-go system to a partially or fully funded system are not seriously debated among government officials ... reform will become more difficult as political power shifts from the working population to the retired population.'[39]

The difficulty in switching to a fully funded scheme is that today's workers have to shell out twice over, paying for today's retirees and building up funds for their own pensions when they retire. Simulations by economists David Miles and Andreas Iben show that with a rate of return on the new funded scheme of 5 percent (much lower than the rate assumed by Feldstein for the US), it would take until the 2030s for the combined rate to fall below the rate payable under the pay-as-you-go scheme. The heaviest losers would be 30–40-year-olds, if the transition began in 2001.[40]

Calculations like these spell out why a wholesale switch to a fully funded scheme is politically impossible. But such simulations necessarily make a crucial assumption: that tomorrow's pay-as-you-go pension commitments will be honored. If they are not going to be, then losses are simply being drawn forward and experienced during working life rather than in retirement. That is why, as in the US, a move towards a partially funded scheme offers the best way out of the European pensions quagmire.

Will European governments grasp the nettle? On past form, it will take a major crisis to bring about genuine reform. Those financial groups circling round those rotting state pension systems may have to keep circling for a while. However, the longer reform is postponed, the bigger will be the eventual collision with reality when the pension bills are presented in earnest. For most people now working – particularly those living in many European countries – the only sensible assumption must be that without reform future governments will at some point renege on the extravagant commitments of pay-as-you-go state pensions.

Don't believe the promises

Partial funding is no panacea, but it is the only realistic way forward. It puts secondary pensions on a firmer contractual base and reduces the pressure on the basic 'pay-as-you-go' scheme, which can then play its primary role of essential social insurance. It offers a much stronger guarantee against the whims of politicians, who are guilty of more serious crimes of misselling than private insurers. The new funded secondary pensions will provide a pool of savings which should promote greater investment and national wealth, so providing more resources for future payouts.

But don't be taken in by the warm words of politicians and the financial services industry about the need to plough everything you can into pensions. The political risk you face with funded pensions is much less than with unfunded ones, but it is still considerable. UK Chancellor Gordon Brown lifted a cool £5 billion from private pensions in his first budget – and got clean away with it, even though the National Association of Pension Funds called it 'the biggest attack on funded pension provision since the war'.[41]

The problem with pensions of all kinds is that they are an extraordinarily inflexible form of saving. They are the longest financial commitment you can make, in which you are betting on the unknowable – both politics and economics – way into the future. Even if you have your own personal or stakeholder pension fund, you are tied hands and feet in terms of how you can use it when you retire. The basic deal is that you have to convert all the fund except a tax-free lump sum into a set of annuity payments for the rest of your life. Drop dead the day after you've signed a standard annuity contract and all the money you have painstakingly built up stays with the insurer, unless it is a joint policy. Those who die sooner cross-subsidize those who live longer.

Yes, for the time being your contributions are tax free, but who's to say the benefits won't be taxed at higher rates in the future? Financial advisers routinely warn you against making investments on the basis of tax relief. Yet they fall silent when it comes to the biggest investment, apart from property, that most of us are ever likely to make. Look at what happened in the US where legislation of the 1980s created 'virtually confiscatory tax rates on pension assets', according to two experts on retirement saving, until subsequent reforms in 1997.[42]

The limits of reform

At the end of the day, pensions reform is essentially a financial fix to a real economic problem. Moves to reverse the tide of early retirement – if they could be achieved – offer a more realistic way of averting the pensions crunch. This is indeed one of the strongest reasons to back the introduction of secondary funded pensions, since they give people a greater incentive to carry on working. Even so, there is a clear danger that they will deliver less than is hoped as the demographic forces undermining traditional state systems also lead to an eventual reduction in returns in the stock market.

Despite this risk, partial funding remains the best way forward. Secondary funded schemes relieve the burden on exclusive pay-as-you-go schemes. The retention of a mixed system continues to deliver a vital element of social insurance and means that you don't have all your eggs in one basket. Sooner or later, European governments will see the light of day and move to enhance secondary funding.

This is one very good reason for optimism about western stock markets in the 2000s. Indeed, stock market performance and pension reform are intertwined. The more likely partial funding is, the more that will sustain stock markets. The better that stock markets perform, the more likely it is that partial funding will become reality. The irony, of course, is that the optimal time to make this move would be in a bear market prior to a recovery.

Partial funding can help avoid a head-on collision between today's unaffordable commitments and tomorrow's harsh demographic realities, but it won't get western populations fully off the hook. Reform cannot deliver miracles and only the disingenuous pretend otherwise. The pensions crunch is still coming soon to a place near you.

Part Three

Shockwaves

9

Richter nine

'OLD AGE IS THE MOST UNEXPECTED OF ALL THE THINGS THAT HAPPEN TO a man,' wrote Russian revolutionary Leon Trotsky when exiled in Mexico. That was before an icepick happened to him. The demographics of the next 30 years may be written in our stars, but the agequake will still come as an enormous shock when it erupts in earnest. Around 2020, tremors will give way to shockwaves. The agequake will hit Richter nine, shaking western economies to their foundations.

2020 is the time when the full bills will be presented for the West's ageing societies. The time when boomers will find out whether their retirement plans have come good – or come unstuck. The time when spending on health will balloon.

With a shortfall of workers and an excess of pensioners, states that have shirked the need for reform will renege on their pension promises. Some European countries could find themselves facing the unthinkable: their economies will start to shrink because of declining numbers of workers. The steady growth in living standards we take for granted will slow to a crawl and may even halt altogether. Ageing on the scale that looms in the early twenty-first century will disrupt western economies and disappoint ingrained expectations of ever-rising prosperity.

The rollercoaster plunges

Ageing will intensify in the West in the 20 years after 2010 at an extra-ordinary rate. At the epicenter of the agequake is the looming imbalance between workers and retirees. You can't eat state pension promises and you can't drink mutual funds. Only people at work can ultimately provide marketable resources to support people who don't work.

That brings us to a key concept. Think of it (unkindly) as the drone to worker bee ratio. More specifically, define it as the ratio of old dependants to the working age population: those aged 65 or more to those aged 20–64. The use of the word 'dependant', incidentally, does not imply physical dependence but a reliance on others to provide economic resources. As I have already argued, health trends suggest that tomorrow's older people will be much more like astronaut John Glenn than the unfavorable stereotype of old age to which so many still cling.

Like any such definition, the old age dependency ratio is rough and ready, but it is a fair approximation if you look at the proportion of the population in each age group that works or wants to work. Some projections include the 15–19 age group as potential workers. However, the extension of full-time education has undermined the validity of this definition. In 2010 only a third of Americans and a quarter of Germans in their late teens will be in the labor force. Any distortion introduced by excluding this age group from the calculation is offset by the inclusion of 60–64-year-olds, despite their low and declining participation rates in the labor force.[1]

Now let's see what lies in store for this key ratio measuring the burden of older people who no longer work on the population of working age. Start with Germany. Over the past three decades, the burden of age has stayed roughly constant, with about one dependant for every four people of working age (see Figure 25). In the first decade of the twenty-first century, the ratio increases as the big generation born in the late 1930s and early 1940s retires. There's then a breathing space, but by the 2020s the burden increases drastically as the bulge genera-

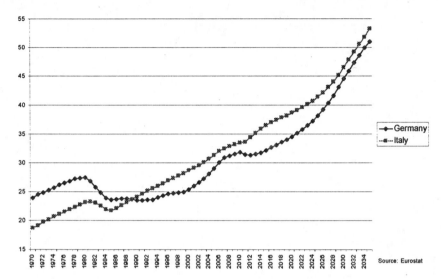

Figure 25 The burden of age in Germany and Italy
Those aged 65 or more as percentage of working-age population, 1970–2035

tion born in the 1960s retires. By 2035, there will be only two people of working age supporting each person over 65.

In Italy, the dependency ratio is already rising sharply. In the early 1990s, it stood at one in four, but by 2008 it will already be one in three. By 2035, there will be fewer than two people of working age to support each person aged 65 or more.

Italy and Germany are the outriders in western Europe. Britain and France get off lightly, by contrast, in the 2000s. In the UK, this is caused by the delayed impact of the baby bust of the 1930s and early 1940s feeding through to the number of retirees. In both countries, however, the respite is temporary, and the dependency ratio starts a steep ascent in the 2010s, although the deterioration is never so extreme as in Italy and Germany.[2]

Yet these distinctions are essentially trivial. In countries at the heart of the European prosperity zone, the 'golden banana' that stretches from Northern Italy through Switzerland, Germany and the Low Countries to Southeast England, the age scales are set to tilt decisively away from the worker bees and towards the drones.

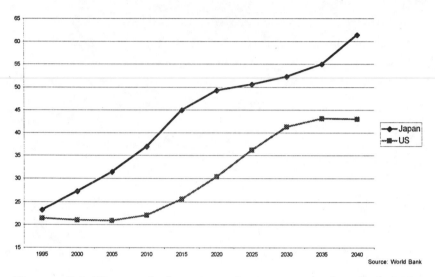

Figure 26 The speed of ageing in Japan compared with the US
Those aged 65 or more as percentage of working age population (20–64)

For Europeans, the agequake hits Richter nine in the 2020s. For Japan, 2020 will mark the point when the shockwaves start to subside after a period of unprecedentedly fast ageing. The easiest way to see this is to compare Japan's trajectory with that of the US (see Figure 26). In 1995, Japan's old age dependency ratio was roughly the same as that of the US. But just two decades later, in 2015, it will have doubled to stand at 45 percent: almost one drone for every two worker bees. By contrast, America's will have risen only marginally to one in four, helped in the 2000s by the small size of the cohort born in the 1930s and early 1940s.

Although the old age dependency ratio is set to reach unprecedented levels, some congenital optimists point out that the ratio has already risen substantially in the postwar era. Will the rise ahead be so much more painful than the rise we have already successfully managed? There is a logical fallacy in this 'it'll be all right on the night' view. If you stick your hand in a saucepan while the water warms up to, say, 40°, it won't burn. Can you deduce that it won't burn as it heats up further to boiling point? Just try it.

At this stage, the determinedly complacent often resort to another counter-argument. If you are worried about the ratio of drones to worker bees, they say, you should include children as well as the elderly as drones. When you look at this ratio, the prospective deterioration in the dependency burden in the decades ahead is less drastic. Indeed, this measure actually falls slightly in the UK and the US between 2000 and 2010.[3]

Again, this offers false comfort. The first is that western societies have already been benefiting from a sharp fall in this total dependency ratio since birth rates fell so sharply in the 1970s. Yet this has been the period when the cost of the welfare state has escalated to breaking point. Even more importantly, parents willingly shoulder the main burden of bringing up children, but society bears the cost of looking after older people. So the increased number of elderly dependants goes to the heart of political economy. Furthermore, as far as parents are concerned, the cost of children has spiraled up, so the decline in the dependency ratio caused by fewer children has not relieved the pressures on their finances.

The speed with which ageing occurs is also vital. It is no coincidence that Japan, the country experiencing the fastest onset of ageing, has been suffering so much from its effects in the 1990s. Adjusting to the downward plunge of the rollercoaster is much more difficult when it's accelerating fast.

Your money or your life

There's a bill to be paid for such adverse demographic trends; and it will be presented in just 15–20 years' time. The US has less of a mountain to climb than many other countries. Yet trustees of the retirement fund calculate that contribution rates will have to jump by over a third in the 2020s to bring social security back into balance. However, even this may be overoptimistic. Two top American demographers argue that the official forecasts of mortality that underpin the pension projection envisage declines in death rates that are 'far too low'.[4]

The social security projections foresee 'implausibly small' gains to life expectancy over the next 75 years, say Ronald Lee and Shripad Tuljapurkar. The official forecast of life expectancy at birth of 81 for both sexes in 2070 implies far smaller gains than have occurred in the US in the twentieth century. Is it really likely that the US will take another 50 years to reach the level already enjoyed by the Japanese?

With each extra year of life expectancy requiring either a rise in contributions or a fall in benefits of 4 percent, the financial implications are sobering. Lee and Tuljapurkar believe that life expectancy will in fact rise to 87 by 2070. This would mean that by 2030 contributions would have to increase by half to balance the books, and would eventually have to double.

Fiscal cardiac arrest

Yet the impending crisis for US social security is as nothing compared to that in store for healthcare. Medicare and Medicaid, the two systems through which most healthcare for older Americans is publicly financed, face a much more profound challenge from ageing baby boomers than social security, says the President's Council of Economic Advisers.[5]

On current projections, outlays on Medicare, currently almost 3 percent of GDP, will break the bank. In 1997, Harvard health economist David Cutler warned that spending would reach almost 8 percent of the economy in 2030 – more than social security at this point. And yet the payroll tax collected to cover Medicare hospital expenditure in 1997 was only a quarter of that for social security. Substantial cutbacks arrested the runaway growth in the programs in 1998. Even so, trustees of the Hospital Insurance Fund which pays for inpatient hospital expenses still expect it to go bust in about 10 years' time.[6]

If you then add the underestimate of life expectancy to the prospects for healthcare spending, the outlook turns truly alarming. 'The long run outlook for the federal budget is deep red, largely due to projections of steeply rising per capita health care expenditures and of increases in the relative size of the elderly population', warn Lee and Tuljarpurkar. So much for all those bright hopes about the dawn

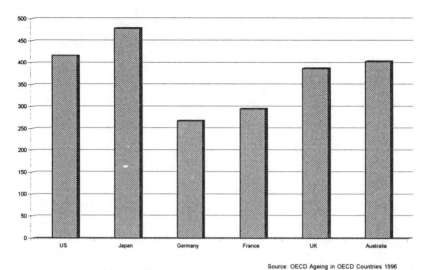

Source: OECD Ageing in OECD Countries 1996

Figure 27 The looming health bill

Spending per head on ages 65 and over as percentage of that at ages 64 or under

of a new era that would see a federal budget of black rather than red ink.[7]

The American way of health is renowned for its profligacy, but the 2010s and 2020s will also be the time when health spending takes wing throughout the developed world. Health expenditure in developed countries for each person over 65 is much higher than it is for the rest of the population. In Britain, the US and Australia it is four times greater; in Japan almost five times more. Such spending rates are barely containable with the current number of older people; they will not be when numbers swell with ageing boomers (see Figure 27).[8]

The end of growth?

Ever since the industrial revolution, western societies have been able to count on continuing economic growth. Not every year: the business cycle sees to that. But like a chart pinned on the marketing manager's wall – the type long satirized by cartoonists – the long-run trend has always been up and away. It's a magic we have come to rely on. A relapse into recession causes misery for the millions who lose their livelihood and plunges state finances into the red.

But when the agequake strikes in earnest, the improvement in living standards we take for granted will slow to a trickle. In 1998, the Organisation for Economic Co-operation and Development calculated the impact of ageing on developed economies in a model that set new standards for its comprehensive, international approach. On the basis of current demographic and productivity trends, it projected a slowdown in growth of per capita income to 1 percent a year in the US and EU in the 2020s – roughly half the rate we're used to. The effect will be to lower living standards in 2030 in the US, the EU and Japan by around a sixth, compared with what we could expect on past growth trends.[9]

Living standards – output per head – are what matter to individuals. But for businesses and investors, growth in actual output is vitally important. Growing economies are more congenial environments for businesses to flourish and investors profit accordingly. On this score, it gets worse: Europe and Japan will, to all intents and purposes, go ex growth.

With population decline commencing in Japan, Italy and Germany within the next 15 years, there will be fewer heads. So even though output per head of population may continue to rise, overall output will virtually stagnate. Japanese growth will decline to little more than half a percent a year in the early 2010s. Where Japan leads, the EU will follow some 10 or so years later (see Figure 28).

The ex-growth era will last for several decades. On the OECD's baseline projection, output in the EU and Japan will continue increasing at around half a percent or less a year until the middle of the twenty-first century. These minimal rates of growth are far lower than those expected in the US, which will continue to expand at about 1.5 percent a year thanks to more favorable demographics.

The root cause of the ex-growth era will be the demographic shift to fewer people in the labor force. If participation rates – the proportion of the working-age population that is economically active – remain

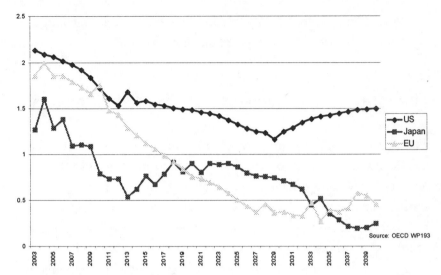

Figure 28 *The great growth slowdown*
Annual percent increase in potential output

constant at 1995 levels, labor forces in Japan and the EU will contract throughout the first half of the twenty-first century. The decline in Japan will be particularly acute in the first half of the 2010s; in the EU in the 2020s. By 2030 Japan's labor force will be 13 percent lower than in 2000; the EU's will be 16 percent lower. By contrast, America's will be 9 percent higher.

An even more pessimistic forecast comes from Tim Congdon, head of Lombard Street Research in London, who believes that living standards in some European economies will cease to grow at all. He is gloomier about the potential for productivity growth than the OECD and he projects continuing falls in labor participation rates. As a result, the positive contribution to growth from productivity will be canceled out by the twin effects of demographics and participation.[10]

If you consider these forecasts over gloomy, then Japan's malaise of the 1990s should make you think again. Growth has slumped from 4 percent in the 1980s to 1 percent in the 1990s. No need to look too far down the identity parade for suspects: adverse demographics have been at work. The working-age population has been declining and the prospect of that decline has pushed down investment.

The longest and deepest bear market in history?

The public finances of most western countries will be in an unholy mess and the West will go ex growth. But does that matter to the army of investors who have signed up to the equity dream? There's been no shortage of experts assuring them that shares always pay off in the long run, whether as their own private investments or as the principal assets of funded pensions.

They could be in for a cold shower. At the end of 1996, Benjamin Meuli, managing director of JP Morgan in London, warned: 'It is arguable that the funded systems existing in the UK and the US have laid the foundation for the longest and deepest bear market in history in the early quarter of the next century, as the retiring baby-boomers start to liquidate their savings by selling them to – who?'

In more muted language, a report for the Group of Ten leading industrial countries on the effects of ageing populations expressed similar worries in 1998. 'Pension managers and individual savers,' said the study, 'need to plan for the possibility of declining equity (and possibly bond) prices at the time when baby boomers are liquidating assets to finance their retirement.'[11]

Because of their scale, private pension funds will be vital in determining when this liquidation gets under way. American pension experts Sylvester Schieber and John Shoven believe that private pension benefits in the US will already exceed contributions by 2006. However, with annual investment income still running at $450 billion, funds will continue accumulating assets. The crunch year when the pension system becomes a net seller is 2024. It is around this time that these experts fear share and bond prices will fall.[12]

Just as the demographic rollercoaster pushes up asset prices as the baby-boom generation bulges in the prime years for accumulating financial wealth, so it will push them down as it plunges into the prime years for dissipating that wealth. Starting around 2010 in the US, somewhat later in western Europe, the boomer generation will cause the number of retirees to bulge as never before.

A downturn in equity prices could come about through an alternative channel to the mismatch between the size of the big baby-boom generation trying to sell assets and the small successor generation of potential purchasers. Each member of the smaller working generation of the future will have more physical capital. This will drive down rates of return on real capital assets, reducing income from equities and property. Certainly, historical experience suggests that just as rapid population increase pushes down real wages and pushes up rents, so declining population depresses rents and raises workers' share of national income.[13]

The demographic signposts signal a prolonged bear market. With so distant a danger, many investors will simply shrug their shoulders, deciding to deal with it when it materializes in the 2020s. Unfortunately there's a snag with this strategy: by then it may be too late. Financial markets are highly effective at discounting the impact of future known shocks. One of the principal reasons that equities have boomed in the 1980s and 1990s is that baby boomers have been able to take a long view. But once they are in their sixties, they will become a lot less sanguine about possible setbacks. On this reading, a financial meltdown could set in a lot earlier than the 2020s, as investors seek to bail out early.

End of the housing dream

What about that surefire bet of the postwar era, investing in your own house? The unpalatable answer is that when the agequake strikes in earnest, property is likely to go belly up. The reason: ageing will greatly increase the numbers of older people who are likely to trade down while reducing the proportion of first-time buyers in the population.

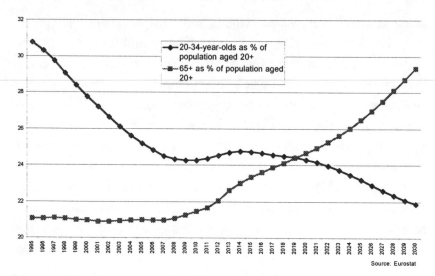

Source: Eurostat

Figure 29 Housing market blues
Downtraders (65+) and first-time buyers (20–34) as percentage of adult population

In the UK, the number of 65-year-olds starts to grow sharply from 2010 onwards as a proportion of the adult population – so much so that by 2020 it exceeds the 20–34 age group. Many retired people stay put, even if the house gets too big for them. But to the extent that they do move, they trade down. The crossing of the scissors of these two age-groups spells blues for the housing market (see Figure 29).

You can expect a similar scenario to play out in the American housing market. US retirement specialist Olivia Mitchell is much more pessimistic about the prospects for property than she is for shares. She thinks that a depression in house prices is possible and recommends diversifying out of home ownership as the main asset that we take into retirement.[14]

The baby-boom generation has been brought up to believe in the value of housing as an investment. Despite the reverses of the past few years in many countries, particularly the UK, this is a belief that most still cherish. But as the later members of the generation come to retire, many of them will be sorely disappointed. This time there will be no crock of gold at the end of the housing rainbow.

Don't bank on inheritance

To the extent that today's retirees have been able to hang on to their assets, could a bequests bonanza let baby boomers off the financial hook? Don't bank on it. While a majority can expect a small legacy, they would be foolish to pin their hopes on inherited money to guarantee a comfortable retirement.

Information about the pattern of inheritance is notoriously unreliable. However, wide-ranging surveys conducted in the US in the 1990s have broken new ground by asking older people about their intention to leave a legacy. These show that many younger Americans will miss out on bequests altogether. Over a quarter of Americans over 70 said they wouldn't leave anything. Two-thirds said there was no chance that they would leave $100,000 or more. Less than a fifth said they were sure to make a bequest of that size.[15]

Although the surveys indicate that Americans now in their fifties are more likely to leave a legacy, the trend to early retirement may negate these more generous intentions. So, too, could gains in life expectancy, which may force older Americans to use up more of their wealth in retirement than they have planned. Some wild figures have been bandied about concerning a deluge of inheritance funds in the US. But Laurence Kotlikoff, an expert in generational accounting, has calculated that American bequests were already 40 percent lower as a percentage of labor income in 1995 than they were 30 years earlier.[16]

The main point to emerge from these surveys of older people is the large number of children who can expect to receive relatively little. Bear in mind, too, that by definition baby boomers come from large families and will therefore have to share their inheritance with their siblings. The harsh truth is that wealth is much more unevenly distributed than income. Among Americans born in the 1930s, the richest 10 percent of households had net worth of at least $520,000, but the typical household in the middle of the range just $100,000, of which $60,000 was in housing equity.[17]

When you read stories about an inheritance boom, take a reality check: a favored few will walk away with most of the loot. Remember, too, that by no means all bequests go to children. Some of the largest don't – take the New York couple Donald and Mildred Othmer who died in the late 1990s. Thanks to longstanding stakes in Warren Buffett's Berkshire Hathaway, they had built up a fortune worth three-quarters of a billion dollars. While some was left to relatives, the vast bulk of the estate was earmarked for institutions like Brooklyn's Polytechnic University and Long Island College Hospital.[18]

Will developing countries save the day?

An alternative scenario is that the new world will come to the rescue of the old. The increasingly well-off middle classes of Asia and Latin America will step into the breach and provide the missing buyers needed by ageing boomers when they try to sell their stocks. This is the line taken by US retirement specialist Olivia Mitchell. In contrast to her pessimism about the prospects for real estate, she is more optimistic about the outlook for equities because of the existence of a global capital market. In early 1998 she told a House of Commons Select Committee: 'Yes, it is true that we have an ageing population in the developed world, but there is a young population in the rest of the world. There is a demand for our assets that presumably the next group will continue to buy.'[19]

Don't bet the farm on this rescue plan. At present, Chile's pension fund is smaller than that of Ford; and it has less than 1 percent of its assets invested overseas. Although there is often capital flight from emerging economies, many investors, like those in developed countries, will prefer to keep their money at home, where they are not exposed to exchange-rate risk and are familiar with the investment risks. More important, the same demographic forces that make the 2020s a crunch decade for the West are at work in the two most developed of the developing countries, Latin America and emerging Asia.[20]

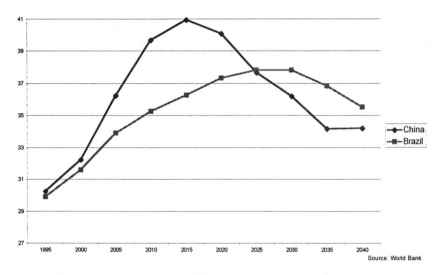

Figure 30 Twin peak ratios in emerging economies
40–59-year-olds as percentage of adult population

Asian trends afford little comfort for those hoping that investors there will bale the West out of the demographic pit it has dug for itself. In the first decade of the twenty-first century there will be a strong impulse to financial markets as the key ratio of 40- and 50-year-olds to the adult population rises. In the key country, China, it shoots up by a third – from around 30 percent in 2000 to 40 percent in 2010 (see Figure 30). However, what goes up must come down; and what goes up that fast usually falls back before long. The ratio reaches a pinnacle in 2015 and then starts an abrupt fall as the big cohorts initially making up the 40–59 bulge move into their sixties. A similar pattern occurs in South Korea.

In Latin America's most populous country, Brazil, there will be a more gradual but still substantial rise in the relative size of the 40–59 age group. However, the ratio stabilizes in the 2020s. In Chile, the ratio also increases fast in the early 2000s, but actually declines after 2010.

The implication is clear. Savers in developing countries will certainly help to underpin western equity markets in the first decade of the twenty-first century. In the 2010s, they should also help to sustain stock markets as growing wealth compensates for the deceleration in the growth of the key saving group of 40- and 50-year-olds. But in the 2020s, the shockwaves of the agequake will start to ricochet through key emerging economies – earlier in some of the most successful ones like Chile and South Korea. Even if today's more backward countries in Asia and Africa do begin to advance in a big way, their starting point of wealth is so low that it seems unlikely they can step into the breach.

The gamble on investing overseas

An alternative approach is for investors to bank on high returns in fast-growing emerging economies. The collapse of so many emerging markets in 1997–8 makes this seem a shattered dream, but the setback should prove temporary. With economic growth in the developed world juddering to a virtual standstill in the 2020s, the most dynamic economies should be today's most under-developed countries.

The case for optimism is simple. Precisely because they are coming from further behind, developing countries have greater scope for fast growth. One of their principal disadvantages – their shortage of capital – is also their advantage, because the pay-off from investment is potentially so much greater.

Add favorable demographics and you have the makings of a starburst of catch-up growth for the world's economic stragglers: those that have been last shall be first. As we saw in Chapter 3, the demographic 'gift' from an age pyramid that bulges in all the right places can be substantial. The countries that will benefit most are where you might least expect them – in Pakistan and Bangladesh.

That's the upside – but it's wishful thinking to pretend there isn't a downside. The majority of developing economies have consistently failed to hit the high road of catch-up growth. Far from countries automatically converging on the economic leaders since the war, divergence has been the rule. The countries that have been able to exploit their lack of economic development have been relatively advanced in their social capabilities – governments that are not hopelessly corrupt and peoples that have passed first base in education. Nigeria has enormous potential – but will its leaders ever allow that potential to be exploited?

If you look at FDI inflows – investments made by companies – which the World Bank has shown are correlated with growth, South Asia, sub-Saharan Africa and the Middle East were bypassed in the 1990s. In *The Wealth and Poverty of Nations*, economic historian David Landes insists on the importance of culture – something economists too readily overlook. 'If we learn anything from the history of economic development, it is that culture makes all the difference.'

Overseas investment makes sense in theory. But for it to work in practice a lot of things have to go right. You are making a bet on future international relations. If all works out for the best, it will be like the girl with the curl on her forehead: very, very good. If all goes pear-shaped, it will be perfectly horrid.

Whatever the outlook for individual investors, overseas investment will be no panacea for the depressive impact of ageing on western living standards. The OECD finds only a modest offset from such an attempt to 'beat demography'. The build-up in foreign assets required to compensate for the effects of ageing is implausibly large.[22]

New economy?

Rather than looking to developing countries to carry the ageing white man's burden, a more reliable way forward is to shift productivity growth up a gear in the West so that a smaller number of worker bees can sustain a larger number of drones. Hopes for a quantum leap forward in efficiency to coincide with a new millennium have been fueled by the apparent emergence of a 'new economy' in America in the 1990s. Even so sober a figure as Alan Greenspan, chairman of the US Federal Reserve, has speculated about a possible productivity breakthrough. In 1997, he asked whether 'current developments are part of a once-or-twice-in-a-century phenomenon that will carry productivity nationally and globally to a new higher track'.[23]

What Greenspan had in mind is a convergence of technologies based on computers, which will unleash a broad-based technological advance similar to the one that underpinned the swift productivity growth of around 3 percent a year in the 1950s and 1960s. This post-war growth in labor efficiency was not based on brand new inventions and innovations, but on the delayed exploitation of known techniques that became mutually reinforcing across industries; for example, the productivity gains in the oil and transport industries achieved through supertankers and superhighways.

For supertankers, read the plummeting cost of computer power; for superhighways, read the Internet. In the 2000s, e-commerce is expected to spread like wildfire, slashing costs by cutting out interme-diaries and creating global markets at the click of a mouse. In 1994, 3 million people, most of them in the US, used the Internet. In 1998, 100 million around the world were using it. By 2005, if not earlier, this could rise to a billion. Technological innovations orchestrating a convergence between telecommunications, broadcasting and comput-ing will speed the process. According to the US government, within 10 years the vast majority of Americans will be able to interact with the Internet from their TV sets, watch television on their computers and make telephone calls from both devices.[24]

As if these potential improvements from the IT revolution were not enough, the US has currently been benefiting from the initial positive effects of an ageing workforce on productivity. The 1990s have seen a decline in the number of 20-year-olds, whose productivity is relatively low. Meanwhile, the number of prime-age workers in their late thirties and forties has been swelling.[25]

Demographic pressures may also be promoting higher productivity in another way, as companies respond to a tight labor market by trying to raise labor efficiency. This potential was first spotted by economist Lawrence Summers as long ago as 1990. In a paper for the Brookings Institution, he and fellow economists established that nations whose labor forces were growing more slowly made faster efficiency gains than those whose workforces were expanding more quickly.[26]

Fast forward from 1990 to the end of that decade. Summers, by now deputy Treasury secretary, has definitely put on a turn of speed. More importantly, the American economy seems to be following in his trail. Productivity – output per hour worked – rose in 1996 and 1997 at around 2 percent a year – double the trend rate since the early 1970s. In line with Summers' earlier views, this improvement has coincided with a marked deceleration in the rate of labor force growth as the baby bust of the 1970s feeds through to the working-age population.

Looking ahead to the twenty-first century, ageing populations will create incentives for a switch in investment from physical to human capital; from machines to education and training. Maxime Fougère and Marcel Mérette at the Canadian Department of Finance argue that this switch could offset some of the most adverse demographic effects on growth arising from a decline in the labor force. True, there will be fewer workers, but they will be better qualified and thus more productive.[27]

Old truths

These arguments suggest there may be a mild improvement in the early 2000s from the sluggish rate at which labor efficiency has been increasing since the 1990s. But the case for a sustained productivity breakthrough – one lasting decades rather than a few years – remains flimsy. Indeed, all the good work from an upward shift in the next few years is likely to be undone in a subsequent offsetting downward shift.

Unlike the postwar upsurge, there is no backlog of existing technologies waiting to be exploited after a prolonged period of depression and war. Indeed, the upturn in US productivity growth in 1996 and 1997 could simply turn out to be a blip, reflecting the strength of the economy: efficiency tends to move in tandem with growth in the short term as more output is squeezed out of the existing labor force and machines. A sharp rise in productivity in the mid-1980s and in 1992 was greeted in like fashion as a long-term breakthrough, but was not sustained. An analysis by the Bank of England largely backed this cyclical explanation of the much-touted productivity uptick.[28]

American economist Paul Krugman of MIT is sceptical about the idea of a 'new economy'. He points out that Silicon Valley employs only one-third of a percent of all American workers; and IT only about 3–4 percent. Comparing past predictions of technological utopias with present realities, he says that 'we live in an age not of extraordinary progress but of technological disappointment'.[29]

Of course, information technology packs a punch an order of magnitude greater than the number of employees. Its impact has been most spectacular in the US, where the IT sector grew between 1993 and 1998 at double the rate of the national economy. But it is a mistake to consider IT in isolation. Employment may be growing in the high-tech sector, but it continues to shift out of automated manufacturing into labor-intensive services where productivity is necessarily lower – think of all those Starbucks cappuccino bars or the growing army of domestic helpers.[30]

As for the supposedly favorable impact of a smaller workforce on productivity, this fails to take into account the fact that it will also be a progressively older one. In the 1990s, the ageing of the labor force has helped US productivity as workers have moved into their prime years for individual effectiveness at work. As we saw in Chapter 7, however, age–earnings profiles indicate that productivity declines after the age of 50. This suggests that the rising number of 50-year-olds in the workforce in the 2000s will act as a brake on future productivity growth.

Innovation in Europe and Japan will also suffer from the deficit of people in their twenties. You only have to think of Silicon Valley's computer nerds and the Microserfs of Seattle to see the link between innovation and youth. Tomorrow's generations of new workers may be stuffed to the eyeballs with qualifications and 'human capital', but there will be fewer of them. This matters, because the more people there are, the more knowledge and knowhow will be created. As that early numbercruncher of 'political arithmetic' William Petty wrote in the seventeenth century: 'It is more likely that one ingenious curious man may rather be found among 4 million than 400 persons.'[31]

Pulling it all together, a sustained upward shift in productivity growth seems highly unlikely. For a country like the US at the cutting edge of economic efficiency, the best that can be expected is a mild improvement over the next few years, followed by a reversion to a trend increase in productivity of around 1 percent. A more likely scenario is that the reverse will shunt productivity growth below 1 percent a year.[32]

Japan and the European Union are still behind the US in productivity, so they should be able to increase labor efficiency somewhat faster than America. Management consultants McKinsey argue that the shortfall is such that there could be a spurt of growth, particularly in the UK over the next 10 years. However, the roadblocks they identify on the path to higher productivity are ones that would require wrenching social change to remove – for example, an all-out assault on restrictive land use and planning regulations, which hold back productivity in hotels and supermarkets. Such deregulatory reforms are easier to advocate than to execute. A more sober assessment is offered by eminent economic historian and growth accountant Angus Maddison, who sees 'little potential for significant narrowing of the productivity gap' between the US and other advanced countries over the next 20 years.[33]

Deaf ears

This takes us back to the only realistic answer: if we are living longer, we have to work longer. The OECD has run simulations on how to avert the coming slowdown in living standards, feeding in a package of measures ranging from debt stabilization to deregulation. The reform that makes the key contribution is later retirement. In Europe, there is particularly large potential to mobilize older workers under the existing age of retirement.[34]

Unfortunately, the solution of later retirement may turn out to work better in simulations than in practice. Quite apart from the resistance of ageist employers, many individuals will be reluctant to rally to the call. New American research into the history of retirement, extending back to Union army veterans, suggests that the reveille to work longer will fall on deaf ears. No one doubts that perverse incentives have developed in the past 25 years which push older employees out of the workplace. However, the new research shows that the trend to earlier and earlier retirement goes back long before that and that people place much more value on free time than on income as they pass 60.[35]

Indeed, the proportion of American retirees citing a preference for leisure as their main motivation for leaving the labor force rose from 3 percent in 1941 to 48 percent in 1982. Retirement income levels have become progressively less important in determining the retirement decision. With mass tourism and entertainment becoming more and more affordable, the opportunities to enjoy oneself in retirement without spending a fortune have never been greater.

Live longer, work longer is the logical solution to the agequake. It is the favored proposal of western governments. But the solution runs counter to a deep-rooted, longstanding and understandable reluctance to spend the last period of a longer life chained to work. If ageing baby boomers do carry on working, it will be on their terms, a part-time and low-key engagement that is likely to boost output only marginally.

Timing is everything

Does it make any sense at all to look so far forward into the future? What workable strategies can be plotted when there are so many uncertainties? I believe that forward planning on this scale does help provided you use it to keep your bearings and set an overall direction.

One conclusion you can draw even now is that the 2020s and indeed the latter part of the 2010s are going to be a tough decade for investors unless a lot of things go right. If you see economic miracles spreading to South Asia, the Middle East and Africa in the next few years, you can be more confident about things going right. The demographic transition in many developing countries to an optimal age structure for economic growth, combined with economic catch-up, are the strongest antidote to the downdrafts in asset markets from ageing in the developed world. Companies with a stake in these burgeoning economies will thrive and emerging middle classes will join a now global equity culture.

If you see developed countries taking decisive action to sort out unaffordable pay-as-you-go state pensions and to increase the participation rates of older people, then again you can be a lot more confident about the future. There will be less risk of sudden tax raids on pensions to stave off default.

But even if you see these necessary reforms occurring, it seems to me that baby boomers should be starting to diversify their portfolios out of domestic equities by around 2010. Thereafter, they should be planning to realize a good chunk of their equity gains by purchasing bonds, which is in any case a sensible strategy for older people. Given the political risk in government bonds because of a possible struggle between the generations, they should also consider buying high-class corporate bonds. To gain some protection against political risk, they should be seeking to buy assets that are internationally tradable and are not tied into political and tax jurisdictions.

A similar strategy should be adopted with housing. The relatively buoyant sector when boomers come to retire will eventually be smaller homes, though not necessarily ones packaged for the elderly because of the attendant social stigma. However, demographic influences are set to create an eventual overhang of large family houses. The secret of success will be to trade down early and buy into the most favored locations.

The downward plunge of the demographic rollercoaster will shake western economies and shatter expectations. No one can fully insulate themselves from such an event. But through sensible forward planning, you can position yourself to protect as much of your wealth as possible. There is no point in being an ostrich, still less when you know that the ground will eventually move under you.

10

New age

REMEMBER THE NEW WORLD ORDER THE COLLAPSE OF SOVIET
Communism was supposed to usher in? It didn't happen – but the agequake will generate a new world *economic* order. Rapid ageing will
diminish the power of Europe and Japan in the twenty-first century,
while the economic clout of slow-ageing countries such as India will
grow enormously. The combination of increasing labor forces in developing countries and a declining number of workers in the ageing societies of the rich industrial democracies will redraw the economic power
map in the early twenty-first century, with major implications for
national security.

Developed countries are conducting a dry run for the whole world
in confronting the new demographic specter: one of imploding rather
than exploding populations. But the most profound change of all, one
that will eventually affect everyone on earth, is the dawn of a new age
when humanity is no longer young.

Rising suns set and setting suns rise

At the start of the 1990s, Michael Crichton's thriller *Rising Sun*
depicted a US at bay to an all-conquering Japanese business invasion.
No matter that the Tokyo stock market had already fallen like a stone

since its peak at the end of 1989: Americans needed a new economic demon to replace the fallen Soviet 'evil empire'.

With Japanese companies buying up large chunks of central Manhattan and Hollywood studios, Japan was the natural candidate. Its economic star had been in the ascendant ever since the war with an average annual growth rate in GDP of 7 percent between 1950 and 1990. True, Japan's growth rate had fallen back from the stunning 9 percent rate between 1950 and 1973, but in the ensuing period to 1990 it had still run at 4 percent a year.[1]

With the Japanese economy grounded on the demographic rocks for most of the 1990s, the *Rising Sun* scenario seems as outdated as only past fashions in paranoia can be. The sun in the East has been eclipsed in the 1990s by the sun in the West, the reborn 'new economy' of the US. There is a good chance that Japan will stage a recovery in the 2000s, as it shakes off the straitjacket of a producer-based manufacturing economy and reorientates itself towards services and consumers. Beyond that, adverse demographics point to further setbacks.

The agequake will turn another big-time postwar winner into a loser. Like Japan, Germany lost the war but won the peace. During the postwar miracle – from 1950 to 1973 – GDP grew at an annual rate of 6 percent. In the next 20 years, growth fell back to a stodgy 2 percent, but Germany was still viewed as the powerhouse of Europe, even though the economy was bowed down by excessive welfare spending and a sclerotic labor market.[2]

The lights are programmed to go out in the powerhouse. Germany is likely to have a good start to the twenty-first century, but after around 2010 it will face the problems of a declining working-age population. A ranking of 146 individual countries' growth potential to 2020 put Germany at 144th, ahead only of Italy and Belgium. The study, by economic research consultancy Lombard Street Research, highlighted the importance of unfavorable demographic trends, principally the contraction in the labor force.[3]

An unexpected winner – of sorts – in the developed world will be the UK. Britain is set to age considerably less than many European countries; and in any case there is less pressure on the public finances because state pensions are less generous and private pensions more widespread. This should improve the UK's competitive standing compared to the rest of the EU. In Lombard Street Research's ranking, it comes sixth among the 15 EU countries in its growth potential to 2020.

Ireland comes top of the EU class. The favorable demographic trends that have helped turn the country into a 'Celtic tiger' will be sustained into the twenty-first century. The burden of age remains stable until 2010, with only one person aged 65 or more for every five people of working age. By contrast, the German ratio will then stand at one in three. The Irish dependency ratio does then start to deteriorate, but fairly gradually: in 2020, it will be one in four. A continuing expansion in the population of working age, helped by further immigration as more of the Irish diaspora return, should ensure that Ireland continues to sprint ahead.[4]

The US century (continued)

Remember how the US was going to bow out in the twenty-first century? Don't hold your breath. The US will remain the preeminent global economic superpower for many years to come, thanks to more favorable population trends than in any other major developed economy. Previous warnings of decline failed to give sufficient weight to the demographic factor. In *Preparing for the Twenty-First Century*, written at the start of the 1990s, Paul Kennedy saw Japan as better placed to face the new millennium than the US. While he acknowledged that Japan faced adverse demographics, he failed to anticipate the damage that rapid ageing would wreak on the Japanese economy.[5]

Unlike Japan and the European Union, the American economy will continue to grow quite strongly throughout the first half of the twenty-first century thanks to continuing expansion of the labor force. Under the OECD's baseline scenario in its modeling of the impact of ageing, economic growth in the US will decline only very gradually from its current trend, between 2 to 2.5 percent a year, to 1.25 percent in 2030; after which it picks up again.

This continued American preponderance owes much to the US's willingness to admit immigrants, which has also helped keep birth rates much higher than in other developed countries. Sheer scale of population does not automatically lead to greater geo-economic clout. But when the world's economic leader enjoys strong population growth, the combination is a potent one.

The euro's sternest test

A key question is whether European monetary union will buckle under the pressure of the demographic strains. The correct policy response to the pressure of ageing is to cut budget deficits and repay debt over the next 15 years, so creating some leeway for borrowing when the burden of age mounts sharply thereafter. Essentially this is an enforced policy of national saving which brings forward the burden of ageing and imposes it on today's rather than tomorrow's working population. But if the European Central Bank (ECB) pursues a tight monetary policy to gain credibility, it will force national governments to relax fiscal policy, the very reverse of what's needed. They will repeat the lurch into deficit finance that occurred in the early 1990s when the German Bundesbank kept interest rates too high for comfort across Europe.

Even if the overall correct policy mix of tight fiscal and loose monetary policy is pursued, the ECB could face an intractable task because of the very different problems that individual countries within Europe face in sorting out the pensions mess. In 1998, the French budget balance needed to swing by some 4 percent of GDP into the black to prevent a build-up of pension debt; however, the UK required no adjustment at all.[6]

Optimists argue that just as the Maastricht criteria for entry into EMU forced governments to take unpopular steps to curb spending and raise taxation, so the advent of the euro will push them further towards more fundamental reform. A more pessimistic assessment is that the entry criteria into Euroland were fudged with one-off measures like Italy's 'euro tax', and that once countries make it into the monetary union, governments will relax. More fundamentally, there has never been an enduring monetary union in history without a political union, as none other than Otmar Issing, European Central Bank chief economist, has warned. EMU is bound to lead eventually to a much greater sharing of resources through common taxes and spending.

This could turn the imbalance between the implicit liabilities of state pensions in different member countries into a lethal political cocktail. Unfunded state pensions are not scored in countries' balance sheets as formal debt, even though they involve future commitments that are usually more onerous than the interest on existing borrowing. For example, the IMF has estimated the present-day value of future pension commitments between 1995 and 2050 at over 110 percent of GDP for France and Germany. The cost of these implicit pension liabilities is thus almost double the Maastricht limit for gross government debt. By contrast, the IMF estimated the present-day value of future pension commitments in the UK at just 5 percent of GDP.[7]

In 1996, the House of Commons Social Security Committee warned that if the UK joined the single currency British taxpayers could be called on to help finance the pay-as-you-go pension obligations of other EMU members. This seems highly unlikely, but the imbalance in pensions liabilities could take its toll as euro interest rates were pushed up to help fund these huge pension commitments. Probably the most serious risk is that countries facing particularly severe imbalances will seek a way out through inflation, an effective tax on today's generations. Laurence Kotlikoff and Willi Leibfritz, experts on generational accounting, warn that 'this may place significant stress on the union and lead to its eventual collapse'.[8]

Short-term renaissance, long-term decline

As EMU turned from blueprint to reality in the late 1990s, it was increasingly viewed as a long overdue kick up the pants of the moribund European economy and welfare state. The hope has been that this 'supply-side shock' will force through urgently needed reforms, from more realistic pension funding to greater liberalization of the labor market and deregulation of key industries. If these hopes become reality, then the euro will spur a burst in productivity and economic growth in the first decade of the twenty-first century.

There is undoubtedly the potential for a European renaissance. The introduction of secondary funded pensions could spur the development of financial markets, increasing the pressure on European companies to lift returns and improve productivity. Such a pension reform would help bring down the tax burden on workers.

Labor market reform could tackle the structural obstacles that have kept unemployment far too high. If Europe could bring down unemployment to American rates, this alone could boost GDP by around 1 percent a year for a decade. More realistically, if the EU could bring it down to, say, 7.5 percent from the 10 percent rate prevailing in mid-1998, this would allow output to grow by an extra half a percent in the 2000s.[9]

Deregulation could also boost the European economy. For example, the OECD calculates that deregulating the electricity industry, airlines, road transport, telecommunications and distribution could push up GDP over time by 4 percent. If other sectors like public administration and professional services were also reformed, the total gain could be double that. Add to all this the fact that the baby boomers of the 1960s will be entering their most productive years, and you have the makings of a virtuous circle.[10]

But there remain real doubts over whether Europe will exploit the potential for a strong decade of economic growth. Progress in reforming pensions has been derisory and there seems little enthusiasm for labor market reform. In Germany, Chancellor Schröder has revived the discredited solution of early retirement to deal with the unemployment crisis. As for the prospects for deregulation, we have been here before. The reforms resemble an exercise that the European Commission conducted in the late 1980s about the impact of the single market on growth. Then, as now, supply-side reforms were predicted to galvanize a one-off gain of 5 percent of GDP which never materialized.[11]

Beyond 2010, the European Union faces daunting challenges. In the OECD's benchmark or 'business-as-usual' scenario, EU growth is forecast to decline to under half a percent a year in the 2020s as unfavorable demographics cause the labor force to shrink. In some ways this prospective slowdown is even more extraordinary than Japan's. The climacteric ahead will bring to a halt a century and a half of sustained economic advance.

When tortoises beat hares

In the new world economic order, slow-ageing tortoises will overtake fast-ageing hares. The tortoise's slow ageing means that its workforce is expanding fast. In addition, its potential for growth is high because it is coming up from behind. The hare's fast ageing means that its workforce is stagnant or contracting. Its potential for growth is low because it is already at the frontier of economic advance.

In the next 50 years, the tortoises will be India, Indonesia, Brazil, Mexico and Turkey. Together with smaller slow-ageing countries, their share of world output will grow from 29 percent at the start of the twenty-first century to 46 percent by 2050. Meanwhile, the fast-ageing hares – the US, the EU and Japan – will be slipping behind. In almost an exact role reversal, their combined share of global GDP will fall from 46 percent to 28 percent (see Figure 31).[12]

The other countries that are ageing quickly – principally China – gain some ground by 2020 but then slip back so that their share of world output remains virtually the same, at just over a quarter, in 2050 as at the beginning of the century. As early as 2015, China will catch up with the US with roughly 17 percent of GDP, says Angus Maddison, an

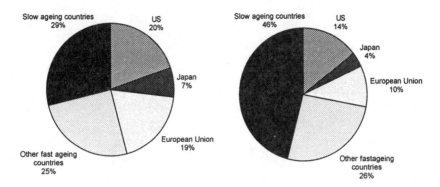

Figure 31 Shares in world GDP, 2000 and 2050
Source: OECD, GDP at 1995 purchasing power parities

authority on economic growth. Individual Americans will of course remain greatly more prosperous because of the disparity in populations. China will then pull ahead, but its bigger share of world GDP will still be outweighed by the US's advantage in wealth and international influence. The UK was able to exercise continuing global leadership long after its economy had been overtaken by America's. By that token, the US will still be the preeminent economic superpower well after China has caught up with it. Even so, China's role in the world economy and its geographical leverage will certainly be enhanced, says Maddison.[13]

Russian cirrhosis

Russia's chances of economic regeneration are gravely threatened by the population trends that have turned the country into a demographic disaster zone. Russian men are dying in middle age at an unprecedented rate for a developed society, as the country drinks itself not just into oblivion but towards extinction. 'The current death rates present the clearest possible threat to the national security of Russia,' a special report to President Boris Yeltsin concluded in 1997.[14]

As the twentieth century started, Russia's population was swelling dramatically thanks to the highest fertility in the world. As it ends,

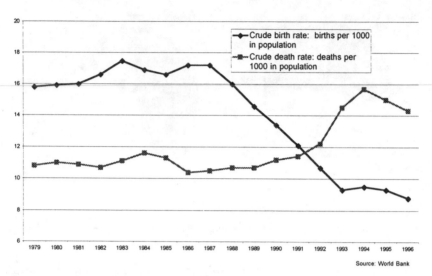

Figure 32 Russia's demographic crisis
Falling birth rate, rising death rate

Russia's population is falling equally dramatically and fertility is among the lowest in the world. The population decline started in 1992, the first such fall in peacetime history, as births plunged and the number of deaths shot up. Deaths have been outnumbering births by almost a million and immigration has not been sufficient to bridge the gap (see Figure 32).[15]

Life expectancy fell between 1987 and 1994 for men by over 7 years to 58, the lowest level for males in a developed country; in some parts it was 49, a level comparable with some parts of sub-Saharan Africa. The sex differential in life expectancy soared to a record 13 years as Russian men hit the bottle and keeled over in an epidemic of heart attacks and strokes.[16]

Shortly before he won the 1998 Nobel Prize for economics, Armatya Sen argued that mortality trends should be considered alongside the usual index of economic success and failure, the amount of national income per capita. He pointed to the speed with which life expectancy deteriorated in Russia after 1989 as a object lesson: mortality responded with extraordinary swiftness to declining economic welfare and the bankruptcy of the Soviet healthcare system.[17]

Throughout the 1990s, false hopes were peddled about Russia's chances of economic regeneration. The tide was supposed to be turned in 1996, but the economy continued to shrink. In 1997, there was an astonishing bull run in Russian shares as the market outperformed all others in the world. In August 1998, these hopes were shattered as Russia defaulted on loans and the stock market collapsed.

Those smart investment bankers who ended up losing a pile in Russia would have done better to have inspected the mortality statistics than their spreadsheets filled with bogus projections of profits in what turned out to be shell companies. Advice to long-term investors (rather than revolving-door speculators): don't believe the economic forecasts; look at the vital statistics, the key population numbers, and monitor health trends. Only when there are clear signs that Russia is surmounting the immediate demographic crisis should you consider dipping your toes into these troubled waters.

Sooner or later, the enormous potential of applying modern technologies in Russia will be realized. But the task facing reformers is made harder by such unfavorable demographics. Russia will be exposed to the full shockwaves of the agequake without the buffer of 50 years of prosperity. Far from worrying about the threat posed by Russia to the West, security analysts will be agitated by its growing incapacity to act as a bulwark against China in the East.

If Russia can get to grips with its problems, there is a flickering light at the end of the demographic tunnel in the immediate future. Although the birth rate collapsed in the 1990s, it hovered around replacement level in the 1980s. As a result, Russia has a higher proportion of its population due to join the workforce in the 2000s than have its European neighbors. These new cohorts will have none of the mental blocks of older generations born and bred in Soviet times. If anyone is to realize the enormous potential of applying modern technologies to Russia, it will be this new generation.[18]

New world order

As the scales of demographic and economic power tilt away from the West, its true weight in the world will at last register. The impact will be felt most acutely in Europe. This will give a political impetus to European integration that could outweigh the economic problems arising from an ageing EU.

The rise in population in developing countries in just the next 10 years is the same order of magnitude as the total increase in the West in the past two centuries. Between 1998 and 2050, Europe and North America's share of world population will slip from 18 to 12 percent. At present there are 10 countries with over 100 million inhabitants. On the UN's central projection, a further eight will join their ranks by 2050, including Mexico, the Philippines, Vietnam and Egypt.[19]

More importantly, this increase in population is likely to be matched across much of the developing world by fast economic growth, as rapid fertility decline creates more favorable age structures – the so-called demographic gift. While western investors can't take this for granted, the world's two most populous countries, China and India, should complete their transition to fully developed economies in the next 50 years. On current UN projections, each will number 1.5 billion people by 2050.

This will be the real new world order – one in which an ageing, economically sluggish West is ringed by more youthful and economically buoyant countries. One in which the West – with the exception of the US – inevitably cedes power to the developing world.

United we stand, divided we fall

Global institutions will have to adjust to the new world economic order that the agequake is producing. The International Monetary Fund and World Bank are dominated by the US, which often prefers to act indirectly via these institutions rather than in its own name. The Group of

Seven industrial nations, set up at the urging of President Giscard d'Estaing in 1975, is an exclusive club of rich countries, to whose annual summits Russia has grudgingly been admitted.

These arrangements are as archaic as London clubs like the Carlton that won't admit women as members. Is it sensible to exclude China from attempts to run the world economy? At the 1998 annual meeting of the IMF in Washington, bankers and politicians, scared witless by the prospect of an economic meltdown, talked of the need for a new 'global financial architecture'. Gordon Brown, British Chancellor of the Exchequer, styled himself as a Christopher Wren for our times with his call for a world financial regulator. But as so often with grand phrase making, the reality was more prosaic. There was no serious intention to open the doors of world economic policy making to developing countries.

This must change in the future. The virulence with which Asian flu spread to threaten the most serious setback to the world economy since the second oil shock of the early 1980s shows that globalization is a two-way street, making the West more vulnerable to developing countries as well as enhancing its stake in them. In the twenty-first century, an ageing West will be more and more dependent on the future success of the developing world. While overseas investment cannot 'beat demography', it can certainly help. As we saw in Chapter 9, overseas buyers offer the best hope of mitigating a future age-related slump in share values.

Environmentalists remind us that we all live and sink in 'lifeboat Earth'. The analogy also holds true for the global economy. As Japan and the West age, they will become more and more reliant on the economic health of the developing world. That reality will need to be buttressed by new institutions that bring power sharing to the international arena.

Precipitate ageing in the developing world

The West may be affected first, but it is essentially conducting a dry run for the rest of the world. The agequake won't stop rumbling throughout the twenty-first century – it will merely strike elsewhere. What ultimately lies ahead for the developing world is an even more profound upheaval.

One commonly used measure of the speed of ageing is the length of time it takes for the proportion of the population aged 65 and over to double from 7 to 14 percent. France, the first country to control fertility, took over 100 years, Sweden 85 years. The US is expected to take 68 years, reaching the 14 percent threshold in 2012. Britain took 45 years, reaching that level in 1975.

By contrast, it took just 26 years for Japan to make this transition, from 1970 to 1996. It will take China one year longer, starting in 2000. Population ageing will even more precipitate in some countries. Using the same 7 to 14 percent indicator, Thailand will take just 21 years, starting in 2006 (see Figure 33).[20]

The agequake will strike developing countries with even greater force because the decline in fertility has been so much more pronounced and faster than in the West. Countries have started further up the demographic gears and crashed down them much more quickly. For example, the fertility rate is now estimated to have halved in Bangladesh in just 15 years, from around 6 children per woman in the early 1980s to 3 in

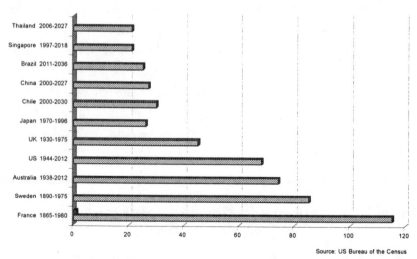

Source: US Bureau of the Census

Figure 33 The acceleration of global ageing
Number of years required for 65+ to rise from 7 to 14 percent of population

the late 1990s. By contrast, the transition in most western countries was from lower rates of fertility and occurred more gradually.

Take Kenya, long written off as a hopeless case of incorrigibly high fertility. In the late 1970s the fertility rate was indeed astonishingly high at just over 8 children a woman. Yet by the late 1990s, it had fallen to 4.5. The UN now expects it to fall to 2.8 by the early 2010s; my guess is that the Kenyans will surprise us by even sharper reductions in the next 10 years.

With the exception of the Philippines, fertility has dropped faster in every country in East and South-East Asia than it did in Japan. By the 1990s, fertility in China was comfortably below the replacement level. While these measures of fertility are subject to changes in the tempo of childbearing – women postponing the time when they have children – there is little evidence that the decline in most developing countries has been caused by such a distortion.[21]

A side effect is mounting alarm about a marriage squeeze caused by a surplus of prospective grooms over brides still more extreme than the one now facing British men. In South Korea, men in their late twenties will outnumber women in their early twenties by over a quarter in 2010. As in the UK in the 1990s, the rapid decline in fertility means that at any stage there will tend to be a surplus of older men over younger women. This mismatch is exacerbated by the preference of Korean families for sons and the ability to achieve that nowadays through selective abortion aided by modern techniques of identifying the gender of an unborn child. Demographer Nicholas Eberstadt warns that both China and South Korea 'are poised to experience an increasingly intense, and perhaps desperate, competition among young men for their country's limited supply of brides'.[22]

Asian versus multicultural values

The more farsighted governments in Asia are already wrestling with the impending arrival of the agequake. Most think they have a secret weapon: Asian values. Their hope is that the strains on the state will be minimized because children will look after their ageing parents. This looks over-optimistic. Filial duty has its limits in the East as well as the West.

Take Japan. It is true that many older people continue to live with their children, but there has been a decisive shift in the past 25 years towards the western pattern of living in separate households. Since the end of the 1980s there has also been a sharp fall in those who agree that supporting their parents is a child's natural duty. Government attempts to shift responsibility for caring for the elderly back to families will fail, say Naohira Ogawa and Robert Retherford of the East-West Institute in a recent study. Changes in social attitudes, in particular the weakening values of filial duty, increased employment of women and declines in co-residence, all point to 'a continuing decline in the ability and will-ingness of the Japanese family to provide care for the elderly'.[23]

The Confucian tradition inculcating filial duty will come under attack as the age pyramid bulges at the top. Veneration of age is a value rooted in millennia of agricultural societies where the old were rela-tively few and controlled valuable resources of knowhow. It will be shaken to its foundations when the old start to outnumber the young and when today's expertise commands a premium over yesterday's experience.

As the world ages rapidly but at uneven speeds in the twenty-first century, Asian values will prove less valuable than multicultural ones: the preparedness to allow substantial immigration and to integrate immigrants into the host community. In the Asian crisis of 1997–8, racial tensions contributed to Indonesia's collapse, as the key Chinese community came under attack. Japan's problems are particularly acute because of its reluctance to admit immigrants. Such attitudes contrast sharply with American openness, highlighted in the new quota intro-duced in 1996 which actively seeks to increase the diversity of countries sending immigrants to the US.[24]

The US is the key test case in terms of immigration. The prize is a great one. Immigration is the one demographic way to relieve the most serious effects of ageing in the immediate future. But creating a genuinely multiracial society is an enormous challenge. 'White flight' from city centers in America and the mushroom-like growth of gated communities testify to the strains. Veteran economist Walt Rostow believes that the urban problem is the US's number one national security problem. 'If we succeed in mastering the current urban problem of our country, we shall strengthen our hand on the world scene. We shall demonstrate that we can be a truly multiracial society.'[25]

Global new age

As the agequake spreads throughout the world, the new age of humanity will begin: one when we will no longer be young. More and more of us will spend longer with our children as adults than as youngsters. This is an astonishing development set against the broad span of human history. In Roman times, a family with more than two adult children was exceptional. The Antonine Emperor Marcus Aurelius and Faustina had 12 children but only one son, Commodus, survived to adulthood. No wonder he was a stoic, consoling himself and others with his *Meditations*.[26]

Within the past century, we have moved from the large family – an exceptional episode in the history of humanity – to what historian Peter Laslett calls 'the beanpole family'. Children today no longer have lots of brothers and sisters, but are far more likely to have living grandparents and great-grandparents. In Victorian times a child aged 5 had only a one in four chance of having a grandfather alive. Today virtually all 5-year-olds have a living grandfather.[27]

In beanpole families there are extended and more intense relationships between parents and children and between siblings. But the lateral reach of families has contracted enormously. My father was one of seven surviving children who scattered across the world as part of the Irish diaspora. As a result I have lots of cousins. But my twin children have only three cousins. So it goes with most modern families. The sepia prints in the family album that could be a small school class change to color videos of today's pocket-sized families.

The implications of this global new age are as hard to grasp as they will be far-reaching. Could it ultimately herald the end of wars? This may seem an outlandish idea, but there is a well-established link between population explosions, an excess of young men and foreign adventures. Naoki Tanaka, President of the 21st Century Public Policy Institute in Japan, blames the wars of the early twentieth century on 'demographic surpluses'.[28]

Another reason to expect a more peaceful world in the long run is the growing numerical importance of older women thanks to their greater longevity. Francis Fukuyama, best known for proclaiming the end of history, has recently speculated about the way in which international relations will change in a more feminized world. He points out that that older women will become 'one of the most important voting blocs courted by mid-21st century politicians ... it seems likely that they will help elect more women leaders and will be less inclined towards military intervention than middle-aged males have traditionally been'. However, in the near future, they will face developing countries that are much younger and still headed predominantly by men. As he says, 'an unfamiliar world'.[29]

The global new age may eventually be more peaceful but it will be less dynamic. Each new generation reinvents humanity in its own image. Think of this process of generational renewal as a running bath in a Russian hotel – one without a plug. In the past, the bath emptied quickly and was refilled quickly. But now the fertility taps are only half on and an ill-fitting mortality plug means the bath is draining away much more slowly. The decelerating rate of generational turnover is a recipe for more stable but less adaptable societies.

This rigidity was anticipated in a classic thought experiment by sociologist Karl Mannheim 60 years ago. He imagined a world of one immortal generation – a bath with no taps and a plug that works. How could this race of immortals match the effects of generational refreshment? His answer was that they would need perfectly elastic minds and would have to learn to forget. The continuous emergence of new human beings 'alone makes a fresh selection possible when it becomes necessary; it facilitates re-evaluation of our inventory and teaches us both to forget that which is no longer useful and to covet that which has yet to be won'. Lack of experience might seem a disadvantage, but it 'means a lightening of the ballast for the young; it facilitates their living in a changing world'.[30]

Generations at war – let battle commence?

Set against the long-term prospects for a more peaceful world is the more imminent danger of social tensions within countries. The 2020s will be the decade when the threat of conflict between the generations is most serious, particularly in those countries that have failed to reform pay-as-you-go pension schemes. Under this scenario, the old will use their voting power to insist that younger workers fork out to pay for their pensions. But the young will resist with their economic power by pushing up real wages for services that the old have to pay and evading contributions wherever possible, so that the gap between the legitimate and the black economy grows ever wider.

In a recent international comparison of generational accounts, economists have totted up a huge bill facing future generations around the world if all the commitments of public spending are to be met, including the servicing of national debt. The imbalance is most acute in Japan, where future citizens will have to pay over two and a half times more net taxes (taxes less benefits) than current generations. In Germany and Brazil, the tax burden on future generations will be almost double what it is for today's.[31]

Proponents of the idea of generational warfare ascribe such imbalances to greed, short-sightedness or whatever term of abuse comes most readily to hand. But as Figure 34 shows, the source of these imbalances comes predominantly from demography. If future populations were the same, in size and in age structure, as today's, Germans and

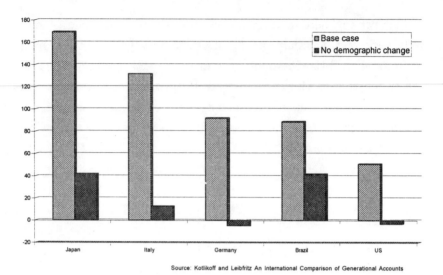

Source: Kotlikoff and Leibfritz An International Comparison of Generational Accounts

Figure 34 Passing the generational buck
Percent increase in net tax burden on future generations

Americans would not be passing the generational buck: today's generations would actually be asking future ones to pay less. The imbalances in Japan and Italy would be whittled away to manageable amounts.

The accounts highlight the potential for generational conflict in countries that fail to tackle the imbalances by pushing up taxes or cutting benefits now or in the near future. As I have argued earlier, there is something bogus in the notion of generational conflict, since the warring generations comprise families, with all the cooperative and altruistic bonds that implies. However, this attenuating influence will be less effective in the future because of the rising number of single people and the break-up of families through divorce. In her review of generational differences towards politics in Florida, Susan MacManus found that to date these are largely a matter of the intensity with which views are held. But she goes on to warn that 'tomorrow, we are more likely to find different generations supporting policy priorities that are diametrically opposed to each other as the nation undergoes its graying metamorphosis and the economic realities associated with it sink in'.[32]

This casts a shadow over pensions of all kinds. State pensions are likely to be reined back at short notice. Private pensions face the danger of tax raids. Baby boomers could find themselves paying higher tax rates when they draw their pensions than the tax rates they avoided when they made the pension contributions in the first instance. Demographer Alfred Sauvy spoke of 'the silent struggle between the adult generation and old age', which manifests itself in the level of interest rates or the rate of inflation. Without reforms, that struggle could turn out to be a noisy one in the early twenty-first century.[33]

Hard choices on medical care

Another potential battleground is medical care. Ageing will give an added twist to the steady escalation of healthcare costs in developed societies. The US already spends one dollar in every seven on health bills, but that will rise to one in four by 2050 on present trends.[34]

Does any society really want to spend a quarter of its national income on medical care? It seems unlikely. But if we are to spend less then we will have to curtail treatments. 'The dominant factor in the growth of medical care costs over time is the increasing quantity of services, not the price of given services,' writes David Cutler, an American expert on the economics of healthcare.

If we are to curb the runaway growth of health spending, we will therefore have to curtail the number of services that are provided. That's rationing by any other name, although rationing is a practice that dare not speak its name – not if politicians have anything to do with it. An early sign of the kind of decisions that will be taken was British Health Secretary Frank Dobson's decision to restrict NHS prescriptions for Viagra, despite its medical advantages.

Throughout the West, governments will try to shift the burden for non-essential medical expenses away from the state. In the US, you can expect further reforms to Medicare that will increase the amount of money that older people have to pay for healthcare. More generally,

Cutler argues that choice-based insurance, which allows people to decide what medical care services they want insured, is the 'only option that may help reduce medical care costs in the long run'. That option is strewn with difficulties, ranging from 'adverse selection' – the less healthy choosing the most generous scheme and the more healthy opting out – to fundamental issues of equity. But the alternative, a relentless rise in the medical burden, is likely to prove even more unpalatable.

Social panic?

Rather than generational wars, there could instead be a backlash against the modern values that have created the agequake. If ageing and population decline intensify, social panic might break out. At its most extreme, the future could resemble *The Handmaid's Tale* by Canadian novelist Margaret Atwood, a dystopian vision in which the feminist revolution is overturned and women are forced back into breeding. Such pronatalist policies would be combined with pressure on people to discharge their 'demographic debts' by having children.

Such ideas may be seen as unthinkable but in 1997, Werner Fasslabend, the Austrian defense minister, asserted that women had a patriotic duty to have at least two children to increase the number of earners. The Austrian family minister said that the retirement age should be raised for childless women. The proposals caused uproar among women's groups and were swiftly dropped.[35]

Pronatalist policies don't have to be vindictive. They can take the shape of tax incentives and general support for the family. The drawback is that they don't seem to work. A package of incentives introduced in Singapore in the late 1980s has failed to raise fertility, which remains well below replacement rates. But it is Sweden that offers the most telling example of the difficulties of sustaining higher fertility rates through fiscal incentives.

Sweden has been supporting the family since the end of the 1930s, pioneering such practices as maternity leave and children's allowances.

This did not stop the birth rate from plunging in the 1970s in common with that in most of Europe. However, in the late 1980s and start of the 1990s, Sweden stepped out of line, chalking up a mini baby boom by today's standards (see Figure 35). Fertility had been falling since the late 1960s. But in the 1980s it rose sharply and went above the replacement level of 2.1 in the early 1990s, well above the average fertility rate in the EU. The increase spanned both older and younger women and involved increases in the number of second as well as first children.[36]

One key reason for this mini baby boom was a new form of support for families called the 'speed premium' on the next child. This apparently minor reform introduced in 1980 meant that mothers continued to enjoy paid parental leave based on their income before the first child if they had a second child soon afterwards. This speed premium led many women to have a second child much more quickly than before. The incentive worked because most women knew that if they delayed, parental leave for their second child would be related to their subsequent income, likely to be in part-time work and therefore lower.

But even as Swedish demographers were hailing the ability of this new pronatalist policy to change behavior, the ground was shifting

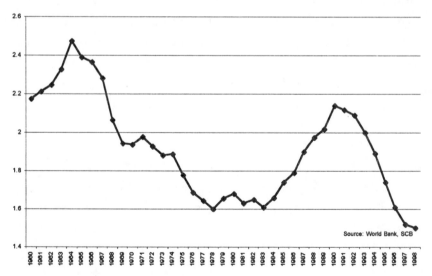

Source: World Bank, SCB

Figure 35 The Swedish experiment
Total fertility rate (births per woman)

under them. The rise proved short-lived. Fertility plummeted as swiftly as it had risen, falling to 1.5 in 1998, the lowest in Swedish history. The swings in fertility – from 1.6 in 1983 up to a peak of 2.14 in 1990 and then back down again – were the most intense in any western country in the last three decades.[37]

One point to make about this episode is that the baby-boom peak barely took fertility above the replacement level, about 2.1 births per woman. Even so, the fiscal incentive to have children may simply have compressed fertility into a brief boomlet which then gave way to slump. A study of pronatalist incentives in operation in the 1970s and 1980s in 22 industrialized countries found that maternity-leave benefits had no significant effects. More generous child allowances did have a positive impact, but it was nothing to write home about. Indeed, in Anglo-Saxon countries like the US, Australia and the UK, higher cash benefits had no effect at all. The overall conclusion was that even a substantial rise in the value of family allowances would only marginally increase the fertility rate.[38]

In conditions of a social panic, society might resort to less gentle methods than higher child allowances to restore birth rates. While these might work temporarily, the history of social attempts to control fertility shows that coercion is as ineffective in the long run as it is abhorrent. Brutal measures were employed by dictator Nikolae Ceausescu to try to increase the birth rate in Romania, leaving a pitiful legacy of unwanted children. But after the regime fell in 1989 the birth rate collapsed: in 1992 the number of abortions was three times the number of live births.[39]

In East Germany the incentives were more subtle, such as easier access to housing and 'baby years' – leave for the mother on full pay with the guarantee of keeping her job. They too created a temporary bulge – the notorious 'Honecker mountain' (after the East German leader who introduced them). But fertility never recovered to replacement levels and plunged at a record rate after reunification to unprecedently low levels.[40]

The main problem that pronatalist policies will encounter in the future is that they will intensify the financial pressure on younger generations. However much fiscal support the government provides, it will still be only a fraction of the private cost of bringing up children. Yet it is members of these generations who will also have to shoulder a bigger burden as the bumper generation of baby boomers retires. The danger is that we have unwittingly created a demographic vicious circle in which a constantly rising burden on successive generations causes a progressive decline in birth rates; which then intensifies that burden. Policies to promote higher fertility are a feeble antidote to such powerful incentives to bail out of the family business.

Confronting the sterility of modern capitalism

There is an inherent paradox in any book about the future. The more convincing your scenario is, the more likely it is that you will be wrong, because society and individuals will take avoiding action. I have sought to convey some of the ways in which individuals and governments can react to the approaching agequake. What is clear is that nothing short of a revolution in our working lives will overcome the sterility of modern capitalism.

It seems strange that in an era which insists on the priority of education, which accepts that investing in skills is as important as investing in physical assets, that we neglect the ultimate resource: ourselves. In the modern hubris of market economics, we have lost sight of a truth that traditional societies never overlooked: that the most essential investment of all is to replace ourselves. We have created an economic system that threatens our demographic future.

We have also created societies in which for the first time in human history resources flow up to the old rather than down to the young — and on a massive scale. Contrary to received wisdom, research by Californian demographer Ronald Lee has shown that in hunter-gatherer and agricultural societies resources flow down from the older to the younger. It is only in modern societies like the US with extended retirement and public pensions systems that the reverse is the case. There has been a fundamental reversal in the direction of traditional wealth flows.[41]

Reforms will have to tackle the fundamental mismatch between people's desired mix of work and leisure and what is actually on offer in the workplace. The present system crams work into people's middle years, making children even more of a burden – so helping to create the agequake – while resulting in a surfeit of leisure in later years. Women are heavily penalized if they want to work part-time to enable them to look after children, while older workers are not usually offered a reduction of working hours in their fifties and sixties. For their part, older workers are not generally prepared to accept lower earnings, even if this reflects the reality of their declining productivity.

Governments talk endlessly about the need to support the family. But talk is cheap, action expensive. In Britain, a welcome increase in child benefits is being mainly paid for by a rundown in the married couple's tax allowance, which further undermines the fiscal support for marriage. New subsidies for paid childcare are intended to help low-income families and single parents. But most women want to look after their own young children where possible, and choose to do so when offered a cash homecare allowance, as in Finland. In general, policies are shaped by a narrow economic perspective. 'There is little discussion of the incentives created either for or against marriage, family stability and committed parenting,' say Shirley Dex and Robert Rowthorn of Cambridge University. 'We appear to think that we can buy love and care for our children in unlimited quantities as a perfect substitute for our own care.'[42]

Reform does not mean pronatality policies, which are likely to prove ineffective and are in any case a particularly odious form of social engineering. Rather, it means ending policies and practices that are powerfully *anti*-natality. Instead of loading ever greater burdens on young people – asking them to contribute to pensions in their twenties and to pay off student debt when they should be saving for a house – we should be seeking to relieve the financial pressure on them.

Nor will reform entail a return to the traditional model of the male breadwinner and the little housewife back at home. The Scandinavian new man is proving a better guarantor of population stability than the macho Italian male. Intriguingly – though maybe not so when you consider the severity of ageing in Japan – this is now recognized by the government, which has manned the revolutionary barricades, calling for an end to the 'fixed division of roles between men and women and the inflexible employment practices which prioritize work over family'.[43]

This social and economic imbroglio will not be fixed without far-reaching changes. What is required is a drastic shake-up in working practices to allow women and men more flexibility to combine work with the upbringing of children, society's investment in its demographic future; and to extend their working lives on their own terms rather than curtail them as they live longer. So far no government in the world has had the courage to contemplate such a change, which would involve confronting the prevailing business culture head on. One way or another, it will have to happen if we are to avoid the full force of the agequake.

New age, new expectations

Throughout the lives of everyone living today, populations have been growing sharply and have remained relatively young. We stand on the cusp of a new era, when many populations are poised to decline and to age at unprecedented rates. These changes are welcome in many ways. They relieve the pressure on the environment. They reflect greater longevity, surely a triumph to be savored. The reduction in birth rates allows women to play a much fuller part in society and the economy.

But the transition from one historical era to another often passes through treacherous territory. Adjusting to the new age of humanity will require wrenching, often painful reforms at which we have so far balked. Life in an era of declining and ageing populations will be totally different from life in an era of rising and youthful populations. A new age calls above all for a new mindset. The new millennium is an apt moment to change the way we view our future and to start preparing in earnest for the agequake.

Appendix: Key terms

THE GENERAL METHOD I ADOPT IN THIS BOOK IS TO COMBINE demographic projections about the age structure of populations with *current* patterns of activity as they relate to age and *cohort* trends in economic and social behavior. In many aspects of our economic behavior, we are true to our age, as we form households and bring up children, then become empty nesters and eventually retire. However, often there are also strong cohort shifts in behavior, like women's move into the labor market. Assessing which is likely to be the most dominant factor in the future is a matter of judgement.

In the graphs, I define **adult population** as people aged 20 and over.

I use the term **average age** throughout to describe the median age: the age which splits the population in two.

Cohort describes people born in a particular year or period as they pass through their lives. Sociologists argue that particular formative experiences when a cohort is young can create a generation with distinct attitudes and behavior.

The **total fertility rate** or **TFR** is the average number of births that women would have provided that they live to the end of their reproductive years and conform to the current age patterns of fertility. The advantage of this standard measure of fertility is that it enables us to track fertility in timely fashion, comparing behavior across populations of widely varying age structures. However, it is an artificial measure, which can give a distorted reading of underlying fertility when a new cohort of women changes the timing of births.

Life expectancy measures the number of years for which you can expect to live at different ages – it is often quoted at birth – given prevailing survival chances across the age spectrum.

Lifespan can have two distinct meanings: one is the maximum time that human beings or other species can live; the other is the average lifespan that one can expect to live.

The **replacement rate** is the number of births per woman needed to ensure that populations neither grow nor decline in the long run in the absence of net immigration. For this to occur, every mother needs one daughter who herself survives to have children. The fertility rate required to ensure this in developed countries is 2.1 births rather than 2 births per woman, mainly because more boys are born than girls (roughly 105 for every 100).

The principal sources that I have used for demographic projections are: The UN *1998 Revision of World Population Prospects*; for the UK, the 1996 based projections carried out by the Government Actuary's Department (GAD); for the US, population projections of the Bureau of the Census issued in 1996; Eurostat, 1997, for the UK and other European countries; the World Bank in *World Development Indicators* (WDI), 1998. Throughout, I have used the central projections, unless specified in the text. Other principal sources include the UK's Office for National Statistics (ONS), the Organisation for Economic Co-operation and Development (OECD) and the International Labour Office (ILO).

References

Chapter 1 – Boom, bulge and bust

Except where otherwise specified, population figures – total numbers, average (median) age, total fertility rate – come from *World Population Prospects: the 1998 Revision*, issued by the UN in October 1998, medium-variant projection.

1   Peter E. Drucker, 'The Future That Has Already Happened', *Harvard Business Review*, September–October 1997, pp 20–23, Drucker's own italics.

2   Projections for years of population peaks are based on official population data from Japan's National Institute of Population and Social Security Research and the EC's Eurostat, in both instances the medium or baseline projections.

3   World Health Organization (WHO) *The World Health Report 1998*, 'Life in the 21st Century' p 1; Simon Field, *Trends in Crime Revisited*, Home Office, 1998.

4   Tim Parkin, *Demography and Roman Society*, John Hopkins University Press, 1992, p 84; national sources for life expectancy in England and the US.

5   WHO, *op. cit.*, p V.

6   *Statistical Abstract of the United States*, 1997, 117th edition, p 14; Ansley Coale, 'How a Population Ages or Grows Younger' in Ronald Freedman (ed.) *Population: The Vital Revolution*, 1964.

7   The median age of the world population will rise to 43.5 in 2050 in the UN's low-variant projection.

8   McNamara said 'the threat of unmanageable population pressures

is much like the threat of nuclear war' in 1973: cited in Allen Kelley, 'Economic Consequences of Population Change in the 3rd World', *Journal of Economic Literature*, 1988, p 1685.

9   The Brazilian data comes from Dr A. Kalache at the WHO.

10   UN Expert Group Meeting on Below-Replacement Fertility, New York, 1997, pp 32–9.

11   Californian Department of Finance, 17 December 1998. Estimates of when the US will become the second and third biggest Spanish-speaking nation based on WDI, World Bank 1998, for Spain, Colombia and Argentina and US Bureau of the Census, *Population Projections*, 1996, Table 2 Medium projection. *The Economist*, 'America's Latinos', 25 April 1998, cites comparisons of purchasing power of US Hispanics with Mexican economy.

12   ONS Population Estimates Unit: 26.6% of women aged 30–34 in England and Wales were single (never married) in 1996. Answers to the General Household Survey indicate that 10% of women aged 30–34 were cohabiting: ONS, *Social Focus on Families*, 1997, p 15. Note, however, that cohabiting couples are more than four times likely to split up as married couples: ESRC Research Centre on Micro-social Change, *Changing Households, British Household Panel Survey 1990–1992*, 1994, p 61.

13   WHO, *op. cit.*, p 102.

14   Benjamin Meuli, managing director J.P. Morgan, in letter to *Financial Times*, 7 November 1996.

Chapter 2 – The future that's happened

Except where otherwise specified, population projections – life expectancy, median age, TFR   –   come from *World Population Prospects: The 1998 Revision*, medium-variant projection; historical data are drawn from the UN or official national sources.

1   www.centenaire.com.

2   *The Economist*, 'Jeanne Calment', 16 August 1997; National

Research Council (NRC), *Between Zeus and the Salmon: The Biodemography of Longevity*, National Academy Press, 1997, p 250.

3   *Philosophical Transactions of the Royal Society*, Series B, 'Ageing: Science, Medicine and Society', 1997, p 1802; National Institute of Aging (NIA), 'In search of the secrets of aging', www.nih.gov/nia.

4   WHO, *op. cit.*, p 102, based on INSEE projections for France.

5   Peter E. Drucker, *op. cit.*

6   Ansley J. Coale, *op. cit.*, esp. pp 49–50; Nathan Keyfitz, 'Changing Vital Rates and Age Distribution', *Population Studies*, 1968, pp 235–51.

7   Kenneth Manton, Eric Stallard and Larry Corder, 'Changes in the Age Dependence of Mortality and Disability: Cohort and Other Determinants', *Demography*, 1997, p 135.

8   S.J. Olshansky and Bruce Carnes, 'Demographic Perspectives on Human Senescence', *Population and Development Review*, 1994, pp 57–80.

9   Richard Rogers, 'Socio-demographic Characteristics of Long-Lived and Healthy Individuals', *Population and Development Review*, 1995, pp 36–8.

10   NRC, *Between Zeus and the Salmon*, pp 4, 28; NASA, 'Facts: Voyager Mission to the Outer Planets', www.jpl.nasa.gov.

11   NRC, *Between Zeus and the Salmon*, pp 195–203.

12   Kenneth Manton, Eric Stallard and H. Dennis Tolley, 'Limits to Human Life Expectancy: Evidence, Prospects and Implications', *Population and Development Review*, 1991, pp 603–37; NRC, *Between Zeus and the Salmon*, pp 32–3.

13   Kenneth Manton *et al.*, *op. cit.*, pp 617–18; Kenneth Manton, Eric Stallard and Larry Corder, *Demography*, 1997, pp 135–57.

14   Data on strokes and heart disease from National Institutes of Health at www.nih.gov; UN Working Group, *Projecting Old-Age Mortality and its Consequences*, February 1997, p17; NRC, *Between Zeus and the Salmon*, pp 13, 58–61, 260–1.

15   ONS, *Living in Britain, Results from the General Household Survey: 1996*, 1998, p 157; House of Lords Select Committee on Science

and Technology, 'Resistance to Antibiotics and other Antimicrobial Agents', HL Paper 81-I, pp 49, 51, citing evidence from the Association of the British Pharmaceutical Industry and SmithKline Beecham.

16   The initiative is the 'Longevity Assurance Genes' Program; NIA, *op. cit.*, 'The Genetic Connection'; statement by Richard Hodes, Director, NIA, to Congress on Fiscal Year 1999 President's Budget Request, 1998.

17   NIA, *op. cit.*, 'Biochemistry and aging'.

18   NIA, 'Two new studies suggest that calorific restriction in monkeys may extend their life and health', 2 October 1997.

19   Statement by Dr Harold Varmus to Congress on Fiscal Year 1999 President Budget's Request for the NIH, March 1998.

20   Quoted in *Financial Times*, 'America's pursuit of knowledge', 21 February 1998; statement by Dr Richard Klausner, Director, National Cancer Institute, to Congress, March 1998; WHO, *op. cit.*, p 5.

21   Statement of Dr Claude Lenfant, Director of NHLBI, in evidence to Congress, 1998.

22   Woodring E. Wright *et al.*, 'Extension of Life-span by Introduction of Telomerase into Normal Human Cells', *Science*, 16 January 1998; 'Scientists extend the life span of human cells', UT Southwestern news release.

23   NIA statement by Richard Hodes, *op. cit.*: 'the correlation between telomerase activation and cancerous growth has stimulated many scientists to view telomerase inhibition as a potential new approach to cancer therapy'.

24   Statement by Dr Harold Varmus to Congress, *op.cit.*

25   Ansley J. Coale, *op.cit.*, p 52; *Statistical Abstract of the US*, p 14.

26   John Ermisch, 'Easterlin, Home Economics and Fertility', *Population Studies*, 1979, p 55; '1996- based national population projections for the UK', *Population Trends*, Spring 1998, pp 44–5.

27   Antonio Golini, 'Levels and Trends of Fertility in Italy', in UN, Expert Group Meeting on Below-Replacement Fertility, New York, November 1997.

28 UN, *The 1998 Revision*, constant variant projection, based on fertility rates in the early 1990s.

29 For example OECD, *Ageing in OECD Countries*, 1996, p 103.

30 Gigi Sandow, 'Coitus interruptus and the Control of Natural Fertility', *Population Studies*, 1995, pp 28–9, 36, 40.

31 Adam Smith, *Wealth of Nations*, Penguin Classics, 1987, p 173.

32 Gary Becker, A *Treatise on the Family*, Harvard University Press, 1993, ch 5, especially pp 135–44.

33 Diane Macunovich, 'Relative Income and the Price of Time: Exploring their Effects on US Fertility and Female Labor Force Participation', *Population and Development Review*, Supplement, 1996, p224: 'probably the most crucial factor in completed family size, as well as in period measures of fertility, is the timing of the first birth. The earlier this occurs, the higher will be completed family size on average.'

34 Fiona McAllister with Lynda Clarke, 'Choosing Childlessness', *Family Policy Studies*, 1998, p13; Richard Leete, 'The Continuing Flight from Marriage and Parenthood among the Overseas Chinese in East and Southeast Asia', *Population and Development Review*, 1994, pp 818–19.

35 UN, *Projecting Old-Age Mortality and its Consequences*, p 13.

36 World Bank, WDI, 1998.

37 Robert Retherford and Norman Luther, 'Are fertility differentials by education converging in the US?', *Genus*, July–December 1996.

38 Figures for fertility of women aged 40–49 are for 1994, with the exception of the UK (1995), from UN Expert Group Meeting on Below-Replacement Fertility, November 1997, pp 46–8.

39 Shanna Swan *et al.* in *Environmental Health Perspectives*, National Institute of Environmental Health Sciences, 1997; Dr Stewart Irvine, 'Evidence of Deteriorating Semen Quality in the UK', *British Medical Journal*, 4 Februrary 1996; Niels Skakkebaek *et al.*, 'Relation between Semen Quality and Fertility: a Population-based Study of 430 First-pregnancy Planners', *The Lancet*, 10 October 1998, pp 1172–7.

40 NRC, *The New Americans*, National Academy Press, 1997, pp 34, 40, 50–52. The NRC estimates that illegal immigration into the US is running at approaching 300,000 a year and that gross emigration is about 300,000 a year. Official figures from the Immigration and Naturalization Service are for legal immigrants only, but can give a distorted picture of the underlying level of immigration since they include naturalizations of people already living in the US. For Germany, see *Trends in International Migration*, OECD, 1997, pp 105–7.

41 Massimo Livi-Bacci, *A Concise History of World Population*, Blackwell, 1997, p 137.

42 David A. Coleman, 'Contrasting Age Structures of Western Europe and of Eastern Europe and the former Soviet Union: Demographic Curiosity or Labor resource?', *Population and Development Review*, 1993, pp 533–5, 544–5.

43 OECD, *The World in 2020*, 1997, p 65.

44 OECD, *Trends in International Migration*, 1998, p 29.

45 On disparity in earnings see NRC, *The New Americans*, pp 176–7.

46 NRC, *The New Americans*, p 351 for estimate of $80,000 net present value of immigrants' fiscal contribution; for a view from California that stresses the costs of immigration, see Kevin McCarthy and Georges Vernez, *Immigration in a Changing Economy*, Rand, 1997.

47 Social & Community Planning Research (SCPR), *British and European Social Attitudes*, Ashgate, 1998, p 14; *The Guardian*, 27 April 1998, 'German neo-Nazis grab vote in East'.

48 John S. Lapinski *et al.*, 'The Polls – Trends Immigrants and Immigration', *Public Opinion Quarterly*, Vol 61, 1997, pp 360–61; 'When two tribes make a third', *Financial Times*, 12 September 1998.

Chapter 3 – Financial rollercoaster

1   William Gale and John Karl Scholz, 'Intergenerational Transfers and the Accumulation of Wealth', *Journal of Economic Perspectives*, 1994, pp 146–7,155–6. There is great controversy over the precise importance of lifecycle wealth in relation to bequests, caused by definitions of when households are formed, how contributions to university fees should be treated and whether transfers should be capitalized to include subsequent interest payments on them.

2   Group of Ten, *The Macroeconomic and Financial Implications of Ageing Populations*, ch 3, p 5. Helmut Reisen at the OECD Development Centre calculates that demographics account for about a fifth of the rise in the Standard & Poors price/earnings ratio between the early 1980s and 1996. The equation, which doesn't take into account the role of demographics on inflation, is set out in *Institutional Investors in the new Financial Landscape*, OECD, 1998, pp 338–42.

3   Richard Hokenson, *Generations*, Donaldson, Lufkin & Jenrette, September 1997. The immediate reason for the rise in inflation may have come from loose fiscal and monetary policy; but the pressure on governments came from the underlying demographics, both within western economies and globally through commodity prices as the rate of world population growth rose to a peak.

4   Douglas Lee, 'Savings at a new low – baloney', *HSBC Washington Analysis*, June 1998. In August 1998, the Bureau of Economic Analysis revised down the personal savings ratio by almost three percentage points when it excluded mutual fund distributions of capital gains from personal income, reclassifying them as retained corporate earnings.

5   Group of Ten, *op. cit.*, ch 3, p 6 on potential reduction in bond yields as governments cut deficits; for international trends in domestic savings 1992–7, see Table II.2 and Graph II.5 in Bank for International Settlements (BIS), Annual Report, 1998, pp 19–20.

The generally disappointing levels of household savings are not that surprising given this push to increase government saving. A study by the IMF in 1995 showed that about half any government move to saving or dissaving is offset by the private sector. See Paul Masson, Tamim Bayoumi and Hossein Samiei, 'International Evidence on the Determinants of Private Saving', IMF Working Paper 95/51.

6   Investment Company Institute (ICI), *Trends in Mutual Fund Investing*, February and November 1998; US Federal Reserve Flow of Funds Accounts, release 11 December 1998. Total financial assets of mutual funds stood at $5.37 trillion at the end of November 1998, total financial assets of commercial banks were $5.5 trillion at the end of September 1998.

7   ICI, *Mutual Fund Shareholders: the People behind the Growth*, 1996, pp 3–4, 19. The survey excluded households who only held mutual funds via 401(k) retirement plans.

8   ICI, *op. cit.*

9   ICI, *op.cit.*, p 22; 'Thirtysomethings fuel pensions boom', *The Times*, 21 January 1998.

10   Employee Benefit Research Institute in Washington, DC.

11   NBER, *Economic Reporter*, Summer 1996: as assets in the 401(k) plans grew between the early 1980s and early 1990s, contributors maintained the level of their other financial assets and those people eligible for a 401(k) plan have saved more in financial assets than those ineligible for such a plan. On cohort effects, see James Poterba, Seven Venti and David Wise, 'Implications of Rising Personal Retirement Saving', NBER Working Paper 6295, November 1997, which projects that the cohort born in 1959 will have a 401(k) balance of $91,600 in today's money when they retire, while the cohort born in 1969 will collect $125,500.

12   David Hale, *How the Mutual Fund Boom Is Changing the US Economy; Has America's Stock Market Boom just Begun or how the Rise of Pension Funds Will Change the Global Economy in the 21st Century*, Zurich Insurance, March 1998.

13 David Coleman (ed.), *Europe's Population in the 1990s*, Oxford University Press, 1996, pp 11–14.

14 Deutsches Aktieninstitut on German shareholdings as proportion of household wealth; Bernhard Brinker and Michael Sautter, 'Mutual Funds in Germany: Evaluating Opportunities', *McKinsey Quarterly*, 1997: 2.

15 Ulrich Baumgartner and Guy Meredith (eds), *Saving Behaviour and the Asset Price 'Bubble' in Japan*, IMF 1995, pp 51–3; Lester Thurow, *The Future of Capitalism*, Nicholas Brealey Publishing, 1996, p 197; the respective valuations of Japan and the UK based on the FT/S&P/Actuaries World Index end March 1998.

16 Cited in W.W. Rostow, *The Great Population Spike and After, Reflections on the 21st Century*, Oxford University Press, 1998, p 130.

17 Paul Krugman, *It's Baaack! Japan's Slump and the Return of the Liquidity Trap*, Brookings Panel on Economic Activity, September 1998.

18 W.W. Rostow, *op.cit.*, p 131.

19 On past successes of procrastination (and failure of far-reaching reforms) see Peter F. Drucker, 'Defending Japanese Bureaucrats', *Foreign Affairs*, September/October 1998.

20 On details of Big Bang reforms: 'Reform plans gather pace', *Financial Times*, 15 July 1997.

21 *Equity-Gilt Study*, Barclays Capital, 1998. Same source for subsequent details on UK equities.

22 Jeremy J.Siegel, *Stocks for the Long Run*, McGraw-Hill, 1998, pp 13–15; *Equity-Gilt Study*, p 53.

23 Published in *Wall Street Journal*, 21 April 1998.

24 *Equity-Gilt Study*, p 36; Richard Disney, Paul Johnson and Gary Stears, *Asset Wealth and Asset Decumulation among Households in the Retirement Survey*, Institute for Fiscal Studies, May 98.

25 Erik Hurst, Ming Ching Luoh, Frank Stafford, 'The Wealth Dynamics of American Families 1984–94', Brookings Papers on Economic Activity 1, 1998, Table 3, p 276.

26   The Bank for International Settlements calculates that falling import prices brought consumer price inflation down by half a percentage point per annum in the US between the end of 1995 and 1997 – see BIS, *op. cit.*, pp 24–5.

27   W.W. Rostow, *op. cit.*, 1998, p 79.

28   BIS, *op. cit.*, p 119.

29   David Bloom and Jeffrey Williamson, 'Demographic Transitions and Economic Miracles in Emerging Asia', NBER Working Paper 6268, 1997; see also Matthew Higgins and Jeffrey Williamson, 'Age Structure Dynamics in Asia and Dependence on Foreign Capital', *Population and Development Review*, 1997.

30   Martin Baily *et al.*, 'The Roots of Korea's Crisis', *McKinsey Quarterly*, 1998:2, pp 76-83.

31   Research by Barry, Peavy and Rodriguez, *Emerging Stock Markets: Risk, Return and Performance*, ICFA 1997, in a comparison from 1975–95, cited in Alex Brown, 'Life Is a Lemon and I Want my Money back', 19 November 1997.

32   Burton Malkiel and J.P. Mei, *Global Bargain Hunting: The Investor's Guide to Big Profits in Emerging Markets*, Penguin, 1998, pp 16, 124–5.

Chapter 4 – The new property game

1   Alan Holmans, 'Where Have all the First-time Buyers Gone?', *Housing Finance*, No 25, February 1995, pp 8–9.

2   Holmans, *op. cit.*, pp 9–11. This estimate excludes 'right-to-buy' purchases by council tenants.

3   John Muellbauer and Anthony Murphy, 'Booms and Busts in the UK Housing Market', *Economic Journal*, 1997, p 1704 for repossessions estimates; Fionnuala Earley, *Ten Years after the Housing Boom*, Council of Mortgage Lenders, April 1998, cites estimates of 1.9 million in negative equity in early 1991.

4   For an overview of the forces affecting the housing market, see

Stewart Robertson, 'The Future of the UK Mortgage Market: A City Analyst's View', *Housing Finance*, August 1998.

5   GAD principal projection shows 23–25 age group falling from 2.6m to 2.1m between 1995 and 2002.

6   Marie Heiborn, 'Demographic Factors and the Demand for Housing', *Economic Studies*, 40, Uppsala University, 1998; Muellbauer and Murphy, *op. cit.*, p 1723.

7   DETR, *Projections of Households in England to 2016*, 1996, p viii. The projected annual growth is over a fifth down on the rate of increase in the 1980s.

8   ONS, *Living in Britain: Results from the 1996 General Household Survey*, 1998, Table 2.1, p14; Eurostat, *Social Portrait of Europe*, 1998, p 53.

9   DETR, *op. cit.*; Netherlands National Household Forecasts 1996 reported in Council of Europe, *Recent Demographic Trends in Europe*, 1997, p 240. The number of one-person households will rise from 2.1m to 3.3m; the total number of households will rise by 21% to 7.9m..

10 DETR, *op. cit.*, p xiv.

11 Alan Holmans, *Housing Demand and Need in England, 1991–2011*, Joseph Rowntree Foundation, pp 31–2, 70–71. His main projection shows an increase in owner-occupier households of 2.7m against an increase in households of 3.6m. The increase in owner-occupier households could be as high as 3.4m under alternative projections.

12 Alan Holmans, *op.cit.*, p 43.

13 Town and Country Planning Association (TCPA), *The People – Where Will they Go?*, 1996, pp 42–3: 'While there is little doubt that a large increment of small households will eventually lead to a overall requirement for more small units, there is no easy or automatic equivalence. The question is further complicated by rising incomes and rising expectations, which may well mean that one person households will demand larger dwelling units, including houses with gardens.'

14 National Association of Realtors, *The Home Buying and Selling Process: 1997*, July 1998.

15 DETR, *Housing and Construction Statistics*, Table 10.17 shows that of purchases by existing owner-occupiers, 48% of advances completed by building societies in 1977 were to 25–34-year-olds; this fell to 38% in 1997. There was a rise from 28 to 33% in the share of 35–44-year-olds and a rise from 14 to 18% in the 45–54 age bracket. The figures are based on mortgage lending, so purchases financed wholly by equity are not included, but such purchases are relatively insignificant for people aged 25–44.

16 ONS, *Social Focus on Families*, 1997, Table 1.5, p 12: in spring 1996, 64% of men and 61% of women between 35 and 44 were couples with dependent children; 36% of men and 23% of women aged 45–54 fell into this category.

17 FPD Savills, *Residential Research Bulletin*, No 25, Spring 1998.

18 FPD Savills, *op.cit.*, cites price rises of 192% and falls of 65% in parts of Bristol 1995–7.

19 Nicola Düll, 'Population Aging and German Economic Performance', in Barry Bosworth and Gary Burtless (eds), *Aging Societies The Global Dimension*, Brookings Institution Press, 1998, p 218.

20 Joint Center for Housing Studies of Harvard University, *The State of the Nation's Housing: 1998*, pp 7, 13–14: the number of empty nesters without adult children living with them is estimated to rise by 3.2m.

21 John Ermisch and Stephen Jenkins, *Housing Adjustment in later Life: Evidence from the British Household Panel Survey*, University of Essex, ESRC Research Centre on Micro-social Change, 1997, pp 1, 6, 21; 'Home sweet home for the empty-nesters', *Financial Times*, 25 July 1998.

22 Andrew Cochera, 'Vacation and Investment Homes', *Housing Economics*, November 1997; Michael Carliner, 'Second Home Construction', *Housing Economics*, July 1998.

23 American Resort Development Association, *The Vacation Ownership Industry*, 1998.

24 Russell King, Anthony Warnes and Allan Williams, 'A Place in the Sun', *European Urban and Regional Studies*, 1997, p 117; Alan Holmans, *op. cit.*, pp 13, 35–7.

25 I owe this information to John Karevoll, database analyst with Acxiom/Dataquick, who conducted a search on transactions up to mid-November 1998.

26 Interview with G-U Krueger; and Gerd-Ulf Krueger and Wei Wang, 'Multi-ethnic Housing in Southern California', *LUSK Review*, 1998, pp 138–41.

27 This and the subsequent analysis about minorities comes from Harvard Joint Center for Housing Studies, *op. cit.*, and George Masnick, *Understanding the Minority Contribution to US Owner Household Growth*, Harvard Joint Center for Housing Studies, November 1998.

28 DETR, *op. cit.*, p ix; *Household Growth: Where Shall we Live?*, 1996, p 11; *An Economic Assessment of Recent House Price Developments*, Dublin, pp 3–4, 50–51.

29 NRC, *The New Americans*, pp 59–61.

30 NRC, *op. cit.*; Huw Jones, *Population Geography*, Paul Chapman Publishing, 1990, p 244; TCPA, *op. cit.*, pp 43, 79–80.

31 William Frey, 'Minority Magnet Metros in the '90s', *Population Studies Center*, University of Michigan, 1998, Report 98-418, Tables 1, 3; Harvard Joint Center, *The State of the Nation's Housing: 1998*, p 6.

32 Harvard Joint Center, *op. cit.*, p 7, Table A10, p 33.

33 *ibid.*, p 12.

34 *ibid.*, Table A-9, p 32 for regional house price movements.

35 TCPA, *op. cit.*, pp 5, 105.

36 NRC, *Demography of Aging*, National Academy Press, 1994, pp 326–7, 330–1. UK Census figures show that the migration rate of people 60+ in 1990–91 was less than 40% for that of the population as a whole – see Anthony Warnes, 'Migrations among Older People', *Reviews in Clinical Gerontology*, 1996, p 102.

37 NRC, *Demography of Aging*, pp 352–5.

38 US Bureau of the Census, *65+ in the US*, 1996, P23-190, projections from 1993. The eight states are Nevada, Arizona, Colorado, Georgia, Washington, Alaska, Utah, California. Only in Arizona was the proportion of 65+ to the population higher than in the US in 1996: see *Statistical Abstract of the US 1997*, p 33; *Population Projections for States by Age*, December 1998, www.census.gov/population/projections/state/stpjage.txt, for contribution of 65+ to population growth in Arizona, Nevada and Utah 1995–2015.

39 Russell King, Anthony Warnes and Allan Williams, 'International Retirement Migration in Europe', *International Journal of Population Geography*, 1998; *A Place in the Sun*, pp 116, 131.

40 Anthony Warnes, *op.cit.*, p 112: the figures are for state pensions paid in January 1995. Russell King *et al.*, *A Place in the Sun*, pp 120–21.

41 Nicola Düll, *op. cit.*, p 214.

42 The estimate of 6% living in age-restricted communities comes from Harvard Joint Center for Housing Studies, *op. cit.*, p15.

43 Jack Lessinger, *Penturbia: Where Real Estate Will Boom after the Crash of Suburbia*, 1991, pp 16, 23.

44 Anthony Warnes, *op.cit.*, p 101; Russell King *et al.*, *International Retirement Migration in Europe*.

45 Russell King *et al.*, *International Retirement Migration in Europe*; CPRE, *Urban Exodus*, 1998, pp 6, 54–9.

46 FPD Savills, *The Emerging Residential Investment Sector*, Summer 1998, on long-run trend in house prices.

Chapter 5 – The new business game

1   Harvard Joint Center for Housing Studies, *op.cit.*, Table A-11, p 34: household numbers for 1995 are consistent with the *1995 Current Population Survey*.

2   US Department of Commerce, *Consumer Expenditure Survey 1995*; ONS special run of Family Expenditure Survey data by 10-

year age bands shows virtually even spending per household among 35–44- and 44–55-year-olds.

3 ONS special run of Family Expenditure Survey data by 10 year age bands shows net housing and household services peaking among 35–44-year-olds.

4 Mintel International Group, *Marketing to 45–64s: The Boom Years?*, 1998, p 58; ONS, *Family Spending*, 1997, pp 39–41: spending on soft furnishings in households headed by 50–64-year-olds is 27% higher than all households; on white goods (kitchen/garden equipment, household hardware) it is 29% higher; per person in household it is 44 and 47% higher respectively. Spending at restaurants per person is 42% higher in households headed by 50–64-year olds compared with all households.

5 'Pfizer Impotence Pill Seen as Milestone', *Wall Street Journal*, 31 March 1998; 'Take one before bedtime', *Financial Times*, 7 May 1998.

6 Survey commissioned by Biotechnology Industry Organization (BIO), 1998, 'Living Better as well as Longer: Biotechnology Leads the Way', reporting a symposium into ageing research at the New York Academy of Science, www.bio.org.

7 PaineWebber, *The New Millennium American*, September 1998, p 4.

8 BIO, *op. cit.*; 'Activation of telomerase in normal human cells extends their life-span', Geron Corporation, 13 January 1998, www.geron.com; 'CSIRO discovery fights cell ageing', 31 July 1997, www.csiro.au; the Beta Peptide Foundation Pty Ltd has developed products including beta alistine'.

9 Victoria Ward, 'Acquiring a Taste for Looking Good', *Financial Times Pharmaceuticals Survey*, 16 March 1998.

10 'Alpha Hydroxy Acids for Skin Care: Smooth Sailing or Rough Seas?', *Food and Drug Administration*, March/April 1998.

11 Freedonia Group, *World Nutraceuticals*, September 1998; CSIRO, 'A Cup of Tea May Protect against Skin Cancer', 30 April 1998; MAFF, *National Food Survey*, 1997, Table 2.10, p13.

12 'Positive assessment in the Netherlands Brings New Flora Pro-activ Closer to Market', Unilever, 17 December 1998.

13 *Re-inventing Drug Discovery*, Andersen Consulting, 1998, p 1.

14 Ranking of AstraZenica and Aventis based on MIDAS database of IMS: AstraZeneca ranked third on pro forma sales in year to end June 1998.

15 Morgan Stanley Dean Witter, *The Competitive Edge*, 1998, p 127; British Biotech sought to rebut the allegations in its circular to shareholders, 19 May 1998.

16 Advanced Tissue Sciences, news release 12 October 1998: at this juncture it was licensed for use in Canada and the UK; interview with Professor Suggett.

17 'Merrill offers £3.1bn for MAM', *Financial Times*, 20 November 1997.

18 For this and subsequent paragraph, Marshall Carter, annual stock-holders' address, AGM 15 April 1998; 'State Treasurers and the Challenge of Pension Finance', November 1997.

19 Goldman Sachs, *Asset Management in the 21st Century: New Rules, New Game*, April 1998, pp 1–2, 27.

20 'Prudential of US Set to Float', *Financial Times*, 13 February 1998; 'Prudential Moves to Go Public', *Wall Street Journal*, 16 February 1998.

21 Donald Marron cited in 'Bullish on his Prospects', *Financial Times*, 10 November 1997; 'Banking on the Value of Cross-selling', *Financial Times*, 7 April 1998.

22 'Thundering Herd Moves into Japan', *Financial Times*, 13 February 1998; 'US Group Sees its Demographic Chance,' *Financial Times*, 19 February 1998; 'Financial Big Boys of the West Go on a 'Dating Frenzy', *Financial Times*, 12 August 1998.

23 ONS, *Social Focus on Families*, Table 1.5, p 12, based on women 45–54 in couples; Mintel, *Marketing to the 45–64s*, p 20.

24 Research International Qualitatif (RIO), *Connecting with Baby Boomers*, 1997, pp 18-21.

25 ONS, *Family Spending*, 1997, p 41; Russell King *et al.*, A *Place in the Sun*, p 118.

26 Passenger Shipping Association (PSA), *Annual Cruise Review 1997*, 1998; Princess Cruises.

27 PSA, *op.cit.*; IRN Travelstat.

28 PaineWebber, *op.cit.*, pp 3-4

29 US Bureau of the Census, 'Estimates of the Population of Metropolitan Areas', MA-96-9, December 1997, www.census.gov; for this and subsequent paragraph, Las Vegas Convention and Visitors Authority, LasVegas24hours.com.

30 OFLOT, *Social Research Programme*, June 1996 to March 1997, p 8.

31 SMMT, *UK Car Registrations by Segment*; MG and Porsche for age of customers.

32 'New Generation of Beer Drinkers is Enigma to Marketers', *New York Times*, 18 April 1998; Whitbread, *1997 On-trade Report*, p4. In the UK, the number of 20–29 year old men fell from 4.8m in 1990 to 4.2m in 1997: ONS Population Estimates Unit.

33 This and subsequent material on Whitbread comes from *Whitbread Briefing Book*, March 1998, pp 2–5, 8, 13; *1997 On-trade Market Report*, pp 3–5, 23, 26, 36; Annual Report and Accounts 1997/8; 'The Leisure Industry Report', *Leisure Week*, 1997, pp 29–31, 47–9.

34 Mintel, *Marketing to 45–64s*, p 67. There was a 14 percentage point increase in the number of 45–54-year-olds eating out between 1993 and 1997 and an 8 percentage point increase in the number of 55–64-year-olds.

35 Sporting Goods Manufacturers Association, *Sports Participation Index*, 1997, p 14; Fitness Products Council, *Tracking the Fitness Movement*, 1997.

36 ONS, *Family Spending*, p 39 for age profile of spirits and liqueur consumption; ONS, *Consumers Expenditure on Alcoholic Drink*.

37 The McDonald brothers launched the first fast-food menu in 1948; they had been operating before then. On press criticism, see for example 'McDonald's Plans to Overhaul Menu as "adult-oriented" line does poorly', 'How to save McDonald's', *Wall Street Journal*, 19 March 1998.

38 1997 annual report, www.mcdonalds.com.

39 'Can McDonald's Regain its Golden Touch?', *Business Week*, 9 March 1998.

40 US Department of Agriculture Economic Research Service for data on food consumed away from home as proportion of all food expenditure.

41 Euromonitor, *Fast Food: the International Market*, May 1998: specifically spending on fast foods is little more than a tenth of the American level in Germany and France and under a fifth in the UK.

42 Levi Strauss news releases, 3 November 1997 and 29 September 1998, for details of closures in US and subsequently in Europe.

43 Levis Strauss press releases, 17 June and 17 November 1998, on Hard Jeans ad campaign.

44 Nike fourth quarter and fiscal 1998 earnings and second quarter fiscal 1999 earnings 30 June and 17 December 1998, www.nike-biz.com, 'Athletic Footwear: a Mature Industry', 20 March 1998, www. sportlink.com.

45 ONS, special ten-year age band run of Family Expenditure Survey 1996–7; GAD principal projection shows the number of 25–34-year-olds declining by 1.75m between 1995–2005, while the number of 55–64-year-olds rises by 1.25m.

46 Richard Hokenson, *Generations*, pp 42–4.

47 *UK Blue Book*, 1998, Table 6.5, 1996, pp 270–71, Table 1.7 pp 34–5. US consumer spending rose by 4.3% a year between 1982 and 1988 and by 2.9% a year between 1991 and 1997. Consumer spending on goods as a proportion of total expenditure fell by 2–3 percentage points between the mid-1980s and 1990s in Britain and by about 1 percentage point in the US: *Blue Book*, 1996, p 77, *Economic Report of the President*, 1998, Table B-17, p 301.

48 Corporate Intelligence on Retailing, *Consumer Spending Forecasts for Western Europe 1998–2005*, 1998.

49 OXIRM/Jones Lang Wootton, *Shopping for New Markets: Retailers' Expansion across Europe's Borders*, November 1997, pp 8, 17.

50   Metro website, 'Wal-Mart in German stores acquisition'; *Financial Times*, 10 December 1998.

51   OXIRM/Jones Lang Wootton, *op.cit.*, p 3; Tesco news release on expansion into Thailand, 18 May 1998.

52   Jones Lang Wootton/OXIRM, *op. cit.*, p 39 on Galéries Lafayette; 'Toys 'R' US' Repositions Worldwide Business', news release, 16 September 1998.

53   Morgan Stanley Dean Witter, *op. cit.*, p 187.

Chapter 6 – Cultural revolution

1   BBC Radio 3, 13 September 1997.

2   In academic jargon, social change is a composite of lifecycle, cohort, and 'period' or general trend effects. In Melissa Hardy (ed.), *Aging, Social Change and Conservatism*, Sage Publications, 1997, Duane Alwin produces evidence of the stability of people's political attitudes beyond their early thirties. He argues that the principal reason for the swing towards political conservatism in America comes from general political change, embraced by all generations – 'period' effects – rather than the ageing of baby boomers.

3   Mintel's study of 45–64-year-olds in 1998 found respondents in all groups agreeing that they felt much younger than they actually were, and certainly more so than their parents at the same age: Mintel, *op. cit.*, p 135; 'Fresh Will by Diana Could Have Saved Tax', *The Times*, 24 November 1997: quite a high estimate, since the Government Actuary's Department projects life expectancy for 36-year-old women of 80.6 (estimates for England and Wales, 1994–6).

4   Y&R Brand Futures Group, *Future Dialogue No 3*, December 1997, www.brandfutures.com.

5   American Society of Plastic and Reconstructive Surgeons, *National Clearinghouse of Plastic Surgery Statistics*, releases 13

April 1998, www.plasticsurgery.org, for this and subsequent paragraph.

6   Life expectancy for men at 63, the average age of retirement in the UK, is 16 years; for women at 60, the official age of retirement, is 22.5 years: *Interim Life Tables for 1994–96*, Government Actuary's Department; on comparisons between pensioners and families with children, see DSS, *Households Below Average Income*, 1996, pp 125–8.

7   The Carnegie Inquiry into the Third Age, *Final Report: Life, Work and Livelihood in the Third Age*, Carnegie UK Trust, 1993, pp 3–5.

8   Strictly speaking, the economic ages of man number four: three as adults and one as young dependants; 'Botany with Bellamy', *Financial Times*, 8 August 1998.

9   Data (p-2).gif at jin.jcic.or.jp.

10   Norman Ryder, 'The Cohort as a Concept in the Study of Social Change', *American Sociological Review*, 1965, pp 844, 855.

11   For this and following paragraph, Roger Jowell and Alison Park, *A Disengaged Generation?*, Citizenship Foundation, December 1997, pp 22–4; see also *Changing British Households*, p 75, for similar findings on distinctive cohort attitudes towards cohabitation.

12   John Bynner (ed.), *Twenty-somethings in the 1990s*, Ashgate Press, 1997, pp 100–102.

13   Personal communication from Norval Glenn; Paul Amato and Alan Booth, *A Generation at Risk*, Harvard University Press, 1997, pp 10, 219; *Wall Street Journal*, 5 August 1998, defining older Americans as 65+ and young adults as 18–34.

14   Laurence Kotlikoff and Willi Leibfritz, 'An International Comparison of Generational Accounts', NBER Working Paper 6447, March 1998, Table 2, with education treated as government consumption. The definition of taxes is net of benefits, the calculation assumes a discount rate of 5% and labour productivity growth of 1.5%.

15   For a critique of generational accounting, see Robert Haveman, 'Should Generational Accounts Replace Public Budgets and

Deficits?', *Journal of Economic Perspectives*, 1994, pp 95–111; and Robert Eisner, *The Misunderstood Economy*, Harvard Business School Press, 1995, pp 121–9.

16 Laurence Kotlikoff and Willi Leibfritz, *op. cit.*, Table 8; Robert A.George, 'Stuck in the Shadows with You: Observations on Post-Boomer Culture', in Richard D.Thau & Jay S.Helflin (eds), *Generations Apart*, Prometheus Books, 1997, p 27.

17 David Thomson, *Selfish Generations?*, The White Horse Press, 1996, pp 52, 236.

18 Susan A. MacManus, *Young v. Old*, Westview Press, 1996, p 247. MacManus finds that all age groups tend to back spending priorities that serve their particular age-related interests.

19 William Gale and John Karl Scholz, *op. cit.*, p 152; figures are in 1986 dollars; John Logan and Glenna Spitze, 'Self-interest and Altruism in Intergenerational Relations', *Demography*, 1995, pp 358, 362.

20 The rising gradient of ill health is evident in male patient consulting rates by age: ONS, *Morbidity Statistics from General Practice, 4th National Study*, 1991–2, pp 25–7; see also health–age profiles for Dutch 40–64-year-olds in Marcel Kerkhofs *et al.*, *Age-related Health Dynamics and Changes in Labour Market Status*, CERRA, 1998.

21 *Changing Households*, pp 207-8; David Coleman and John Salt, *The British Population*, Oxford University Press, 1996, p 228; American Association for Retired Persons, *Family Caregiving in the US*.

22 Theodore Roszak, *America the Wise: Longevity, Revolution and the True Wealth of Nations*, Houghton Mifflin, 1998. pp 1–2, 240–45, 104–107.

23 Floris Wood (ed.), *An American Profile: Opinions and Behaviour 1972–1989*, Gale Research, 1990, pp 313–19; *Changing Households*, pp 263, 288–9.

24 DETR, *Projections of Households in England to 2016*, Table 1, p viii; GAD news release 7 January 1999; ONS, *Living in Britain*, p

12: 8% of families with dependent children where the head of family was aged under 60 contained one or more step children in 1996.

25 'Structure and Distribution of Population', *Population Trends*, No 81, Autumn 1995, pp 7–8; 'The Ethnic Minority Populations of Great Britain: Their Estimated Sizes and Age Profiles', *Population Trends*, No 84, Summer 1996, pp 33–5; David Coleman and John Salt, *op. cit.*, p 517; they also assume a decline in fertility to replacement level; '1996-based national population projections for the UK', *Population Trends*, No 91, Spring 1998, p 45.

26 Marian Storkey, Jackie Maguire, Rob Lewis, *Cosmopolitan London*, London Research Centre, June 1997, pp 16–18, 42–3.

27 NRC, *The New Americans*, pp 31–4, 40, 52, 95, 113–23. The study estimates 800,000 legal immigrants, 300,000 emigrants and about 275,000 illegal immigrants, making 800,000 net inflows.

28 NRC, *op. cit.*, pp 113–23: the projection assumes continuing net immigration at current levels, current rates of intermarriage, both first and subsequent generations, and current rates of ethnic affiliation among the descendants of mixed marriages; on Tiger Woods, London Research Centre, *op. cit.*, p 39.

29 OECD, *Trends in International Migration*, 1998, pp 23–4, 111; NRC, *op. cit.*, p 35.

30 'America's Nostalgia Boom', *Business Week*, 23 March 1998.

31 'VW's New Beetle', 5 January 1998, 'VW's new Beetle Print Campaign Wins Grand Prix Award', 25 June 1998, dealer.vw.com.

32 'Over 50 and over here', *The Guardian*, 18 May 1998; 'Special K Abandons Thin Models', 8 Feburary 1998, advertising.tqn.com.

33 Tony Moss, editor of *Reportage*; Horst Stipp, 'Why Youth Rules', *American Demographics*, May 1995; David Lewis and Darren Bridger, *The Soul of the New Consumer*, Nicholas Brealey Publishing, 1999.

34 'She-TV, Me-TV', *New York Times*, 22 July 1998.

35 On the contrast between UK and Australian TV programs in the international market, see 'UKTV blues', *The Economist*, 12 December 1998.

36 Glenn Firebaugh in personal communication; RIO, *Connecting with Boomers*, pp 21, 81–2, for aversion to high tech.

37 For this and following paragraphs, Walker Smith and Ann Clurman, *Rocking the Ages*, HarperBusiness, 1997, p xvii, 6, 8–10, 14, 88, 102.

38 RIO, *Connecting with Baby Boomers*, pp 31–3.

39 *Geographical Mobility March 1995 to March 1996*, Bureau of the Census P20-497, November 1997.

40 Stephen Cutler, 'Aging and Social Change', in Jeffrey Michael Clair and Richard Allman (eds), *The Gerontological Prism: Developing Interdisciplinary Research and Priorities*, Baywood Press, forthcoming.

41 M. Kent Jennings and Richard Niemi, *Generations and Politics: a Panel Study of Young Adults and Parents*; *American Profile, op. cit.*, pp 309–10, which shows sharp falls between 1973 and 1989 in Americans aged 35–45 answering that sharing a home with grown children is a bad idea.

42 Janine Lopiano-Misdom and Joanne de Luca, *Street Trends*, HarperBusiness, 1997, pp 97, 100–103, on 'reverse marketing' strategies.

43 Salzman quote from fastcompany.com/online/03/ future.

44 William Frey, *Minority Magnet Metros in the '90s*, Michigan University Population Studies Center, 1998; Janine Lopiano-Misdom and Joanne de Luca, *op. cit.*, pp 35–8.

45 'The New Immigrant Experience', *New York Times*, 22 July 1998.

46 'McDonald's expands into Mexican food', *Financial Times*, 11 February 1998.

47 Projections for Hispanic share of Los Angeles County from California Department of Finance, County population projections, December 1998, www.dof.ca.gov.

48 Blair interviewed on *A Day to Remember*, Channel Four, 18 April 1998; 'Snapshot of Gerhard Schroeder in Hot Pursuit of Voters', *New York Times*, 3 August 1998, where Schröder is quoted as saying: 'Certainly, this is a change of generation. It's a question of who

has the strength to mould the creative forces into the next millennium.'

Chapter 7 – Work makeover

1 Eurostat baseline projection.
2 International Labour Office (ILO), *Economically Active Population 1950–2010*, 1996.
3 ILO, *op. cit.*, Vol 4, p 117.
4 OECD, *Employment Outlook*, 1998, pp 197–9: male employment/population ratio.
5 ILO, *op. cit.*, Vol 1, p 52.
6 OECD, *The Transition from Work to Retirement*, 1995, p 48.
7 OECD, *op. cit.*, pp 24–7.
8 Interview with outplacement consultants, BBC Radio 4, *Fired at Fifty*, 13 April 1997; speech by Howard Davies, June 1997, to the Employers' Forum on Age.
9 For this and subsequent two paragraphs, 'Tackling Age Bias: Code or Law?', *Equal Opportunities Review*, July/August 1998, pp 32–7; the survey in the *Sunday Times* was of jobs advertised October 1997 to March 1998.
10 James Arrowsmith and Ann McGoldrick, *Breaking the Barriers*, Institute of Management, 1996, pp 27–8, 38–9 for survey findings and respondents' answers.
11 OECD, *op. cit.*, p 34.
12 *ibid.*, p 80, on percentages of Austrians 55–64 receiving invalidity benefit.
13 Axel Börsch-Supan and Reinhold Schnabel, 'Social Security and Retirement in Germany', NBER Working Paper 6153, 1997, pp 20–21, 30–31.
14 London Fire and Civil Defence Authority, Briefing no 28, December 1998; interview with Tony Ritchie.
15 For this and comparison with retirement in private sector in next

paragraph, Audit Commission, *Retiring Nature*, 1997, pp 5, 14, 16, 23.

16 'Early Retirement Is on the Increase', *IDS Pensions Bulletin*, May 1998; Sarah Tanner, *The Dynamics of Male Retirement*, Institute for Fiscal Studies, May 1998; David Wise, 'More Older People Living Longer, Working Less', in *Facing the Age Wave*, 1998, pp 15–18.

17 OECD, *Economic Outlook*, June 1998, pp 185–6; the 'implicit tax' occurs when discounted costs of obtaining benefits exceed the discounted gains; it is expressed as a proportion of gross earnings.

18 Séan Rickard, A *Profits Warning: Macroeconomic Costs of Ageism*, Employers Forum on Age, 1998; World Bank, *Averting the Old Age Crisis*, OUP, 1994, p 323; the calculation assumes that the labor force participation rate in 1990 was held constant at the rate of 1960.

19 Richard Disney, *Can We Afford to Grow Old?*, MIT Press, 1996, p 72.

20 OECD, *Maintaining Prosperity in an Ageing Society*, 1998, pp 4–19, 33–41.

21 The Law Society, *Age Discrimination and Employment Law: a Report of the Employment Law Committee*, 1996, p 2.

22 Bernard Casey, *Incentives and Disincentives to Early and Late Retirement*, OECD, 1997, p 7, for employers' ranking of factors discouraging recruitment and employment of older workers.

23 'Demographics and Leadership Philosophy', *Journal of Management Development*, 1998, reported in 'Senior Heads Hold Balance of Power,' *Financial Times*, 8 September 1998.

24 *Changing Households*, p 165, shows sharp decline in job and employer mobility with age; Bernard Casey, *op. cit.*, p 8, for relative sickness absence rates by age; workers in 14 developed countries aged 55+ are half as likely again to be away sick from work as those aged 25–54.

25 OECD, *Maintaining Prosperity in an Ageing Society*, p 77.

26 Dominic Cadbury, 'The Oldies and Skills Sent Packing', *Financial*

Times, 31 May 1997; Bernard Casey, *op. cit.*, p 10, on French employers.

27   Association of Graduate Recruiters, January 1999.

28   'Paint by Numbers: in Pay Scales, Life often Imitates Art', *Wall Street Journal*, 28 May 1998.

29   'Workforce Ageing in OECD Countries', *OECD Employment Outlook*, 1998, pp 130–31 on the problem older people face through overcommitment to job-specific skills; James Arrowsmith and Ann McGoldrick, *op. cit.*, pp 12, 16, on managers' attitudes.

30   Günter Rommel *et al.*, *Quality Pays*, *Macmillan Business*, 1996, pp 44–7.

31   'On the Shelf without even Being Consulted', *Financial Times*, 22 June 1998.

32   Sumantra Ghoshal and Christopher A. Bartlett, 'Play the Right Card to Get the Aces in the Pack', *Financial Times*, 28 July 1998.

33   ILO, *op. cit.*, Vol 4, pp 48–9, 90–91, 117–18, 138–9.

34   OECD, *Employment Outlook 1998*, Table E, p 206, for part-time working among women.

35   'Growing Pains from an Excess of Success', *Financial Times*, 12 May 1998; 'Congress Likely to Allow more Foreign Engineers', *New York Times*, 25 July 1998.

36   World Bank, *Global Development Finance*, Vol 1, 1997, p 27.

37   James Arrowsmith and Ann McGoldrick, *op. cit.*, p 46, on managers' attitudes in SMEs.

38   'Universities Embrace Distance Learning for Busy Professionals', *New York Times*, 29 July 1998.

39   Bernard Casey, *op. cit.*, p 21–6.

Chapter 8 – Pensions crunch

1   UK estimates: *We All Need Pensions*, Report by Pension Provision Group, DSS, 1998, pp 89, 93; for US estimates (for median household): Pensions evidence from Dr Olivia Mitchell, 28 January

1998, pp 1, 5, Social Security Committee Session 1997–8.

2   The story is well told in Burton Malkiel and J.P. Mei, *Global Bargain Hunting*, p 85.

3   Ida May Fuller: www.ssa.gov/history.

4   Arnold Wilson and G.S.Mackay, *Old Age Pensions*, OUP, 1941, p 14, my italics. On the other hand, the Bismarckian system was not pay-as-you-go: this change was introduced in the 1957 reforms. See Herbert Giersch (ed.), *The Fading Miracle*, CUP, 1994, p 81.

5   Arnold Wilson and G.S. Mackay, *op. cit.*, p 19. The relevant life expectancy measure is for adults, not at birth: for men aged 20 and 40 in England and Wales in 1901 this stood at 61.3 and 65.8 respectively, according to figures from GAD.

6   Quoted in World Bank, *Averting the Old Age Crisis*, p 105.

7   The effective return on a pay-as-you-go pension system is the sum of labor force and real earnings growth. Real earnings per hour rose at an annual rate of 0.6% in the business sector 1970–96 compared with 2.8% 1960–70: *Economic Report of the President*, 1998, p 338.

8   Richard Disney, *op. cit.*, p 85; 'Too Soon to Samba', *Financial Times*, 6 October 1998.

9   OASDI, Annual Report, 1998, pp 3, 33–4, 122–2.

10   Trustees' quotation in Social Security Administration, *A Summary of Annual Reports*, 1997, p 39.

11   Nicola Düll, *op. cit.*, Table 4-12, p 165; Philip Davis, *Can Pension Systems Cope?*, Royal Institute of International Affairs, 1997, p 12.

12   The pension contribution rate was set at 20.3% in January 1998: OECD, *Economic Survey of Germany*, 1998, p 148; see also OECD, *op. cit.*, 1996, p 68.

13   A similar assessment of merits of funded versus pay-as-you-go schemes is given in Group of Ten, *op. cit.*, ch 2, p 11.

14   *We All Need Pensions*, p 8, on shares of British retirement income.

15   On pension fund assets as % of GDP: Group of Ten, *op. cit.*, ch 3, p 1; Salomon Smith Barney, *Private Pension Funds in Latin America*, December 1997, p 3.

16   OASDI, *op. cit.*, p 28.

17 Gary Evans, *Red Ink*, Academic Press, 1997, pp 142–4: in 1993, the old age fund was due to be exhausted in 2043; in 1995, the date had been brought forward to 2031!

18 'Shuffle up the Pension Path', *Financial Times*, 20 November 1997.

19 James Banks in presentation to NIESR conference 4 December 1998 on the population forecasts for Serps stopping short in 2008; Alan Budd and Nigel Campbell, 'The Pension System in the UK', in Martin Feldstein (ed.), *Privatizing Social Security*, 1998, p 111 for estimate of current spending projection on Serps compared with original.

20 Treasury Select Committee, *The Mis-selling of Personal Pensions*, Ninth Report, November 1998, especially paras 25 and 26.

21 Sheetal Chand and Albert Jaeger, 'Aging Populations and Public Pension Schemes', IMF Occasional Paper 147, 1996, pp 14–17.

22 Agar Brugiavini, 'Social Security and Retirement in Italy', NBER Working Paper No 6155, September 1997; for estimate of pensions spending as percentage of GDP, OECD, *Economic Survey of Italy*, 1998, pp 61–2.

23 OECD, *Ageing in OECD Countries*, 1996, p 102.

24 The total contribution is 13%, with 3% covering health and survivor's insurance and administrative costs.

25 Address by José Piñera to Cato/Economist Conference, London, 1997.

26 Salomon Smith Barney, *Pension Funds in Latin America*, 1998, pp 6, 8 on spread of Chile model in Latin America; World Bank, *Averting the Old Age Crisis*, p 128, on Peru's record.

27 Sebastian Edwards, 'The Chilean Pension Reform: A Pioneering Program', in Feldstein, *op. cit.*, p 45, for administrative costs; Salomon Smith Barney, *op. cit.*, 1997, p 107, on sales and marketing budgets; Rubio quoted in 'Mexican Pension Groups Grab Customers', *Financial Times*, 21 April 1997.

28 Chile pension fund returns cited in Salomon Smith Barney, *op. cit.*, 1998, p 127; Robert Holzmann, 'Pension Reform, Financial Market Development and Economic Growth: Preliminary

Evidence from Chile', IMFStaff Papers, 1997, pp 167–75; Chilean central bank study cited by Dmitri Vittas of World Bank at Cato/Economist Conference 1997.

29 ONS, *Population Trends*, Spring 1998, Table 6, p 57, for proportion of population of pensionable age in Britain.

30 OASDI, *op. cit.*, pp 85, 108, 105.

31 Report of 1994–1996 Advisory Council on Social Security, 1997.

32 Martin Feldstein and Andrew Samwick, 'The Transition Path in Privatizing Social Security', in Feldstein, *op. cit.*, pp 215–64.

33 John Geanakoplos, Olivia Mitchell and Stephen Zeldes, 'Would a Privatized Social Security System Really Pay a Higher Rate of Return?', NBER Working Paper 6713, pp 11–18, 36.

34 *Economic Report of the President*, 1997, p 113, on volatility of equity returns; David Miles, 'The Implications of Switching from Unfunded to Funded Pension Schemes', *National Institute Economic Review*, 1998/1, pp 84–5.

35 For this and details of proposals in subsequent paragraphs: DSS, *Partnership in Pensions*, 1998, pp 3–8, 40–44, 49, 62.

36 Sheetal Chand and Albert Jaeger, *op. cit.*, p 18.

37 Quoted in 'Germans Squabble over Welfare Crisis', *Financial Times*, 21 November 1997.

38 Kurt Biedenkopf and Meinhard Miegel, *Von der Arbeitnehmerrente zur Bürgerrente*, 1997, pp 2–4. Their assessment of rates of return is backed by Axel Börsch-Supan and Reinhold Schnabel, *op. cit.*, p 2, who say that rates of return will be negative for all cohorts born after 1970.

39 Axel Börsch-Supan and Reinhold Schnabel, *op. cit.*, p 32.

40 David Miles and Andreas Iben, *The Reform of Pension Systems: Winners and Losers across Generations in the UK and Germany*, 1998.

41 Peter Murray, NAPF chairman, 2 July 1997.

42 John Shoven and David Wise, 'Keeping Savers from Saving', in David Wise (ed.), *Facing the Age Wave*, 1997, p 59.

Chapter 9 – Richter nine

1   ILO, *op. cit.*, vol 96-4, pp 47, 167 for labor participation rates by age group.

2   The OECD defines the old age dependency ratio as 65+/15–64, but factors in less immigration than Eurostat's baseline projection. On this definition, the ratio also deteriorates to 1 in 2 by 2030 in Germany, Italy, and Switzerland: see OECD, *Ageing in OECD Countries*, p 102.

3   OECD, *op. cit.*, defining the dependency ratio as those aged 0–14 and 65+ as a percentage of 15–64-year-olds.

4   OASDI, *op. cit.*, p 22; Ronald Lee and Shripad Tuljapurkar, 'Death and Taxes: Longer Life, Consumption, and Social Security', *Demography*, 1997, pp 67–81, also for ensuing paragraphs.

5   *Economic Report of the President*, 1997, p 120; nearly two-thirds of medical spending for the old is financed publicly.

6   David Cutler, 'Medical Care Reform for an Aging Society' in David Wise (ed.), *Facing the Age Wave*, 1997, p 96; social security spending is projected at 6.8% of GDP in 2030, OASDI, *op. cit.*, p 187; '98 Medicare Growth Slowest since Program Began in 65', *New York Times*, 12 January 1999; Social Security and Medicare Boards of Trustees, Summary of 1998 Annual Reports, April 1998, p 9.

7   Ronald Lee and Shripad Tuljapurkar, another version of the paper 'Death and Taxes', http://arrow.qal.berkeley.edu/papers/rlee/death-tax.

8   OECD, *op. cit.*, p 53.

9   OECD, *The Macroeconomic Implications of Ageing in a Global Context*, WP193, March 1998, especially pp 13, 16, 17, 24, 47, 49, 64. The projections I cite here are based on the OECD's reference or 'business-as-usual' scenario.

10 'The Decline and Fall of the Modern European State', *Lombard Street Research Monthly Economic Review*, December 1997.

11 Group of Ten, *op. cit.*, ch 3, p 6.

12 Sylvester Schieber and John Shoven (eds), 'The Consequences of

Population Aging on Private Pension Fund Saving and Asset Markets', in *Public Policy towards Pensions*, Twentieth Century Fund, 1997, pp 236–4.

13 Allen Kelley and William Paul McGreevey, 'Population and Development in Historical Perspective', in Robert Cassen (ed.) *Population and Development: Old Debates, New Conclusions*, Overseas Development Council, 1994, p 117.

14 Pensions Evidence from Dr Olivia Mitchell, *op. cit.*, p 16.

15. James P. Smith, *Inheritances and Bequests*, Rand, April 1998; the paper draws on the AHEAD and HRS surveys conducted by the Institute for Social Research, Michigan University in the 1990s. Values are expressed in 1992 dollars. The AHEAD survey samples 70-year-olds while the HRS samples 50-year-olds.

16 Laurence Kotlikoff speaking at NIESR conference, 4 December 1998.

17 1998 HRA Report, www.umich.edu/~hrswww/overview/hrarr.html.

18 'A Lifetime of Patient Investing Yields a Stunning Bequest', *New York Times*, 13 July 1998.

19 Pensions Evidence from Dr Olivia Mitchell, *op. cit.*

20 Figures for Ford and Chile pension funds, *ibid.*, p 14; Salomon Smith Barney, *Private Pension Funds in Latin America, 1998 Update*, p 126, estimates Chile pension funds at $30bn, compared with the $40bn that Dr Mitchell cites for the Ford pension fund.

21 World Bank, *Global Development Finance 1997*, Vol 1, Figure 3.4, p 31; David Landes, *The Wealth and Poverty of Nations*, 1998, p 516.

22 OECD, WP 193, *op. cit.*, pp 27–9. The reference scenario shows foreign investment income contributing less than 0.25% p.a. in growth of living standards for the OECD.

23 Alan Greenspan, *Monetary Policy Testimony and Report to the Congress*, 22 July 1997.

24 US Department of Commerce, *The Emerging Digital Economy*, 1998, pp 7, 10.

25 ILO, *op. cit.*, Vol IV, p 47.

26 Lawrence Summers *et al.*, 'An aging Society: Opportunity or Challenge?', *Brookings Papers on Economic Activity*, 1990:1, pp 40-1: the effect was strongest, however, for the period 1960–73.

27 Maxime Fougère and Marcel Mérette, *Population Ageing and Economic Growth in Seven OECD Countries*, Canada Department of Finance, March 1998.

28 *Bank of England Quarterly Bulletin*, August 1998, p 214.

29 Paul Krugman, 'Why Most Economists' Predictions Are Wrong', *Red Herring*, June 1998.

30 US Department of Commerce, *op. cit.*, p 4 on IT growth.

31 William Petty quoted in Julian Simon, *The Ultimate Resource 2*, Princeton University Press, 1996, p 372.

32 One reason to expect a short-lived increase in productivity growth is that the Bureau of Labor Statistics is changing its calculation of consumer prices in a way that brings down inflation, but is not backdating the adjustments; the effect is to mechanically push up productivity growth. See Nicholas Oulton, 'The Implications of the Boskin Report', *National Institute Economic Review*, 1998/3, p 95: 'there will appear to be a significant improvement in US economic performance over the recent past, even though no genuine improvement has actually occurred'.

33 McKinsey Global Institute, *Driving Productivity and Growth in the UK Economy*, 1998; Angus Maddison, *Chinese Economic Performance in the Long Run*, OECD, 1998, p 98.

34 OECD, WP 193, *op. cit.*, pp 31, 60, 25–6, 57.

35 Dora Costa, 'The Evolution of Retirement: Summary of a Research Project', *American Economic Review*, May 1998, pp 232–6.

Chapter 10 – New age

1 Angus Maddison, *Monitoring the World Economy 1820–1992*, OECD, 1995, p 183.

2   *ibid.*, p 181.

3   Eurostat baseline projection for working age population, defining it as 20–60; Lombard Street Research, *Tigers 2020*, MIR 65, July 97.

4   Calculations based on Eurostat baseline projection, defining old age dependency ratio as 65+ to 20–64.

5   Paul Kennedy, *Preparing for the Twenty-First Century*, Fontana, 1994, pp 138, 152–7, 322–5.

6   Sheetal Chand and Albert Jaeger, *op. cit.*, p 17 for benchmarks of primary surpluses needed to stabilize pension and other government debt; OECD, *Economic Outlook*, December 1998, Table 32, p 222 for primary balances in 1998.

7   Chand and Jaeger, *op. cit.*

8   Social Security Committee, *Unfunded Pension Liabilities in the European Union*, House of Commons Session 1996/7; Laurence Kotlikoff and Willi Leibfritz, *An International Comparison of Generational Accounts*, *op. cit.*, p 12.

9   According to Okun's law, an observed statistical regularity, GDP needs to grow at 2% above trend to bring the unemployment rate down by 1 percentage point. In mid-1998, standardized unemployment rates stood at around 10% in the EU, and below 5% in the US.

10 OECD, WP 193, *op. cit.*, p 27: the OECD envisages such gains occurring over a longer period than the 2000s.

11 'Germany Awaits Revision of Tax-cutting Proposals', *Wall Street Journal*, 9 November 1998 for report of Schröder's early retirement proposal; Cecchini Report, *The Benefits of a Single Market*, p 84.

12 OECD, WP 193, *op. cit.*, pp 9, 65, based on the reference or 'business-as-usual' scenario: China accounts for more than 70% of the fast-ageing region.

13 Angus Maddison forecasts that China will overtake the US by 2015 in *Chinese Economic Performance in the Long Run*, OECD, 1998, pp 17, 97. In 2015, output per head in China will be roughly a fifth of US levels.

14 'Russian Demography: a Case for Dostoyevsky', *International Herald Tribune*, 9 June 1997. In 1995, 15-year-old Russian boys had a 47% probability of dying before the age of 60; in the UK the probability was 12%: World Bank Development Indicators 1998.

15 Jean-Claude Chesnais, *Le Crépuscule de l'Occident*, Robert Laffont, p 194; Council for Europe, *Recent Demographic Developments in Europe*, 1997, p 291.

16 WHO, *World Health Report*, 1998, p 122.

17 Amartya Sen, 'Mortality as an Indicator of Economic Success and Failure', *Economic Journal*, January 1998, pp 21–3.

18 Council for Europe, *op. cit.*, pp 285, 145, 364, shows that cohorts aged 5–14 accounted for 16% of the population in 1996 compared with 11% for Germany and 13% for the UK.

19 UN 1998 Revision, *op. cit.*

20 US Bureau of the Census, *Older Workers, Retirement and Pensions*, 1995, p 5.

21 Griffith Feeney, 'Fertility in China: Past, Present, Prospect', in Wolfgang Lutz (ed.), *Future Population Growth in Africa, Asia, and Latin America: What Can We Assume Today?*, 1994, p 121; John Cleland, 'A Regional Review of Fertility Trends in Developing Countries', in Wolfgang Lutz (ed.), *The Future Population of the World. What Can We Assume Today?*, p 57.

22 Chai Bin Park and Nam-Hoon Cho, 'Consequences of Son Preference in a Low Fertility Society', *Population and Development Review*, 1995, pp 74–5; Nicholas Eberstadt, 'Asia Tomorrow, Gray and Male', *National Interest*, Fall 1998, p 64.

23 Naohiro Ogawa and Robert Retherford, 'Shifting Costs for the Elderly back to Families in Japan: Will it Work?', *Population and Development Review*, 1997, pp 75–7, 87–8, 91.

24 OECD, *Trends in International Migration*, 1998, p 180, on the US program offing 55,000 permanent permits to nationals of countries which do not send many immigrants to the US.

25 W.W. Rostow, *op. cit.*, p 158.

26 Tim Parkin, *Demography and Roman Society*, pp 94, 112:

'Generally a family with more than two adult children would have been considered remarkable.'

27 Peter Laslett, *Interpreting the Demographic Changes*, Royal Society, *op. cit.*, p 1807.

28 Paul Kennedy, *op. cit.*, pp 34–5. Tanaka was addressing a Cato conference on pensions in London, December 1997.

29 Francis Fukuyama, 'Women and the Evolution of World Politics', *Foreign Affairs*, September/October 1998, pp 38–9.

30 Karl Mannheim, 'The Problem of Generations', 1927, in Melissa Hardy (ed.), *Studying Aging and Social Change*, Sage Publications, 1997, pp 39–41.

31 Laurence Kotlikoff and Willi Leibfritz, *op. cit.*, Table 8. The imbalance is expressed as increase in lifetime net taxes of future generations as a percentage of those payable by newborns, both amounts in present value terms and assuming a discount rate of 5% and growth in labor productivity of 1.5%.

32 Susan A. MacManus, *op. cit.*, p 251.

33 Alfred Sauvy, 'Social and Economic Consequences of the Ageing of Western European Populations', *Population Studies*, 1948, pp 117–18.

34 David Cutler, *op. cit.*, pp 98–9, 111–12, for this and subsequent citations.

35 'Austrian Minister Wants Childless Women to Retire Later', *The Guardian*, 20 August 1997.

36 H. Gille, 'Recent Developments in Swedish Population Policy', *Population Studies*, 1948, pp 3, 16, 43; Gunnar Andersson, 'Childbearing Trends in Sweden 1961–95', *Stockholm Research Reports in Demography*, no 117, 1997.

37 Britta Hoem and Jan Hoem, 'Fertility Trends in Sweden up to 1996', *Stockholm Research Reports in Demography*, no 123, 1997.

38 Anne Hélène Gauthier and Jan Hatzius, 'Family Benefits and Fertility: an Econometric Analysis', *Population Studies*,1997, pp 295–306. The authors estimate that a 25% increase in the value of family allowances would increase TFR in the long run by 4% or

about .07 births/woman. In Scandinavian countries, the increase would be about double.

39 Marina Adler, *Jounal of Marriage and the Family*, February 1997, p 47.

40 Christoph Conrad *et al.*, 'East German Fertility after Unification: Crisis or Adaptation?', *Population and Development Review*, 1996, pp 331–4, 339; Council of Europe, *op. cit.*, p 150. At its trough in 1993–4, the TFR was less than 0.8.

41 Ronald Lee, 'Intergenerational Transfers and the Economic Cycle: a Cross-cultural Perspective', 1995, http://arrow.qal.berkeley.edu/papers/rlee/ccig. Lee's work overturns John Caldwell's influential theory that high fertility in sub-Saharan Africa is because resources flow up to the parents from children.

42 Seija Ilmakunnas, 'Public Policy and Childcare Choice', in Inga Persson and Christina Jonung (eds), *Economics of the Family and Family Policies*, pp 190–91, on Finland's child homecare allowance; Shirley Dex and Robert Rowthorn, 'Parenting and Labour Force Participation: the Case for a Ministry of the Family', ESRC Centre for Business Research, University of Cambridge, Working Paper 74.

43 Council on Population Problems, Ministry of Health and Welfare, *Trend Towards Fewer Children*, October 1997.

Index